CHOSEN

PATH

GOD'S

CHOSEN

PATH

The autobiography of
Dr. William Cameron Mason, Pastor Emeritus,
Asbury United Methodist Church
Tulsa, Oklahoma

A BOLD TRUTH Publication
Christian Literature & Artwork

DEDICATION

To my beautiful wife, Jayne,
and
to my wonderful children,
Peggie Ann Nash,
Robin Jayne Tanner,
William Cameron Mason II,
and
William Randal Mason

God's Chosen Path
Copyright © 2019 by William Cameron Mason
ISBN 13: 978-1-949993-23-3

FIRST EDITION

BOLD TRUTH PUBLISHING
(Christian Literature & Artwork)
606 West 41st, Ste. 4
Sand Springs, Oklahoma 74063
www.BoldTruthPublishing.com
boldtruthbooks@yahoo.com

Quantity sales special discounts are available on quantity purchases by corporations, associations, and others. For details, contact the publisher at the mailing address or email above.

Formatting and design by Aaron Jones.

Printed in the USA.
01 20   10 9 8 7 6 5 4 3 2 1

PERMISSIONS

CONTENTS

Tom Harrison, Senior Pastor, Shares His Story

ACKNOWLEDGMENTS

I wish to acknowledge and thank the following wonderful and generous people for their contributions to this book.

Readers and Consultants
Dr. James V. Heidinger, II, President and Publisher emeritus of Good News

Barbara Davis, Former Human Resources Director, Asbury United Methodist Church

Victoria Williamson, Retired Executive Assistant to the Senior Pastor, Asbury United Methodist Church

A. B. Steen, Retired Chief Executive Officer, T. D. Williamson, Inc., Tulsa, Oklahoma

John Westervelt, Retired Research Engineer, Amoco Research Laboratories, Tulsa, Oklahoma

Asbury United Methodist Church
Dr. Tom Harrison, Senior Pastor
Rev. Guy Ames, III
Angie Brashears, Director of Communications
Betty Logan, Associate Pastor Administrative Assistant
Tera Askey, Print Production Coordinator
Belinda Wilson, Graphic Designer

My family, my church family, and friends for their personal stories, research, encouragement, and support.

Editor
Judy Johnson, Adjunct Professor, Tulsa Community College

Publisher
Aaron Jones, Bold Truth Publishing, Tulsa, Oklahoma

FORGIVENESS

The stories and events of my life are presented chronologically.

For errors in omission, spelling, names, dates, and details, please forgive me.

FOREWORD

Reflections on Bill Mason's book,
God's Chosen Path

It was a deep privilege to be a reader of Bill Mason's book, *God's Chosen Path*, which reflects on his life and ministry. It is a warm and delightful read. I still chuckle at Bill's counsel to husbands-to-be that they remember there is no "Underwear Fairy" that keeps the drawer full of freshly-laundered underwear ready for the next day. What a heart-warming reminder to husbands that they not take for granted the everyday things a wife does to make home a joyful and pleasant place to be.

I have known and admired Bill Mason for many years. He served with distinction as chairman of the Good News board of directors from 1989 to 1992 and then was elected as a life-time honorary member of that board. All of us admired his Christian grace and wisdom as he gave leadership to our board. But to have the chance to read the stories about his life, his early family relationships, his education, his loving marriage to Jayne, his involvement in the family business and then his call to the ministry and service at Asbury United Methodist Church have given me an even greater and fuller appreciation of him as a person and a pastor.

Jesus said to His disciples, "You did not choose me, but I chose you and appointed you so that you might go and bear fruit—fruit that will last. . ." (John 15:16; NIV). Clearly, Bill Mason was called to the Christian ministry. And it is evident that his ministry bore much, much fruit and that the fruit has lasted.

In addition to Bill's own stories, I found myself so very impressed at the notes, letters, and expressions of love and appreciation included in this book. The reader is struck with the fact that these folks at Asbury Church really loved Bill Mason! And as I reflected on that it dawned on me that they loved him because he genuinely loved and cared for them. He clearly felt a pastoral responsibility for his flock. He cared for them, shepherded them, and loved them with unfeigned love.

That love for his flock was reflected in his faithfulness in calling on them, visiting them in their homes, and in his remarkable hospital visitation practice. This is a pastoral gift that laity respond to and will remember for a lifetime. I read recently that our parishioners won't care how much we know until they know how much we care. That's a good reminder for pastors. I believe the folks at Asbury UMC knew that their pastor, Dr. Bill Mason, cared for them deeply. And they loved him for it.

This remarkable ministry was kept passionate and authentic by Bill's attention to his devotional life, characterized by the discipline of early morning prayer and devotional reading. Bill's ministry was one of faithfulness to the biblical message. Putting it all together, you get the ingredients of a beautiful, remarkably fruitful ministry. The appropriate response to this amazingly effective ministry is to say simply, "Thanks be to God!" My heart was saying that again and again. Yours will, too, I am sure.

Dr. James V. Heidinger II
President and Publisher Emeritus of Good News

INTRODUCTION

Knowing Pastor Bill Mason, 1970-2019

In the fall of 1970, I arrived as a sophomore at Oral Roberts University (ORU) after spending the previous five years in Muskogee, including one year of junior college.

President Roberts' new relationship with the United Methodist Church created a natural conduit for other Methodist students to find our way to Tulsa for both our education and our spiritual nourishment. Tulsa United Methodist Churches at the time were healthy, growing, and filled with spiritual opportunities as well as open doors for part-time youth director positions. By my senior year at ORU, I had joined a cadre of Methodist boys who worked with area youth groups. Together we teamed up from time to time to create retreats, seminars, and workshops, and we shared youth group experiences that helped build life-time bonds of friendship. Young men like Adrian Cole, Dub Ambrose, David Burris, Tom Albin, and Tom Harrison worked to help build the spiritual lives of hundreds of young people in those early years. And one young Methodist boy from Magnolia, Arkansas, Billy Joe Daugherty, helped fill one of those positions.

The year after my ORU enrollment, my family followed me to Tulsa as my father received an appointment to pastor, Will Rogers United Methodist Church, which is how I became one of those youth directors, working with the students of the Will Rogers Church. During my senior year, an eighteen-year old from Rose Hill United Methodist Church stepped onto the ORU campus as a freshman and into the role as youth director of Epworth United Methodist Church in West Tulsa. By the end of that year, we had become colleagues in youth ministry and began a life-long friendship.

The overlap of student ministry allowed me to learn from other friends and to see the different ways in which Tulsa Methodist congregations functioned and thrived. The growing list of strong evangelical United Methodist preachers in Tulsa was followed by the growth of those churches as well. Instead of finding mild, vanilla mainline United Methodist preachers, Tulsa abounded with powerful preaching, evangelistic emphasis, and growing Methodist congregations. Rarely did a week pass that I did not hear of the outpouring of God's Spirit influencing a Tulsa congregation. Three younger rising Evangelical Methodist preachers were making their mark on the Tulsa spiritual community. Ray Owen was a long-time friend of my parents who helped to build New Haven United Methodist Church; David Thomas was taking the small Aldersgate congregation to new heights, and Bill Mason had begun moving Asbury United Methodist Church into position to become one of Oklahoma Methodism's strongest congregations.

At that same time, Pastor Mason began putting in place a strong staff, including one young University of Tulsa college student, Bill Clark, who joined our Tulsa team of youth directors. From time to time I would find myself at Asbury for a camp planning meeting or a conversation with Bill Clark and other youth directors. I kept hearing about the growth of Asbury and the powerful influence of Bill Mason. At home, over dinner, my parents talked with appreciation of Bill's influence in opening fresh avenues of ministry for my dad's ministry.

My father found that his long-standing tools could not stop the decline of attendance and membership at his city church; it was the first time he had been appointed to a city church in seven years. The Will Rogers area of Tulsa had begun to experience movement to the South. School busing forced families to move further south to the Memorial and Edison school districts, and the small Union district began to benefit from the southward move. As a result, my dad found it increasingly difficult to draw people back to the mid-town area for worship. Bill Mason's willingness to look outside the Methodist denomination's tools for support encouraged my dad to begin looking to Pastor Mason for ideas such as Evangelism Explosion, Stephen's Ministry, and Bethel Bible Study. The impact of these tools changed the trajectory of Dad's ministry and helped him turn the Will Rogers congregation into a growing church once again.

From this time onward, I saw Bill Mason as one of the pastors that I wanted to learn from and emulate in the days ahead. From time to time, I had the privilege of being with Pastor Mason, whether attending a district gathering, hearing him speak boldly about his concerns for the church, or being present in meetings with my dad. Those days before seminary, rubbing shoulders with Oklahoma's strongest evangelical leaders, had as much if not more impact on my future ministry than did any of the classes I took in my seminary education.

Growing up in the United Methodist Church, I rarely witnessed passionate evangelistic ministry, nor did I witness a seriousness about prayer and the work of the Holy Spirit. Most Methodist laity seemed somewhat pious on Sundays, but come Monday morning, the passion had died. I wanted to be part of ministry that took Jesus seriously 24/7. While my parents were serious about their faith, I rarely saw that same fire in the congregations Dad served, that is until I came to Tulsa in the 1970s. During that time, I witnessed pastoral leaders who were serious about bringing people to Christ. Dr. Bill Mason and Dr. L. D. Thomas set a standard for me that gave me confidence that moving into United Methodist ministry might open doors for me to be part of a serious disciple-making ministry after all.

In the spring of 1974, I began a serious search for seminary education. At the time, Asbury Seminary was not highly recommended for United Methodist seminary students. As an independent school with a bit of a checkered past, most United Methodist leaders discouraged me from attending Asbury. However, two key voices encouraged me to look towards Asbury; one was John Collier, the University of Tulsa Wesley Foundation Director and the other, Pastor Bill Mason. Those voices gave me one of the greatest gifts I have ever received — an education from Asbury Theological Seminary and the confidence that I could be a faithful classically orthodox Christian leader and find meaningful ministry in the United Methodist Church.

In the spring of 1978, I was completing my senior year at Asbury Theological Seminary, preparing to launch my ministerial career, and getting married to boot. We wanted to marry while friends were still in the area, so we scheduled our ceremony the same weekend as graduation. Feeling extremely anxious about pastoral ministry and marriage, I worried about my ability to take a church on my own. I called churches looking for positions as an associate or an assistant, but nothing came available. In March of that year, I called our Tulsa District Superintendent to say that I needed a job. Soon we were sent to Ada, Oklahoma, to serve a two-point charge, Ada Asbury and Ada Francis congregations.

With the Lord's help, those two churches began to thrive and by the spring of 1980, we were actually seeing growth in membership and attendance. One evening the phone rang at the parsonage, and I was thrilled and humbled to hear Pastor Mason's voice on the line. Introducing himself to me, he quickly got to his point. "Guy, I would like for you to come to Asbury to work with our student ministry."

I was quite flattered to say the least to think that Bill Mason wanted me to work with him. However, it did not take me long to answer. Having been burned out in student ministry to the point that I relented to God's call to enter pastoral ministry, I could not see myself going back into the work with students, plus our small churches were beginning to grow for the first time in years. I believed that I still had much work to do in Ada. I thanked Bill for his generous consideration of me and he, always the gracious gentleman, politely received my decline. Some years later I discovered that Bill had turned to a couple of ORU seminary students, one of those, Dick Read, to build his student ministry team. God works in amazing ways as Dick Read is still in ministry with Asbury United Methodist Church.

My next significant interaction with Pastor Mason came

in the early to mid-80's as I received an appointment to pastor the booming Oklahoma City suburb, Mustang, Oklahoma. Mustang, a bedroom community, was the fastest growing town in Oklahoma at the time. People worked in Oklahoma City and came home to get away from the hustle and to place their children in one of the best Oklahoma City school systems at the time. I needed help in organizing and staffing for this small congregation. I knew one pastor who had done what I wanted to do, so I drove up Interstate 44 to meet with Bill Mason. I wanted to learn from him some of the tools he had used to grow Asbury. I loved being at the master's feet as Bill shared story after story, offered resources and advice, much of which I put to use in the next several years. In hindsight, I only wished I had taken more of his advice and stayed longer in that setting before taking the opportunity to move.

For years, our Conference failed to recognize the leadership gifts of Bill Mason, in large part because he stood for traditional/evangelical convictions, while the majority of his pastoral peers tended to be more liberal. Bill received significant criticism because of his strong work with Good News and the Mission Society. The result of this was that time after time Bill was not elected to represent our Conference as a delegate to General Conference. What other liberal pastors had not noticed however, was the impact of the ministry of those few but powerful evangelical pastoral leaders in Oklahoma. Bill Mason, L.D. Thomas, David Thomas, Guy Ames, Jr., Ray Owen, and others opened the door for a new wave of younger evangelical leaders. Soon, the numbers of young evangelical pastors grew to such a degree that we have been able to dominate our Oklahoma Conference leadership and large churches for nearly 30 years. Without the sacrifices of Bill Mason and a few others, the ministry of Tom Harrison, Wade Paschal, Guy Ames, and dozens of others would never have been possible.

And now, after 43 plus years of United Methodist ministry, I have the joy of completing my ministry at Tulsa Asbury United Methodist Church. I see that my life and career have come full circle. A handful of Christian leaders have been used by God to mentor me and encourage me in both my spiritual life and my ministry. One of my greatest delights has been to finish out my years once again in the circle of Bill Mason, Pastor Emeritus, Asbury United Methodist Church. When I think of those upon whose shoulders God has allowed me to stand, one name always rises to the top – Pastor Bill Mason. I am eternally grateful for God's hand in his life and the generosity of his life in serving Christ.

Rev. Guy Ames III
Retired United Methodist Pastor

Meet the Mason Children

I have included stories of my children's births, childhoods, and marriages throughout this book, but for those who may not know my children, I have provided additional information.

Peggie Mason Nash

As a teenager, Peggie modeled while attending Memorial High School. She worked in St. Louis for a summer with Thermo-Jac Clothing and was in the November, 1967, issue of Seventeen Magazine. Peggie was the first of our children to marry. She married Gary Nash, November 26, 1971, and the wedding was held as Asbury. I officiated the service. Peggie and Gary went on their honeymoon and when they came back, Gary bought a monkey for Peggie. She named it, "Harpo." Their apartment manager would not allow a monkey. We had taken the children to the Family YMCA Camp in Colorado, and when we returned, I came into the house from the garage to the utility room. There was something new on the counter that was covered with a cloth. When I peeled up the cloth and peeked in, the monkey was staring back at me. That was a revelation to us all. We had the monkey for about a month, and Jayne made it possible for the cage with the monkey to hang on a hook that was on our porch. The monkey would jump up and down making the whole cage go up and down. Jayne and the children loved it and thought it was funny. After the monkey got out of the cage one time, we didn't know how we would ever get it back in there. It jumped from the table to the top of the kitchen ceiling where it raced around the plate display rack that was built-in the kitchen. Fortunately, we got it back in the cage, and after a short period of being owners of this monkey, Jayne sold it to the wife of the director of the Tulsa Symphony Orchestra. She was from New York and had several monkeys while in New York. She made Jayne promise not to tell her husband what she paid for the monkey, which was twenty-five dollars for the monkey and the cage. To our good fortune, her husband allowed her to keep the monkey, and we were free from it. Everyone was relieved.

Peggie and Gary lived in Norman for three years while Gary finished his degree. Peggie had attended the University of Oklahoma for one year, then she met Gary when her sister, Robin, introduced them. Gary lived down the street from us in our first house in Tulsa. In Norman, Peggie worked for an orthodontist, and with her job and the GI Bill, Gary finished his degree. They returned to Tulsa and both worked. Peggie and Gary divorced after 42 years of marriage. Peggie worked for Dr. Van Nowlin, an orthodontist, for 25 years before retiring.

Peggie is my daughter who people always say she looks like Jayne, and she does. After ten years of retirement, it was necessary for Peggie to go back to work. She chose helping and caregiving as her passion. She continues doing calligraphy on the side. She does so much to help me, especially since I don't drive anymore. She always picks me up for dinners at the church on Wednesdays and helps me with anything I need. She is always smiling.

From Peggie

Bill Mason didn't meet me until I was seven years old. He fell in love with my mother and he got a package deal. His instant family was my mom, me, and my little sister, Robin. He had waited to marry until he was in his thirties and had lived a popular bachelor's lifestyle until that time. I can only imagine how his life changed by adding a wife and two girls in a small house. Things remained that way until eight years later when he balanced out the hormones with Cameron and Randy. When he was called into the ministry, we were excited to move to Dallas so he could go to seminary at Southern Methodist University. Six people were living in an even smaller house with one bathroom. When he graduated from seminary, we had no idea where we were going to live in Oklahoma. We were fortunate to live in Tulsa. People had been telling us that we will probably move every two years, but we stayed in Tulsa and made it our home.

Asbury was meeting in Key Elementary school and the congregation was small. Very quickly the membership grew to hundreds attending. I always felt the love from the wonderful people there. I also knew there were many eyes on me. I felt like I had to be perfect being a PK (preacher's kid). I remember when I was 16 years old and had just gotten my driver's license. I was given permission to drive over to a friend's house. As I was going home, I hit a wet spot in the street where algae had grown. I fishtailed and lost control of the station wagon and jumped the curb. I thought I was hitting the brakes but pushed the accelerator so hard it locked, hit the brake pedal, and broke. I went through people's yards, turned, and went back across the street and hit a house. The house I hit belonged to an Asbury member. She was so sweet to me. She said, "Let's go in the house and call your dad." I kept saying, "He's going to kill me." She assured me that was not going to happen. I felt terrible and knew I was going to be in trouble. When Dad answered the phone, his response was very calm and he wanted to make sure I was okay. That made a huge impression on me that he must love me a lot to only be concerned about my safety at that moment.

I was always known as "Bill Mason's daughter." I guess people knew my first name, but I have always been proud to be his daughter (the one who looked just like Jayne).

As the years go by and he grows older, I get to repay him for raising me in a wonderful Christian family. The roles are reversing, but it is my privilege to take his hand now.

I used to worry about him falling asleep in church, but now I feel he gets a pass for all the years he has loved Asbury. I've always said, "He gets his best sleep in church!"

Love,
Peggie

Robin Mason Tanner

After Robin graduated from high school, she attended Oral Roberts University for a year then got married and had two sons. Robin married Ron Tanner, February 12, 1977, and the wedding was held at Asbury. I officiated the service. They have two sons, Ryan and Stephen. Ryan is married to Rebekah, and Rebekah brought her son, Noah, to the marriage. They live and work in the insurance industry in Oklahoma City. Ryan graduated from University of Central Oklahoma at Edmond. I get to see Ryan and his family two or three times a year. Stephen Tanner is not married and works in Tulsa as a welder after graduating from Tulsa Welding School.

The boys both played sports when they were growing up, and Jayne and I loved going to the games and cheering on the boys and their teams. I miss those days.

Robin is such a blessing and helps me in so many ways and in ways I probably don't know. I love spending time with her and her family.

From Robin

Bill Mason came into my life when I was one year old. I was living with my mother, Jayne, and my older sister, Peggie. After their courtship, Bill and my mom were married. I was too young to attend the wedding, so I took a nap at my grandmother's house. Some of the ladies from the church were watching over me during the time that Bill became my dad. I could have never known the father he would become. After a few years, Dad wanted to formally adopt Peggie and me as his own children. Our biological father did not want him to do that and said, "My daughters are all I have left." Dad respected his wishes.

Many years passed. Peggie had been married for several years. I had been married for about a year and our biological father died suddenly. Dad waited a respectful amount of time and again told our mother, Jayne, that he would like to formally adopt Peggie and me. After a time, the process was done, and Peggie and I were officially his daughters. The judge at the time said it was the first time an individual had adopted adult children so many years after the marriage. At the time and now looking back on it, Dad's decision to adopt Peggie and me was made out of true love for both of us and our mother. I think he also wanted to be legally responsible for us. Peggie and I knew when we were young that this new man in our lives was much more than that. Today, after benefiting from his love and guidance for more than 60 years, Peggie and I know that we were blessed when he came into our lives. Our mother Jayne was also blessed to be chosen and loved by a man who was willing to take on an instant family and the responsibility that it required. Dad is also an amazing grandfather. When our sons were younger, they both played a lot of sports. Mom and dad were avid fans of whatever they were doing. They were always at the games when it was too hot or too cold, rain or shine, cheering on their grandsons. Dad was also never bashful about complaining to the umpire about a call that he thought had been missed. But it was always a respectful complaint. My mother's life, my sister's life, my husband's life, and our sons' lives have all been greatly influenced and enriched from having Bill Mason as the patri-arch of our family. We have all truly been blessed.

Dad, I love you,
Robin

William Cameron Mason II

Cameron played football at Memorial. He went on to the University of Oklahoma for a year and a half, then he dropped out to start a business. Cameron married his high school sweet-heart, and I officiated the wedding. At some point in his career, Cameron ran a mobile operating room for fifteen years.

Cameron had a son, William Cameron Mason III, and we call him "Will." He graduated from the University of Texas at Dallas and presently lives in Frisco, Texas, and sells or-thopedic prostheses. He is married to Robin, and they are parents of my second great-grandchild, a girl born January 17, 2018. Her name is Emery Lane Mason, and everyone is crazy about that baby girl. Will and Robin are expecting a baby in February, 2020, William Cameron Mason IV.

Cameron married Adriane McGregory, March 22, 1997, in Fort Worth, Texas, and I conducted the wedding ceremony. Presently, he works for an engineering and consulting group in Frisco, Texas. Adriane is an insurance specialist.

Cameron and Adriane visit monthly, and our tradition is to have Saturday lunch at Coney I-Lander and watch football all afternoon. Then we go to church on Sunday. I love their visits and our time together.

From Cameron

First of all, I would like to thank Judy so much for taking all this time with my dad to put this book together. It has been very enjoyable hearing all the great memories from Dad and family friends.

My dad's consistency over my lifetime has been amazing. His faith is second to none. The time he spends in the Bible and in prayer for people is mind boggling. He has notebooks that he writes all prayer requests in. He prays daily for every request and never stops until there is a resolution. Over his lifetime, he has filled several of those notebooks. His patience and peacefulness are comforting to me. His role as a father has never wavered. He shows support for us in every situation. As some know, Dad always eats Saturday lunch at Coney I-Lander, and it is something I look forward to every time we come to visit.

Growing up, Dad dedicated so much of his time to the church. I remember Dad was often already gone from the house in the early mornings to visit and pray with people in the hospital before surgery. He missed family evening dinners as well. He is an amazing people person. Dad's busiest day of work was obviously Sunday. He loved his work at Asbury and only took a couple of weeks off a year. He always made our family vacations very special. Looking back, I had a fantastic childhood.

I deeply believe I'm living under a blessing from God for all the good works of my dad. I think scripture backs this up.

Proverbs 20:7
7A righteous man who walks in his integrity — How blessed are his sons after him. (NASB)

Psalms 112:1-3
1 Praise the Lord! How blessed is the man who fears the Lord. Who greatly delights in His commandments.
2 His descendants will be mighty on earth; the generation of the upright will be blessed.
3 Wealth and riches are in his house, and his righteousness endures forever. (NASB)

Psalms 1:1-3
1 How blessed is the man who does not walk in the coun-

sel of the wicked, nor stand in the path of the sinners, nor, sit in the seat of scoffers!

2 But his delight is in the law of the Lord. And in His law, he meditates day and night.

3 And he will be like a tree firmly planted by streams of water, which yields its fruit in its season, and its leaf does not wither: and in whatever he does, he prospers. (NASB)

My wife and I, as well as my descendants, are blessed to have my dad in our lives. The example of his life has been an excellent outline for me.

I can't express how much I love my daddy.

Cam

From Adriane

Bill married Cam and me on March 22, 1997. How many girls are lucky enough to have their father-in-law marry them? Cam and I went with Bill and Jayne twice to Branson, Missouri, for vacation trips. In August, 2015, Cam and I went to Lucerne, Switzerland with Bill. That is one of Bill's favorite places to visit, and I am so grateful for the time with Bill and our trips together. I'm grateful for him sharing his trips with us and the special time together. He always brought peace and joy to me and fun memories together on our trips.

Love,
Adriane

William Randolph Mason

Randy graduated from Memorial and went to Oklahoma State University for a year then went to work.

Randy married Hilde Milch at Asbury in 1982, and I officiated the wedding. Randy and Hilde had a daughter, Jennifer, who is married to Keith Envong. They live in Oklahoma City. Jennifer graduated from the University of Central Oklahoma in Edmond the same year that my grandson, Ryan, graduated. Jennifer majored in Journalism. She has worked as an intern for Oklahoma Publishing Company, and she worked in the headquarters for church denomination in Bethany, Oklahoma, where she received and edited information from all of the field churches of the denomination to distribute to supporters of the different ministries. Presently, Jennifer works in her father's business as the bookkeeper. Jennifer and Keith had my first great-grandchild, Jemma, born August 26, 2014.

Randy is a house remodeler and decorator/interior designer. He also remodels kitchens and bathrooms for people in the Oklahoma City area. He started with no experience and has done no advertising, and all of his business has come to him from word of mouth from his customers. He typically has five jobs going at the same time, and as he completes one or two, clients are waiting for Randy.

From Randy

I am the youngest child in the Mason family. Tulsa and Asbury United Methodist Church are the places where I grew up. Even though Dad was busy as the pastor of a large church, he still made time for his family. I learned kindness and compassion from him. He is not an outdoor person nor an athlete, but he and I joined Indian Guides where we fished and camped. It was fun, but we both agreed fishing and camping were not going to be our hobbies.

I think Dad was trying to teach us about the birds and the bees by having little animals. We started out with rabbits, cats, and dogs, then we had two ugly geese that honked loudly. I think the neighbors asked us to get rid of them.

I had always wanted a horse. Bill Claxton sold us a horse that he had purchased at an auction. He brought the horse to our house thinking we had a place arranged to keep it. The horse stayed in our backyard on 56th street until we could locate a stable. Again, the neighbors weren't too thrilled with that.

As I entered junior high and high school, I found I was good at gymnastics. I began at the YMCA, and then I became a part of the Coca-Cola gymnastics team. Dad was not able to attend my practices or meets, but Mom stepped up for that duty.

My parents always tried to make our growing-up experiences fun and wellrounded. It was probably quite trying at times since I was growing up with long hair and loud music. Mom and Dad never gave up on me, and I always knew how much they loved me.

As I grew older, I tried to show my love for Mom and Dad, and I try now to show my love to my dad. I live in Oklahoma City now, but I try to come visit at least once a month. We regularly talk on the telephone.

I love my dad so much and pray each day for his wonderful life to continue and to be blessed each and every day.
I am proud to be his son.

All my love, Dad,
Randy

GOD'S

CHOSEN

PATH

Part I
Birth to Oklahoma Military Academy

My Birth and Early Childhood

My name is William Cameron Mason. Grandfather Mason's first name was William, and they called him "Will." My mother's family name is Cameron. My dad's last name was Mason, and that is how I got my name. I was born June the fifth, 1927, in Lawton, Oklahoma.

Grandfather Mason was an early day physician in Lawton. I was the first grandchild, and he delivered me as well as my sister, Marilyn, three years later. We were delivered in our home like most everybody was that many years ago. Granddaddy Mason took care of us as long as we lived in Lawton.

Grandfather Mason was a loving man, but I was afraid of his second wife. His first wife had died of cancer. She was a nurse who had manipulated bedpans in those days. A cancer developed from a continuous motion of the bedpan lid hitting her hand. I do not know any of the details since I wasn't born yet, but they did not treat the cancer, and she died. My grandfather married my next grandmother, who also was a nurse.

Typical of nurses, the next grandmother always tried to tell my grandfather how to practice medicine especially when it had to do with me. I was prone to sties on my eyes, and Granddaddy would never lance them. That grandmother would say, "Will, why don't you cut that sty on that boy's eye," and he would say, "Because it hurts!" I hope I thanked him for that wise decision.

I do not have firsthand knowledge of this time of my life. All I know about my birth and early childhood has been told to me by relatives.

My Mother, Bertha Louise Cameron

My mother's name was Bertha Louise Cameron. I have never heard anyone call her "Bertha"; she has always been "Louise" as long as I have been old enough to pay attention to her name. My grandmother had a sister named "Bertha," so I assume that is how Mom got that name.

My Father, Roland Dent Mason

My father's name was Roland Dent Mason. I have no idea where the Roland and the Dent came from, and everyone's dead now who would know, so I have no one to ask. The summer before my dad's senior year at the University of Oklahoma (OU), my dad, mother, and I returned to Norman for the Fall term, and Dad received an electrical engineering degree.

One day my mom wanted to go shopping. Dad said he would look after me. While he was looking after me, he was also working on some of his class assignments until he heard me yelling and crying. He came outdoors where I was playing, only wearing a diaper, and I was covered with red ants. I had sat down in a red ant bed, and apparently the ants didn't like it and started stinging me. Someone had told my dad at some point in his life that for a red ant sting, bluing was a good treatment, so Dad poured a bottle of bluing all over my body. My mother came home to a very blue baby, and I survived.

My mother told me that when I was born and we went back to Norman for Dad to finish college, one day there was knock at the door and it was her brother, Alan. He was a high school student, and he said he had come to Norman for a track meet and asked if he could spend the night with us. He produced a box of Post Toasties from his jacket and told my mother he had brought his own breakfast. My mother invited him in, of course, and he stayed the night. Apparently, this was a habit of Alan's because when he was a student at OU in Norman, he would sometimes scratch on my mother's window screen in the middle of the night wanting to spend the night, and she always welcomed him. When Alan graduated from OU, he became an English teacher and took a position in the hills of Arkansas. There followed a life story about Alan that I feel compelled to make a part of this book.

When visiting Alan one time, I could see that his livelihood was rather meager. He loved classical music which provided him with the bulk of his entertainment. During my visit, I noticed that his record player did not have a conventional needle — rather he found a thorn bush that had large thorns. He would cut off one of the thorns to use as the needle for his record player. Believe it or not, I could not tell the difference between a commercial needle and Alan's thorns.

When World War II broke out, Alan enlisted in the Air Corps; he was trained to be a medical assistant and was assigned to The Fifteenth Air Force stationed in southern Italy. The crew's job was to be on hand when bombers (American and all friendly aircraft) were landing and badly in need of repair. Often, this involved one or more of the crew having to invade the burning aircraft to rescue any airmen who were still aboard. I learned after the war was over that Alan received an Air Force medal for risking his life on several occasions by rescuing personnel from the bombers.

Before returning to the United States, Alan made a career change deciding to become a medical doctor. When he returned to the United States, he had already taken undergraduate courses he would have to take to apply for medical school. He entered OU working on additional undergraduate courses and applied for admission to medical school.

He was accepted and within a short time began medical

school. It was about this time that Alan met, courted, and married Roberta Henson. She worked while Alan was in school. Their first son, Alan III, was born while Alan was in medical school. Alan was an exceptionally good golfer and played as often as time would permit. One Sunday, he was in the winner's bracket in a golf tournament, and his wife wanted to follow him around. Typical of my foolishness, I agreed to babysit their baby after church. I was dressed in my Sunday suit. I didn't know their pediatrician nor did I know anything about their baby. I only learned when I got to their house that they didn't feed Alan III with a bottle but with a shot glass. By the time they got home, I was down to my underwear as I had spilled milk everywhere except in Alan III's mouth where the milk belonged. It was at that point that I made the decision not to babysit anymore.

Roberta loved a cup of coffee before leaving for work and would often leave the cup half full on the breakfast table with cigarette ashes floating around in the coffee. When she returned home from work, she would finish that cup of coffee.

Alan was better than the average golfer and tennis player and taught me what little I ever learned about golf and tennis. Although I never was an accomplished participant in either sport, I enjoyed attempting to play with my friends. Upon finishing medical school and residency, Alan began to practice medicine in Muskogee, Oklahoma. One of the local pharmacists and Alan played golf together, and one day they were joking and the pharmacist said, "I'll pay for kilts and other parts of the Scottish uniform if you will play a round of golf in the uniform at the country club." Alan agreed. The pharmacist ordered the full attire, and Alan kept his word and played in his Scottish attire.

Unbeknownst to any of us, Alan was reading recruitment materials sent out by the Central Intelligence Agency (CIA). The result was that Alan signed a contract to work for the CIA. He and his family were sent to Bangkok, Thailand, to ostensibly be the physician for the diplomatic corps for the American diplomat as well as the King of Siam. They were able to secure a rather comfortable home while living in Bangkok; the house was completely surrounded by a high masonry wall. Three servants were employed: a groundskeeper, a housekeeper, and a cook.

Aunt Roberta was frightened by any kind of reptile. One day she felt the need to go out and talk to the gardener. On her way back into the house, she had to negotiate steps into the house where a large Cobra snake was stretched out and sunning itself. She could not persuade the gardener to kill the Cobra, but he used a long stick to throw the snake over the masonry wall.

Bangkok's residential houses had a number of laws pertaining to their ownership and care. One of the laws made it a criminal act whether intentional or an accident if the house was set on fire. Alan's son, eight-year-old, Robert, was playing in their garage and accidentally set it on fire. Dr. Cameron spent several hours securing Robert's release because the police had taken this young boy away.

Alan loved birds. When he retired from the CIA, they moved to Vienna, Virginia, and Roberta took a job as a secretary with the CIA. Alan had obtained a specialty in psychiatry and began a private practice for counseling. The house in Virginia was on a large piece of land surrounded by trees. There was a tremendous number of birds that gravitated to those trees. Alan felt warmly about those birds except one variety, and that was the blue jay. One day he got an idea of making a hole in the wall in his bathroom so he could point a .22 rifle through the hole in the wall and shoot at the blue jays. Sadly for Alan, the effect of shooting the blue jays sent many of the other birds away.

When Alan died, it was agreed that he would be buried in the cemetery in Wagoner, Oklahoma, where his dad had been pastor of The First Methodist Church of Wagoner, Oklahoma. I went to Wagoner to conduct the internment service for Alan. I arrived early and his sons had prepared a hole in the ground that was about three and a half feet long, and at one end, the hole made a right-hand turn. For the life of me, I could not figure out what the purpose of the hole was until his sons arrived. I asked, "What's this hole for," and they said they were going to bury Alan's five iron beside him. I had never interred a five iron before nor since.

After Alan died, Roberta had occasion to go to Wynnewood, Oklahoma, to visit her sister, Mary, who was quite ill. After being there a few days, Roberta became ill and died; Sister Mary died a few days after Roberta. Instead of having one funeral, we combined the services and had one service for two women. During the service, I read the eulogy and questioned when it read that Roberta had been a secretary for the CIA. Months after the service, one of her children told me that indeed his mother had worked for the CIA.

Back to Lawton and Dad

Dad finished school, received his electrical engineering degree, and we went back to Lawton. The Depression was on, and the only job Dad could find was with Public Service of Oklahoma (PSO) — the company that had the franchise for the electric service in the Lawton area. Some might remember that PSO also owned the ice dock. The electric company usually had the icemaking franchise and stored frozen items.

One day my dad was running the country roads in his truck where PSO had electric lines. He was carrying out his responsibilities and found a three-quarter ton flatbed truck loaded with watermelons stuck in a ditch. The farmer who owned the truck said to my dad, "If you get me out of this ditch, I will give you my watermelons." My dad knew that we loved watermelon, so he pulled the man out of the ditch, loaded up the watermelons, and we were fixed for the summer since we could use the PSO ice dock to keep the watermelons cold.

I do not know why, but Dad left the job with PSO when I was around six years old and opened a bowling alley on Main

Street in Lawton. I expect my Grandfather Mason furnished the money. I do not know if my dad had money enough to do that; nevertheless, I remember visiting it. They had regular-size balls and bowling pins as well as one or two bowling alleys for duck pins where the ball was the size of a grapefruit, and the pins were miniature bowling pins. I was so little that if I took the ball and tried to roll it down the alley to knock the pins down, it made it about two-thirds of the way down the alley before it gave out. I was too little to have the strength to make the ball go all the way.

At one point, my dad decided to try his hand at making home brew (beer). I was taken by the fact that he was making it in our bathtub which was surprising to me since that is not the ordinary use of a bathtub. I don't remember where I bathed during this time. He bottled his home brew in beer bottles and stored them in the top of a bedroom closet. In a few days and in the middle of the night, all of the bottles exploded. I heard the explosion, but I did not know what it was. It was quite a surprise. All of the clothes in that closet smelled like home brew for quite some time.

In Dad's bowling alley, there was also a shoeshine stand. There was room for two or three people to get on this stand and put their feet on little islands. If there wasn't much business, the fella who ran the shoeshine place would climb up there and go to sleep. I can remember being in the bowling alley one day when somebody took the man's shoe polish and put it on the sole of this fella's shoes and lit a match and set the shoes on fire. It didn't take him long to get down out of that shoeshine stand and do a little dance to put out the fire.

Next door to the bowling alley was a theatre, and one day I looked in the alley behind the theatre and there were three elephants standing there. The men taking care of them were hitting them with long leather straps. The purpose of that was to encourage the elephants to go to the bathroom in the alley and not on stage. As a little boy, I found that to be quite funny.

I developed Scarlet Fever and was cared for by my Grandfather Mason. Part of the treatment was to see that no one caught the fever. Anyone who came for a visit or to help mother with housekeeping could come in the front door. When they were ready to leave, they had to wash up in the bathroom and crawl out the bathroom window so as not to get Scarlet Fever. When I recovered from that, I was anxious to get back to waiting for my dad. I knew what time he would be coming home from work, and I waited on the sidewalk by our house watching for him to appear. When I saw him, I would run to meet him saying in a loud voice, "What did you bring me?" He always had something in his pocket — a piece of candy or something. My dad was a quiet man.

In 1932, I started elementary school. One day in class, my teacher came to my desk to help me with a problem. As she was leaning over to help me, I raised my head up and hit her in the nose, breaking her glasses. Rather than scold me, she comforted me since I was so upset for breaking her glasses.

The next-door neighbor's house across the alley had a fairly large hole in the foundation that held the house off the ground. Under that house lived a big white rat. The child who lived there and I learned that if we got some food and held it at the hole, the rat would come out and eat it; we had a pet.

In the neighborhood when I was growing up, I was a short distance from home. Someone had taught me to be afraid of gypsies by saying that they kidnapped little children. I saw some gypsies up the alley looking into the garbage cans to find what they could sell or use. I was trying to find someplace to hide. I saw a washing machine on the neighbor's back porch, and I crawled into that washing machine, and pulled down the lid. Every little bit, I peeked out from under the lid and when I couldn't see them anymore, I crawled out and ran home as quickly as I could.

We lived in Lawton until I was six years old and my sister was three and a half. In 1933, my dad was killed in an accident. He drove a car under a railroad freight car at night and it lodged under the railroad car and drug him a couple of blocks down the way, and the car caught fire. He was burned over most of his body and did not live long.

My Mother and Grandfather Cameron

My mom was quite young when I was born. When my father died, she was twenty-five, and she found herself a widow with two little children with no visible means of support. Her father was a Methodist minister, and she was the second of six children on the Cameron side. All of them had the opportunity to go to college. I don't know how times were economically for others during those days, but things were pretty slim in the Mason household. Dad worked and my mother did not.

My Grandfather Cameron was the pastor of the downtown Methodist Church in Lawton, and since my Grandfather Mason was one of the doctors in Lawton, there were lots of jokes about if my Grandfather Mason couldn't keep us alive, my Grandfather Cameron could bury us. Grandfather Mason could not keep my dad alive.

I didn't know what had happened to my dad until the next day, but someone took me to the hospital, and I remember standing by the bed. I didn't know it was my dad until someone told me. My mom was there; my dad was unconscious. He was completely wrapped in gauze. As a family, we stood around his bed; I didn't say a word, but I observed and listened. Plans were to amputate his leg since there was gas poisoning in his system — which is what took his life. My Grandfather Mason (my dad's father) said they waited too long. I had never been in a hospital before since I had been born at home.

I attended the funeral, and when it was over, we came back to our home. I used to cry every time I told this, but I don't cry anymore. However, I still tell it because I am deeply touched by it. We were back at our house, and my Grandfather Cameron (Papa) was in a rocking chair in our living room and my grieving Mother walked by. Papa took her by the hand

and guided her onto his lap, and he rocked her for a while. That's the kind of tender heart he had. I was exceedingly fortunate to have the grandparents I had except for that second Grandmother Mason who scared the fool out of me.

I didn't know Methodist pastors smoked, but after supper, Papa would go to his rocking chair in the sitting room, and he would take from his coat a nice, long cigar. He diligently trimmed it, and that's all I know about trimming cigars. Finally, he would get that thing ready, strike a match, get it going, and he would start rocking. That's when the good visiting began.

When I was older, my grandfather told stories about when he would go to Annual Conference for the church. Back in those days, Oklahoma had two Annual Conferences due to a transportation problem since they didn't have the rapid transportation then as we do now. But when it came time to elect delegates to General Conference, there was no politicking. Those in charge simply would learn how many delegates for General Conference needed to be elected by either the East or West conferences of Oklahoma. They would pray and ask God's guidance for who He would have represent the two Annual Conferences.

My Grandfather Cameron came to Indian Territory as a young pastor from Mississippi. I don't know how he came to be in Oklahoma, but he served small churches in Oklahoma, and when I would go to visit my grandparents, I appreciated getting to sit and visit with my grandfather. Much of what my expectations were and still are for a pastor and for the church were formed by my Grandfather Cameron.

As I have looked back on my life, I realize from the day of my birth, that God's chosen path for my life was to follow Him.

Mother Goes into Business

Mike Bryan was married to Gladys Mason, my dad's sister, and recently he had opened an office supply store. It was no wider than fifty feet by sixty feet. I presume that when Gladys and Mike were in Lawton for my father's funeral, my mother and my uncle, Mike Bryan, decided to go in partnership on this business. Mother bought a percentage of the business, and that meant we needed to leave Lawton and move to the Oklahoma City area as soon as possible.

When it came time for Mom, Marilyn, and me to move to the Oklahoma City area, we actually moved to Nacoma Park, which is a suburb of Oklahoma City. We moved there because we didn't have any money to pay rent, and we lived with my father's sister, Blanche, and her husband, Jack Needem. I found my aunt and uncle's home an exciting place to live since they had chickens, pigeons, a cow, and a garden — all of which I enjoyed. One day, a snake bit the milk cow on the udder. It didn't kill the cow, but part of the udder fell out since the snake venom killed a part of the udder. My Uncle Jack didn't like blue jays because they would get in his pigeon pen and kill the pigeons. There was always something exciting going on for a young boy.

I went to school one semester in Nacoma Park and met nice neighbors who became friends. Mother, Marilyn, and I stayed in Nacoma Park with family for about six months, then we moved to Oklahoma City where we rented a small place to live. By visiting business schools, Mother was able to find women who had come to the city to go to school who needed places to live; these women became our nannies — one at a time.

My uncle worked on the inside of the business, and my mother was an outside saleswoman and highly successful. Uncle Mike stayed in the store, and Mom went out making calls to sell office supplies.

There are two or three incidences that I have learned about after she died that heightened my enormous respect for her. The first person she called on was a physician in Oklahoma City. Since her father-in-law was a Lawton physician, she thought maybe he would be cordial. When she finally got in to see him, he chewed her out for taking his time. Mom said she walked from Second and Broadway to Twenty Third and

Broadway before she stopped crying, and from that she became determined that she was never going to let a man make her cry again. The second man she called on was an attorney, and his attitude was the opposite. He said, "I'll do anything I can to help you," and that happily picked up Mother's spirits.

Mom worked successfully in the office supply and office furniture business for over 35 years.

Papa Cameron and Rue Mother
in Tipton, Oklahoma

When I was in the fifth grade, I lived with my grandfather, Alan Cameron, pastor of the Methodist church in Tipton, Oklahoma. He eventually served all over the state of Oklahoma. My grandmother, Rue Cameron, had an uncanny ability for making up and telling fascinating stories. She would ask if we wanted the story to be an adventure, a mystery, or a scary story, and she would immediately begin to tell the story. The stories were always filled with Christian principles which influenced my life. When making biscuits, she put a little stool beside her and had me make a small batch of biscuits with her. Teaching me how to do for myself gave me confidence in my abilities. When the family was together, she always fried a chicken for our meal as sometimes my grandfather was paid in chickens. I hid under the table (I am sure everyone knew I was under there), and Rue Mother would always slip me the pully bone because she knew I loved the pully bone.

My Cameron grandparents had five girls, including my mother, and finally a boy, Alan, who was nine years older than I. Papa used to say to Rue Mother that "It is a good thing Alan came along or you would still be wanting to have babies." When Alan was old enough, he didn't want anyone calling his mother "Grandmother," "Granny," or any other name. He taught me to call her "Rue Mother," and subsequently everyone else in the town where they served the church called her "Rue Mother" too.

The bishop frequently moved my grandfather and his family, and I visited Oklahoma towns that I never would have seen had I not been with them.

One of my grandfather's churches was in Chouteau, and that is where my mother was born. That parsonage was so small that Papa was able to find a wooden carton that a piano had been shipped in, and he nailed it over a window of the parsonage, and that was another bedroom. I never heard any of his six children complain about the houses they lived in nor the churches my grandfather served. It was one of the happiest families I have ever known.

Tipton was a cotton town, and I never enjoyed anything quite so much as going in one of the cotton gins in Tipton where cotton seed is stored. A school friend and I would get up and play on a warehouse full of cotton seed, and later I learned that sometimes air pockets could accumulate, and I could have stepped on one of those air pockets and would have been buried alive. Nobody would even know I was in there. I didn't learn that until after I was grown. I never did fall in one of them, but that was God's path for me as He was watching out for me then.

A memory I have about Tipton besides the church was tremendous wind in the Tipton area. The parsonage was a two-story white frame house next to the church. When we would have one of those windstorms, my bedroom would sway back and forth, back and forth, and I thought that was such fun. Of course, the house always stayed upright, but sometimes I wasn't sure that it would.

My great-grandmother, Rue Mother's mother, was small in stature, and she, too, loved to make up and tell stories. One of my favorite stories that Miss Granny told was Billy Owl. When Billy Owl was a little baby, he fell out of the nest, and Mr. Fox was stretched out on the ground underneath the nest. When Billy fell, he fell right into Mr. Fox's mouth, and he gobbled him right down. But along came Farmer Brown carrying an ax, and he chopped Mr. Fox's tummy open, and Billy Owl jumped out. Here I am, 92 years old, and I still remember Miss Granny and Billy Owl. When Miss Granny told her stories, her head would shake back and forth, and I can still see her long earrings jiggling as she told her stories.

Sixth Grade at Cleveland Grade School in Oklahoma City

During my sixth-grade year, I was introduced to Boy Scouts, and I remained active through junior high school and earned my Eagle Scout Award when I was in high school. I remember trying to learn Morse Code and semaphore (a visual signaling system by flags or arms) and not enjoying either one, but I learned enough Morse Code to pass my Eagle Scout test. When I went off to military school at Oklahoma Military Academy (OMA) in Claremore, Oklahoma, I needed three merit badges to complete my Eagle Scout requirements. We had a father in our troop who traveled Northeastern Oklahoma, and he came by to see me three times at OMA to encourage me to get those merit badges. I'll never forget Mr. Karnes and the effort he made to make it possible for me to earn my Eagle Scout Award. The Court of Honor (when I received the Eagle Award) was held in a judge's chamber in Oklahoma City. My mother was presented my Eagle Scout Award since I was away in military school.

Uncle Roy, Wynnewood, and School

I didn't know this at the time, but Mom was concerned that I was going to become overexposed to women in our household because there was a housekeeper, Mother, my sister, and then me. I did not know all of this at the time it was happening, but Mother had four sisters and a brother. In the summer, I would spend a week or two with Aunt Mary, one of mother's sisters, her husband, Uncle Roy, and her family of three girls and a boy in Wynnewood, Oklahoma; I enjoyed that tremendously.

My Uncle Roy, an entrepreneur, owned a grocery store and a meat market.

I went to school in Wynnewood one semester in the seventh grade when my sister had developed an illness I had never heard of before called Saint Vitus' Dance. The only treatment for that was bed rest. Mom knew if I was hanging around the house, I would be pestering Marilyn, and she would not get any rest, so I went off to Wynnewood to school which was an interesting experience.

I had never lived anywhere but Lawton and Oklahoma City. In Wynnewood, I encountered five boys, and every one of them said they wanted to fight me because I was a city boy. I had come to their town from Oklahoma City, and they didn't like it one bit. I talked four of them out of fighting, but the fifth one I couldn't talk out of it. We had a fight; he whipped me pretty good, but after that everything was alright. This boy intimidated me because he always carried a knife called a "frog sticker." It is about twelve inches long, and when closed, it's about six inches. This boy walked around the streets of Wynnewood flipping that frog sticker in the air with the blade open and not even looking at it because he had done it so much that is was natural to him. It scared the fool out of me if I was anywhere near when that boy was flipping that frog sticker.

I had never experienced riding on a school bus to go to another town for a track meet or a speech contest, and I was able to participate in those events. I thought that was neat — especially when a good-looking girl sat by me either going or coming. I liked the coming back better because it was usually dark, and no one could see what was going on in the bus. After that semester in Wynnewood, I went back home to Oklahoma City.

Junior High School

My junior high experiences were the most outstanding of my formal education. Up the block from where we lived, there was a fellow named Pete Wheeler who became a dentist and was my dentist for a number of years. When we were in junior high school, he would walk down to my house on a school day and ring the doorbell, and I would get my books and join him. Pete and I walked across the street and picked up Jack Barry, then Russell Caston, on to Bill Clohessy, Jean Burnham, and we would wait at Jean's house for the Connor twins who came down about four or five houses from their house. We cut through and picked up Violet Ann Angerman, and then we walked one long block to Taft Junior High. We had more fun talking and cuttin' up. No one did anything they shouldn't, and a close fellowship developed over the years. When we arrived home from school, we changed clothes, put on play clothes, and headed up the street to meet in front of the Barrys, Castons, and Noftsgers' houses. We loved to play kick the can, throw the ball over the house, and football. Ann Noftsger played football right in the middle of all the boys. She was tough as nails, and she stood out since she was a girl playing football. When the Barry boys' dad came out and whistled his loud whistle, we all knew it was time to go home. In the summer months, when we would see the milkman and his horse-drawn cart coming, we waited on the curb for him to stop the cart where we were and give us pieces of ice, and oh how we loved those pieces of ice.

One of my memories of junior high is of the sport that I was successful in — track and field. As I look back over my years of track meets, no matter where the track meets were or who my competitors were, I realized that no matter how much publicity I received, I always came in second. I came to the place where I thought of myself as "ole second place Bill."

All of my close friends went on to Classen High School in Oklahoma City, and I went to Oklahoma Military Academy.

After college, Jack Barry opened an insurance agency, and I became a customer.

Jack taught me a valuable lesson. When I had a claim, Jack handled all of the details; I didn't have a thing to worry about. As my children became adults and needed insurance agents, I told them that they should do business with someone who knew them well so that when they needed those services, they would have the assurance their agents would take care of all the details and not put it on their shoulders. I taught them to select carefully the insurance agents chosen to write insurance policies, and let the agents select the insurance companies.

When I was Senior Pastor at Asbury United Methodist Church, Russell Caston's wife went to the effort to set up a luncheon for all of us who were in that close-knit group, and I am so glad she did. To attend the luncheon, I drove to Oklahoma City. Russell Caston didn't live long after that, and then Jeannette, his wife, died shortly after that. One at a time, most of those people have passed away. But the luncheon was such a gift and so much fun. I have been able to attend most all of their memorial services.

Cross Country Hitchhiking Adventure with Jim Owens

As mentioned previously, my mom was concerned about the feminine influence in our household, and when I was in the ninth grade, my mother started talking to me about high school. The summer after my ninth-grade year, I had my heart set on following the wheat harvest. Workers were paid five dollars a day, and that was more money than I had ever heard of. I was hoping to get rich that summer. I was going to come back home a wealthy man. One of my friends, Jim Owens, decided he wanted to go too. Mother wasn't all that thrilled about it, but after she had exhausted all of her reasons why she didn't think we should follow the wheat harvest, she finally said, "Okay, you can do it." I did anything but make big money.

Jim Owens and I started out by taking a bus to Guymon, Oklahoma. We missed the harvest there that had moved on to Kansas, but I was not to be discouraged. We hitchhiked to Woodward then on up into Kansas before we finally found the wheat harvest and found jobs. I was fifteen, and I knew I was going to clean up. There was a place in Kansas where farmers would go to look for men to work for them. I found this man who had a Caterpillar tractor that he used to pull his combine, and he asked me if I had ever driven a Caterpillar. I lied, "Yes, Sir." I had never been close to a Caterpillar. He hired me! The next morning, we were starting to work and that Caterpillar was making lines like a snake. For about a half a day, I couldn't drive the Caterpillar in a straight line to save my life. Driving a Caterpillar against the wind is good because all of that chaff and dust blow away from me. But coming back the other way, the chaff blew down my neck which was miserable, and I didn't like that at all. I worked three days and earned fifteen dollars, and the days included more work after supper when we would go out and shovel wheat grain into the farmer's silo. By the time we quit at 8 or 9:00 at night, that shovel felt as if it was at least as big as a tabletop. The size of that shovel didn't change except in my imagination, but it felt like it kept growing and getting bigger and bigger and bigger until I thought I was scooping up at least a half a barrel of grain at a time. I was old enough to be smarter than that, but I never was so tired at the end of the day in my life as I was after that. Jim and I both worked three days; he was on another farm. We met, and I said, "Jim, I'm not working anymore on a wheat farm." Jim agreed. I never worked so hard in my life. All my dreams about making big money went right out the window. Both of us were embarrassed to go home because I told all my friends about how much money we were going to make.

We asked ourselves, "Where are we going to go now?" We looked at our filling station map that we picked up along the way, and I mentioned that I had some friends living in Denver, Colorado. I thought if we hitchhiked there, Roy and Mary would take us in and feed us for a few days then we would move on. We hitchhiked to Denver, and one guy we rode with was skunky drunk; he sideswiped a car while I was sitting in the backseat of his car, scared to death. I had never been in a car before with a drunk driver. By the time we got to Denver, I was a nervous twit. I thought this guy was going to get us all killed, but we finally got to Denver and to the Leggetts' house about 5:00 in the morning. It was Roy Leggetts' car my dad was driving when he was killed. I said to Jim, "It's too early to ring the doorbell. We'll just sit here on the front porch a little while and wait until Roy comes out to get the paper." However, the neighbor came out to get his paper and wondered why these two rag tag boys were sitting on that front porch. He came over and wanted to know who we were and what we were doing. We told him we had come to visit the Leggetts, and he said, "Well, that's too bad because they are in Oklahoma City visiting the Masons." They had gone there to see my mother. I could not believe it.

Jim got out the map. We decided to hitchhike to Cheyenne, Wyoming, since we had ever been to that part of the United States. One of our hitchhiked rides to Cheyenne was in an oil tanker, and the truck had a flat. The driver told us to get under the tanker while he changed that tire. We assumed we were to get under the tanker since we would be in the shade since it was in the heat of the summer. Oil was dripping from the tank and into my hair, and before I realized it, I was pretty well messed up. When we arrived in Cheyenne, we found jobs since we were out of money. Every time we ran out of money, we found jobs. One time our jobs were tearing down an old brick building. That building was so old, I could take my fingers and pull the bricks out, but it was a job and money.

One night I remember we slept in a fire station. How in the world we got to the fire station, I don't know, but they let us sleep on the fire truck. I slept in the cab of the fire truck which I thought was pretty bad, but Jim slept on a ladder on the back of the fire truck. After seeing that, I decided the seat in the cab was pretty comfortable.

Every day we were gone on this trip, I wrote my mom a postcard, and I always leveled with my mother and told her where we were and what we were doing. Jim was doing the same, but he would kind of flower up the whole trip to make it sound better than it was. It never dawned on either one of us that as soon as our parents got our cards, they would call each other. The Owens lived only a few blocks from where we lived. We finally got into Cheyenne, and there was not much to do for fifteen-year-old boys. We took out the map again and decided we would go to Salt Lake City. We found the highway and got a ride, and in a couple of days, we were in Salt Lake City by evening. We went to the filling station to find out where the highway was that led to New Mexico because I had friends in Ruidoso, Harry and Dot Steinberger, and I figured if we got there, we could live with them for a while. The filling station attendant gave us directions, and sure enough a man was in the filling station filling his tank and said, "I'm heading that way boys, do either of you drive?" Jim told the truth saying, "Oh, I can't drive," and I said, "Sure, I can drive." We got in the car, and the guy got a half pint of whiskey and climbed into the back of the car, drank all of the half pint of whiskey and passed out while I drove the car. We had to get moving, and hitchhiking seemed like a good way to do it.

As I was driving along, I kept hearing a rumbling. I kept looking out the window thinking it was thunder, but there was a big moon and stars. I thought that was a little strange to hear thunder when it was a bright, moonlit night. I finally figured out that we had a flat tire. I got out and changed the flat. We had three flats that night before the sun came up. The guy who owned the car slept all through the night but finally woke up, and I told him what had happened. He said, "You boys go in and order some breakfast, and I'll get the car fixed. I'll come in and buy your breakfast." Instead of coming in and buying our breakfast, he drove off with our suitcases and left us there; we had nothing but what we had on. I was upset and distraught (those are nice words for how I felt). The owners of the place called the sheriff's office, and a deputy came out and talked to us and said, "Boys, it's not likely that we will ever find the fella who took off with your clothes." In fact, he said, "The chances of finding the man and your suitcases are zero to none." We began to realize that this was our destiny.

We started hitchhiking again as we still had the ambition to get to Ruidoso, New Mexico. I observed and learned while riding along the highways in New Mexico, in 1942, that there was nothing on either side of the highways until a little road would appear that went toward a little clump of trees about a mile from the highway, and that's where a farmer lived. When the man who gave us a ride in his pickup came to his road, he turned, let us out, and there we were on the side of the highway. Nobody stopped and picked us up, so we spent the night alongside the road. I happened to have some highway roadmaps in my back pocket, and we wrapped up in those maps to keep warm.

During the night, a military truck full of American Indian soldiers stopped. I was scared to death. I always wanted to be an Indian when I was a little boy, but I was scared of that truckload of soldiers. They were talking in their language as they got out of the truck and were looking at us. I whispered to Jim, "I'm going to play like I am asleep. I'm not going to wake up." Finally, they left, and I was never so glad. I may have been able to sleep some that night, but I'm not sure.

The next morning, I said to Jim, "I'm stopping the next car. I don't care what direction it is going, and we are going to ride with whoever that is." The next car that came by was going back the direction we had come from, and it was a 28-year-old pretty young lady — a school teacher. She had one bench seat in her car, so I sat in the middle, and Jim sat by the door and immediately went to sleep. I felt like somebody had to talk to this lady since she had picked us up — I needed to be polite. I tried to talk, but my head kept nodding up and down from exhaustion. I tried to talk to her, but I kept going to sleep. She took us back to the next town and bought us breakfast. Then she took us to her apartment in Albuquerque where she lived. She volunteered to wash what clothes we had. I let her wash my t-shirt, but I wouldn't let her wash my socks since they had holes in them; I was embarrassed for her to see the holes.

That evening, she took us to dinner and to a movie and let us stay in her apartment that night.

The next morning, she bought our breakfast then took us out to the highway, and we headed back to Oklahoma.

When we got back to Oklahoma City, I had just enough money to get that oil washed out of my hair at the barbershop and a shoe shine before I went home. At age fifteen, it might be surprising that I would care about what my shoes looked like, but I did. Before Jim and I left on this trip, Mother wanted me to go out to New Mexico to the Boy Scout Camp and spend a couple of weeks out there, and I said, "No, Mother, we are going to make too much money harvesting wheat. I can't afford to give the time to that."

Jim Owens would become the head football coach at University of Washington in Seattle.

My Clever Mother and Oklahoma Military Academy

Mother, talked about the idea of how I should attend military school in September. I could hardly wait to get there after making my big money working the wheat harvest which only lasted three days until I quit. Mother had arranged, and I don't know how she did this, but she had arranged for me to go to Claremore, Oklahoma, to Oklahoma Military AcademY for high school. My mother was quite clever, and I thought it was my idea. She took me there, and right after my arrival and check-in, I was taken to the barbershop on the campus and was given a burr haircut. When I arrived at Asbury United Methodist Church, I had a burr haircut. After all those years with a burr haircut, I decided I liked it and would keep it that way.

During the first semester at OMA, students were called "rabbits." Upper classmen harassed us, and anytime we left our rooms, we had to brace which meant that we had to stand erect with our chins against our chests. When we came to a corner, we had to do a square corner. When we went outside, we had to run everywhere and do square corners. I felt like that was rather childish, but I could do it. I had made up my mind that I was going to do anything an upper classman instructed me to do to show I could. I spent three years at Oklahoma Military Academy. World War II was on, and we were going to school three semesters per year. I finished high school and my first year of college by my 18th birthday.

While attending and living at OMA, I had a good time. What I mean by that is that I responded positively or affirmatively to the discipline that they insisted we follow. I was a disciplined type of boy, and in military school, I found I didn't have to worry about what I was going to wear. The bugler would blow a sound on the bugle that indicated that we were to wear no jacket at all, wear a jacket, or wear a heavy coat when it was cold. My life became easier and easier as the military dictated all that I was supposed to do which included Friday nights. We were to get electric buffers and make sure the hall was clean, the hallways and the floors in our rooms were shiny. Inspection was on Saturdays.

I had never heard of men wearing garters, but those were a part of our uniforms. When we fell out for formation, a non-commissioned officer walked up and down behind each one of us and reach down to feel the garter. If he felt it, he would snap it; if he didn't feel it, five demerits.

Every night we would have two hours to study, and if cadets tried to write letters or listen to the radio, or anything but study, we received five demerits. For every demerit, we had to either work or walk off one hour for each demerit. For my first demerits, I did the walking part in a bullring.

We had wooden rifles that we trained with. The government needed the real rifles so they made fake ones for those of us in military school. If cadets walked one hour in the bullring, one demerit would be erased. I got in trouble one time when I went out for football.

Sometimes the coach would keep us longer than it would take for us to go back to the barracks, shower, and get dressed to fall in for retreat. I received five demerits for being late. The coach, Tuffy Klein, had said, "I'll call the office and get them to erase those demerits," but I guess he forgot, and I had to work off those five hours.

The first year I was there, I played halfback, and there was no age requirement to qualify to be on the team. For example, one of the first teams we played was Chillicothe Business School, and the doors for the two locker rooms were side by side. I looked over and here came this bald-headed man out of the Chillicothe locker room, and I thought, "What have I gotten myself into by playing someone that was much older than I." Learning the ropes was sometimes surprising.

It was a mile from the campus to downtown Claremore, and when we had permission to go down to Claremore, I hit it as fast as I could to get downtown. The first stop towards downtown was a soda shop. There was a juke box, and we could get soft drinks, candy bars, and more. We would sit in there and play the jukebox and play like we were back home. Occasionally, I would go to a movie.

I also went out for wrestling. We had a wrestling match coming up, and I was a little bit overweight. The Will Rogers Hotel had a steam room, and I thought I could lose that weight. I had never been in one of those before, and I kept waiting for someone to tell me it was time to get out, and no one did. By the time I got out, I could barely make it back to the campus because I was so dehydrated from all the water weight I lost in that steam room. I had much to learn.

Distant Cousins, Paula Love, and J Bartley Milam

I had good fortune in that the woman who was the curator of the Will Rogers Memorial was a distant cousin of mine, Paula Love, who had been born with some kind of a crippling illness. She welcomed me to come over and relax in the little apartment that they provided the curator. I didn't have to stay in the museum. On the other side of the campus was another relative named J Bartley Milam who was Chief of the Cherokee Tribe on two occasions. I would go there to ride one of the prettiest white horses I had ever seen. OMA, was a Horse Cavalry ROTC Unit when I was there. I didn't realize it, but we were out of date with the Horse Cavalry. The Army was already using jeeps, tanks, and trucks. The horses were saved for parades. But here we were riding horses for military training at least twice a week, and I thoroughly enjoyed riding the horses.

We Had So Much Fun

On certain Saturdays, OMA would have a contest for students. Ten polo balls were put down at one end of the football field; we were at the other end with a gunny sack. The horse had no saddle — only a bridle. The starter would shoot a gun; we would run and jump on horses, ride down, jump off the horses, put polo balls in the gunny sack, jump back on the horse, ride back to the end of the football field, and we did that until we had moved all of the polo balls to the opposite end of the football field. Some of the upper classmen knew some tricks I didn't know right off, and they would ride up beside me and reach down and flip my foot, and I would fly right off the horse landing on all parts of my body. It was funny to them. It wasn't very funny to me, but they all laughed.

While I was at OMA, I was a cadet second lieutenant. One night, I had already gone to bed; we slept in double bunks. One of my friends came by my room after Taps, and he was the officer of the day. He said, "Bill, my girlfriend who lives down in Claremore is coming up and I'm going to meet her at this little pond down in front of our barracks, and she is bringing a friend with her. Do you want to go with me to meet the girls?" I probably thought about that for ten seconds, and I thought to myself, "If the officer of the day is down there, who is going to catch us?" I said, "Yes." I got up, put on my uniform, and off we went. We weren't there ten minutes when the faculty officer of the day showed up. I had forgotten to include him in the equation when I made a decision to go. I had no idea what that girl looked like since it was dark, but it didn't matter since we weren't there any length of time at all. I was busted from an officer to a private.

More Demerits

At Oklahoma Military Academy, if cadets got more than fifty demerits in one semester, we were kicked out of school. The school was always short of cadets and reluctant to kick anyone out. For being out of the barracks after Taps, I received 50 demerits and 100 punishment tours which is the same punishment with a different name, so I had 150 hours of punishment that summer. I mowed yard upon yard of grass and walked bullring after bullring to work that 150 hours off. I was diligent about working off my punishment since I didn't want it hanging on all summer long. After I finished, I went into the cadet first captain's room to report that I had finished that work, and he said, "You did that so fast, you can just do it again." I spent 300 hours mowing yards and walking the bull ring. I'm not sure what I learned from that experience, but I quickly moved on from the experience. I never did go down to the pond anymore — not even if the president of the academy had come to my room to get me. But the president had a daughter, and it was the responsibility of the first captain that she have a date for every dance that we had there. To make sure she did, the first captain would call one of us to his office and say, "You are going to take the president's daughter to the dance Saturday night." I didn't think I had a choice, so I took her to the dance which was quite an experience. I only did that once.

Good Grades

I made the best grades at OMA in all of my academic career, and the reason was one of the rules had to do with study hall every night for two hours. Every night after we finished supper and got back to our rooms, we had two hours to study.

The officers were serious about the study part. I don't know how anybody could help but make good grades if the study rule was obeyed for two hours every night. I obeyed it, and I felt pretty good about my academic prowess.

In addition to the punishment I received the night when I was caught out with my friend after Taps, I had been demoted and was confined to my room. The afternoon I was graduating from high school, my mother came to Claremore so she could see me graduate. She was aware of my demerits and my demotion, so she didn't have any surprises. Two of the orderlies of the guard marched me over to the auditorium where the graduation ceremony was to take place; they stopped at the curtains and let me walk across to get my diploma. They met me on the other side and marched me back to my room. All I could do was wave to my mother. They would not permit me to spend any time with her. That was the toughest part of the punishment.

My rank was eventually restored with all of my responsibilities.

After High School and First Year of College

I finished high school and my first year of college at OMA, and I went straight into the Army. On my 18th birthday, I went from Claremore, Oklahoma, to a camp somewhere in Arkansas to an induction center. The purpose of the camp was to clean us up, fit us for a uniform, give us all else we would need, and send us somewhere for basic training. I was there about three days, and a boy from Arkansas who I had seen hanging around who was there for the same reason said to me, "Do you want to know why they are keeping you here so long?" I said, "I sure do." He said, "So they can teach you to sign your name so you can sign the payroll and get paid." I had finished a year of college and knew how to sign my name, but I didn't tell him that; I thanked him, and he went on his way.

World War II Basic Training in Tyler, Texas

I was sent down to Tyler, Texas. I had heard of Tyler and that it was the Rose Capital. I came to understand that because I did a whole bunch of crawling in the sand there, and I gathered that roses like to grow in sandy dirt. The way the Army taught me to crawl through sand was that they had barbed wire about two feet off the ground. It was a large expanse of barbed wire, and we were to crawl from one end of it to the other end while they fired machine guns over us. That quickly convinced me that I had better keep my behind down if I wanted to get to the other end with my behind. I never violated the height of that barbed wire. One day, they sent us out into the field where they had dug holes in the ground on this big acreage. Two by fours with a sign on the tops of the boards were in each hole, and the sign was a target. They put some of us in those holes and the rest of them were way back where the machine gun line was standing. When they signaled us, we were to hold those targets up, and they would open fire. I learned to keep my head down too. On this particular day, they assigned me to one of those holes, and unfortunately that day I had severe stomach distress. I figured if they wanted to know if I had a problem, they would have asked me. When I got down in that hole, all I found was a rusty can, but I always carried with me a little booklet with paper that I could write notes in, so I was in pretty good shape since I could use those pages for toilet paper. Someone would command me to raise that target, and someone would shoot the machine gun; I would hold that target and pray. They kept us down there for a half a day. When I got back to the barracks, I told the sergeant my problem, and he said, "Well Mason, why didn't you tell me? I wouldn't have put you down there." My thought was, "Well, I've goofed again."

I had four school years of ROTC — two years of basic and two years of advanced. That wouldn't have made me Eisenhower's assistant, but even though I have never been tall, they should have recognized and appreciated my training. However, it didn't make any difference at all, and they made an old boy who was tall and good looking the platoon commander. He had been in Air Force training, but it didn't hold a candle to what training I had. Before our basic training was over, I was having to carry that new platoon commander's backpack; he never could finish a march or carry his own equipment. He flat couldn't do it. That fact did not seem to make any difference to his superiors that he was less able and equipped.

Officer Candidate School

I applied to Officer Candidate School (OCS), and they turned me down and said it was because my vision was not up to standard. I found out later on that the Army could fluctuate the requirements for OCS depending on the supply of lieutenants. They didn't need more lieutenants when I applied, so they passed me over. Up to that point, this was serious for me because I had planned to make the military my career. I had been in military school for 36 months and did well and enjoyed it. I thought it was what I wanted to do, but once they turned me down, I permanently forgot about the idea of being in the Army. It was not God's chosen path for my life.

Part II

Army to First Church Appointment

Aircraft Carrier USS Randolph to Naples

The war ended with the atomic explosions in Japan the last week of my basic training in August of 1945. It was interesting to me how the whole attitude and mood of basic training changed when the war ended. The lieutenants in charge of training were earnest all through our training until the war ended, then they spent all of their time telling jokes. They put us in bleachers out in the field and stood in front of us telling jokes. I was glad when it was time for me to get out of there since that didn't appeal to me.

Even though the war had ended, I still had twelve months to serve. After basic training in Tyler, Texas, I went home on leave before heading overseas. After my leave, I boarded the USS Randolph, an aircraft carrier that had been hit in the fantail by a kamikaze aircraft. I had never been on an aircraft carrier before, and the Navy had made only the necessary repairs to make the ship seaworthy; a troop carrier was made out of the USS Randolph. Bunks were placed on the hanger deck. I never did visit any other decks, so I don't know what they were used for. We were on our way from New York to Naples, Italy. I was fortunate to be heading to Italy and not to Korea as some of the others were.

There were 1,200 enlisted men (GIs) in this group and one

captain, who was in charge of the shipment of troops. Somehow or other, he picked me to be his assistant, but I didn't have much to do until the day before we were to dock. At that time, cigarettes cost five dollars a carton, and the captain said, "I want you to collect money from all of the men on this ship who want a carton of cigarettes. Then come see me and tell me the difference of how many you collected five dollars from and the 1,200 in the group, and I am going to buy the difference." I said, "Captain, may I ask what you plan to do with all those cigarettes?" He said, "When I found out that I was coming overseas, I decided I was going to sell enough cigarettes to buy a new Buick." And I'll declare if he didn't accomplish that on that one trip to Naples.

The toilet facilities on the aircraft carrier were not impressive. In a room as large as a basketball court, a trough had been built around the room and water was pumped from the ocean into the trough with some force behind it. The water went around three walls of the room and out into the ocean. There were pieces of wood cut as wide as the trough, and depending on the size of a GI's posterior, the boards could be adjusted to fit any size. These were the outstanding toilet facilities on this aircraft carrier. One day I was in there, and some old boy came in the door, and he had unrolled a roll of toilet paper. He put it on that stream of water and lit it. The force of the water made the toilet paper go around the trough while burning; whoever wasn't paying attention got a burned behind. That generated laughter, hoops, hollers, and squealing for those who didn't see the burning paper coming. I have never seen soldiers move so quickly in my life.

Midway across the ocean, we encountered a sizable storm. On one of my walks around the flight deck, I noticed that steel I-beams had been placed across the front of the flight deck in a vertical position right where the planes would take off from the ship to fly. I assumed that the I-beams were placed there to keep the GIs from walking off the edge of the ship. On another walk around the deck after the storm, I noticed the Ibeams had been bent backwards and flattened to the flight deck from the force of the heavy sea. That amount of force made a vivid impression on me, and I was thankful I didn't have to be on that flight deck during that storm.

When we landed in Naples, the military personnel stationed in Naples seized every opportunity to warn us to stay in the distribution center and not wander the streets of Naples at night. They told us all kinds of tales about being shot, stabbed, kidnapped, or killed if we went out at night. I decided that was not for me and stayed close.

After two short days in Naples, we were loaded on a train that took us north past Rome until we reached Livorno. There we left the train and were bused to the barracks where we would stay. My assignment was to supervise a group of German prisoners of war while they built barracks for a quartermaster battalion that would join us when the camp was constructed.

We were tested for tuberculosis, and the doctor said if the skin turned red where the shot was given, it meant we had tuberculosis (TB). I tried my best to find any and every medication to put on the test site to keep it from turning red. I did not have TB, but I did not want any questions or possibilities to have to go through that procedure again. I hid out and did all kinds of immature antics, but it was not going to turn red anyway because I did not have TB.

The captain sold enough cigarettes to buy a new Buick and had cigarettes left over. There were a couple of second lieutenants who decided they wanted to buy the cigarettes that were left, so the captain sold them to the second lieutenants. It was in January, wintertime, and those second lieutenants took those cigarettes to their room. They ran out of fuel for their big pot-bellied stove (which was how we kept warm). The only fuel they could find was the gasoline in large canisters strapped on the backs of jeeps. They took one of those canisters and used that gasoline for fuel for their potbellied stove. When they added that gasoline to the stove, there was an explosion. The explosion burned all of their clothes, all of their cigarettes, all they had except the bars on their uniforms. I couldn't help but think maybe poetic justice had been served since all of those cigarettes were burned up.

I learned that we had two warehouses full of German trooper skis that had been seized, and I had never skied before. I also learned I could go to one of those warehouses, get a pair of skis, check out a jeep, go up in the Italian Alps, and ski. The ski lift was a wagon bed; the wheels had been removed, and skids were fastened to the bottom of the wagon. This wagon bed had a rope tied on it that reached to the top of the ski run, and there were some Italian men at the top pulling that rope. As soon as we reached the top, they let it slide back down to pick up the next load. I was embarrassed that somebody would have to work that hard for an absolute novice like me to go up the mountain. I took ski lessons the first morning, and I didn't do well. I skied or more accurately fell down the mountain all morning long. I decided the afternoon would be better spent in the bar drinking Chianti wine. There happened to be an Italian actress and her entourage in the bar, and she invited me to ski with them that afternoon. What an idiot I was since I told her I would. I lost one ski as I was coming down one ski run, and I ended up skiing the rest of the way down on my bottom on the remaining ski that I had. That actress did not speak to me the rest of the day.

Engineering, G4, and Black Markets in Livorno, Italy

We didn't stay long in Naples. We were put on a train for Livorno, Italy, which was right on the coast. "Leghorn" is the English word for Livorno. The next town of any size was Pisa, about twenty miles inland. Once I had seen the Leaning Tower of Pisa, there wasn't much else to do there. After Pisa was Florence, about another forty miles inland.

I was assigned to an engineering battalion in Leghorn. My

dad had earned his electrical engineering degree from University of Oklahoma, so while in school at Oklahoma Military Academy, since I didn't have any idea what I wanted to do for a living, I thought an engineering degree would be a good way to go. I took several freshman engineering courses those two semesters at OMA which appeared on my college transcript. Unbeknownst to me, the Army read my transcript and in so doing noticed these engineering courses on my transcript and assigned me, an 18-year-old smart alec, to an engineering battalion. I didn't realize how fortunate I was because everyone else was being sent to where the fighting was happening. I went to Italy, and bless their hearts, the other GIs went wherever they were shooting at people. I remember being grateful for that turn of events.

Our job in Livorno was to build an American headquarters right on the coast, and we were using German prisoners of war to do the construction work. At 18, I wasn't a construction genius by any stretch of the imagination, but I figured out that digging a hole in sand on the coast and pouring concrete in it for a foundation would not last long. In the meantime, this captain who had financed his new Buick by the sale of cigarettes, called me on the telephone and said, "I would like for you to come work for me." I immediately thought, "This is my chance to not build in the sand." I didn't have any idea what he wanted me to do but I said, "Just send for me, and I will be right there." I transferred to G4 which was Supply. We were responsible for the supplies for the entire Italian peninsula. That was a pushover position. I had never worked in an office as a clerk. As a matter of fact, I had never worked much except for schoolwork. Our living and work conditions were unique. The Italians in Livorno had built a police battalion headquarters which consisted of offices and behind the offices were thebarracks for the policemen. The office building was three stories high, and the barracks were two stories high. The rooms where we stayed were quite nice and had tile floors. The nicest part was the Italian lady who kept the room that I stayed in clean. Every week I would buy a bar of Ivory soap that she would use to wash my clothes, and the other half of the bar was her pay. A half a bar of soap! She ironed my underwear and my socks; those Army woolen socks were sure nice to put on after they had been freshly ironed. It was a nice accommodation, and we had our own mess hall.

In the mornings, I would get up, go downstairs to have breakfast in my casual clothes, then dress in my uniform, and walk across the courtyard to my office where I would spend the day. I had learned about black market cigarettes and soon I found out the lady who cleaned our office was looking for American cigarettes. I started going to the PX once a week which was allowable and bought a carton of cigarettes. I think they were a nickel a pack, and I would put that carton of cigarettes in the file drawer right behind my chair, and the next day there would be twenty-five dollars in that file cabinet. I figured out right away that I didn't need all of that money, so I would put my salary, which wasn't much, in a savings account, and I would live off the twentyfive dollars from selling cigarettes.

The Army made available two hotels in Milano; one was for enlisted men; one was for officers. I remember one of the boys sleeping on the same floor where I was. This hotel was built around a courtyard and at the bottom of the courtyard, there was an opening that went clear to the top of the hotel. This guy was on the third floor and had fallen asleep on the inner wall of this atrium. He fell. Right at the lobby level, the glass panes were about six feet long, and he fell right through one of those glass panes. He didn't hit any of the metal on his way down that was holding it all together. He landed on the floor of the lobby in his underwear, but it didn't kill him. They patched him up, and he did all right.

I could go to Milan and spend the weekend for next to nothing. The Air Force ran an airline from Naples to Rome to Livorno or Pisa then to Milano and back. I could go out and get on an airplane and go to Milano, spend a weekend there, and fly back which I did on several occasions. However, on one trip, we left the airport at Pisa and the pilot couldn't ever find the airport in Milano. I thought there is no way the pilot could not find that big city. I went to the cockpit to help find Milano, but I could not find it either. Subsequently, I didn't make any more trips to Milano.

Florence was a little further away than Pisa, and we made several weekend trips to Florence and had the best times there which included the shops and shopping. Florence was closer to where I was living, and it was a fascinating city in that it was large enough to be entertaining and small enough that I could walk anywhere I wanted to go. Secondly, Florence was known for leather goods. The leather stores were fascinating to me to be able to look at all the amazing pieces of clothing they made from leather, and there were items that I could afford to send as gifts to my family. On one of my visits to Florence, I stayed in a pensione (a place to stay that is usually hosted by family). The elderly proprietor of the pensione told me about the leather shops, where to shop, and where not to shop. She told me about her husband who had served as a Naval Officer in the Italian Navy in World War II. She also gave me names and addresses of other pensiones in other cities that she thought I would enjoy. While staying in the pensione, I learned that cold water was piped into a porcelain tank fastened to the bathroom wall approximately two feet above my head. When I turned on the hot water faucet, a flame ignited instantly under the porcelain tank; then hot water was delivered to the sink immediately. I was impressed with that plumbing system.

When I took my wife, Jayne, to Livorno in 1964, she bought twelve pairs of leather gloves — short ones, medium ones, long ones, white, all kinds of colors. On that trip in 1964, we went from Florence to Venice and it was cold. I said, "Honey, why don't you put on a pair of those gloves," and she said,

"Oh, I can't do that! They're brand new!" She never wore a pair of those gloves. When she died and we cleaned out her chest of drawers, we found all of those gloves still in their white paper envelopes.

While I was in Livorno, coming back from lunch one day, I looked at a bulletin board, and there was an offer of a trip to five major cities in Switzerland, all expenses paid for sixty-five dollars. I was not the brightest boy on the block, but I can recognize a bargain, so I signed up quickly for the trip. On our way to Switzerland, which was north of Livorno, a guide came through with some little business-size cards, and we were to each draw one card, and that would tell us what hotel we would be staying in our first night in Lucerne. I drew a hotel called the Schweizerhof which meant nothing to me. As soon as I arrived and my bag was delivered to the room, I went back down and talked to the concierge and told him my mother's name, telephone number, and all the vital information because I heard that telephone connection between Switzerland and the United States was much better than Italy and the United States.

Unbeknownst to me, the eldest daughter of the owner of the hotel, two months earlier, had married a field artillery captain stationed in Germany. He was from Oklahoma City. I was the second person they had ever met from Oklahoma, and they took me in like a long, lost child. It was from that chance circumstance that a lifetime of friendship was built between the Hauser family and the Masons. I do not remember the number of times I went back to that hotel before I returned to the states as well as the number of times my family and I have been there since my first visit.

I wasn't a Christian when in Italy and in the Army. However, when in Livorno, I did go to church in proportion to how much trouble I might be in at the time. I found a civilian Christian church to attend, and it was a Zwingli Church. I had never heard of Huldrych Zwingli, the leader of the Switzerland Protestant Reformation and founder of the "Swiss Reformed

Churche." He was one of the early Christian leaders responsible for helping to develop organized churches in the southern part of Europe. This was God's chosen path for me at that time of my life.

In this small congregation, there was a German woman. She had come there looking for her husband who was a prisoner of war; she knew he was someplace in Italy. Everything this woman and her husband had owned had been destroyed by bombers, so she had nothing in Germany to keep her there. She began walking from Germany down through the top part of Italy, stopping at every prisoner of war camp looking for her husband. She came to Livorno and visited several German Prisoner of War camps until she found her husband. The Zwingli Church I was visiting took her in and provided a place for her to live and food to eat. Her only contribution to the church as far as I know was being an active part of that Zwingli congregation. I felt badly for this family that was keeping her because they couldn't get any sugar. However, I wore a fatigue jacket most of the time, and the fatigue jackets had large pockets. I found a cloth bag that fit into that fatigue jacket pocket, and I wore that to the dining room to eat. I would empty the sugar bowl in the cloth bag in that pocket, and when the bag was full, I took it to church and gave it to this family that was looking after this woman. As far as I know, that was the family's only supply of sugar that they could get their hands on.

I did make one trip to Rome, but I didn't go any further south than that when I was in the Army.

One of the cities I was able to visit often was Milan which was a fascinating city. I had never been introduced to classical music until then. There was an opera house in Milan, La Scala, that GIs could attend for virtually no ticket charge, and I would go every time I had a chance and listen to the music or whatever was being presented at the time.

Heading Home

It was early December, 1946, and it was time for me to go home from Italy. I had spent a year there and earned enough money to go home and finish college. When my tour of duty was finished, I almost got in trouble. I had a little more money than they paid me in my savings account since I had lived on my cigarettes sales, and I had to explain that. I don't know how in the world I ever did, but I satisfied their questions and they let me have that money to take home.

As I look back, I am grateful for my time in the military; my overseas experience was amazing. That tour of duty, a 12-month tour, was one of the nicest experiences of my life.

Even though it was time to go home, someone said they would make me a second lieutenant if I would sign up for four years. I said, "I heard every word you said, and I'm going home. I'm already enrolled at the University of Oklahoma for my sophomore year."

I boarded a Victory ship in the harbor in Livorno. Mr. Kaiser, a major industrialist in California, built Victory ships, and they were supposed to be for supplies. There were three holds — forward, center, and one in the back. The forward hold was filled with GIs who had broken the law while they were on duty overseas and had been convicted, and they were being sent back to serve their prison sentences. I was in the middle hold. The bunks were five bunks high, and we had to get in the bunks by rotation. One man got in first, and the next man folded the next bunk down, and the bottom of it touched the first man on the nose; then the next man got in, and folded the next one down, and this happened five times until all the bunks were filled with GIs. The first GI could not get out for any reason until every other GI got out and folded back the bunk that was on top of him.

Entertainment on the ship consisted of shooting dice. I've never won anything at gambling, but I watched to see which one of the guys in the circle was winning more often; I would bet with him. I did win a little money that way, but I have never used that "skill" again in my lifetime, but that is how we entertained ourselves coming back home.

We hit some pretty rough seas on our way to New York City. The front end of our ship came out of the water, and when it came down, it made a horrible crashing sound. Then the fantail (back end) would come out of the water, and the propellers (screws) would be completely out of the water and the ship would vibrate. It scared the daylights out of me; I didn't know anything about the ocean. In fact, when I lost sight of land, when we left New York on my trip overseas, I was scared. I had never before been where I couldn't see land. I had been on Grand Lake and a few of the great, vast bodies of water in Oklahoma but never on the ocean. The only time I ever got seasick was on that trip home.

Apparently, while that ship had been docked, they baked enough bread to stock it so as not to have to bake at sea, and they stored it in the freezer. When they took that bread out, it tasted like pork chops, and I couldn't eat it. I spent my days on the top deck, and if I closed my eyes, I could pretend that ship wasn't going up and down, up and down, up and down, up and down. Some of my friends would bring me hardboiled eggs since I could eat those. I lost ten pounds on the trip home.

New York Harbor

As we arrived in New York, I noticed an inch of ice had coated the entire ship; I had stayed on the top deck the entire time since I could not go below with the smell of that bread that tasted like pork chops. It had taken us ten days to come from Italy to New York Harbor. I was discharged from the United States Army at Fort Dix in New Jersey, and I was a pretty happy fellow. I was getting out of the Army; I was going home, and I was already enrolled in my first semester at the University of Oklahoma for my sophomore year.

I was having a little problem with my tooth. I went to the dentist at Fort Dix, and he said, "We better pull that wisdom tooth," and I said, "Okay, let's get it over with." But all this fellow could talk about while he was working on me was how he hated pulling teeth — oh how he hated pulling teeth. I finally blurted out, "Would you just pull that tooth and let me get out of here?" I shouldn't have talked that way since I was a lowly enlisted man, and I'm sure he was an officer, but that was one painful and bad experience I will never forget.

Cousins and Greenwich Village, New York

I had two women cousins who were both married and living in Greenwich Village at the time: Katherine Kaline and Betty Finley. I had some money that I had saved. It was near Christmastime, and I thought I would stay in New York a few days. I love jazz music, so I visited different places that my cousins recommended, and I heard some good jazz musicians and had a wonderful time in New York.

I don't remember who found my first date for me, but my first date was with Maria Pellegrino. I had just arrived from Italy, and I had a date with an Italian woman the first crack out of the box.

While in New York, on opening night of the musical, Most Happy Fellow, I attended with my cousin who was in the cast. After the show, we went to a restaurant to wait for the newspaper to come out with a review of the musical. The restaurant was so cloudy with cigarette smoke, I had to go outside to get some clean air. While on the sidewalk, I looked down the street, and here came a man at midnight with a duck on a leash. He was literally walking his duck. I could hardly believe my eyes. The musical received a good review, and the show enjoyed a long run on Broadway.

Home for Christmas and
the University of Oklahoma

I decided I had better go home for Christmas, so off to Oklahoma I went, and I started back to school in January. That meant that the first semester of my sophomore year was the spring term, which meant that I graduated at Christmastime.

I didn't know how much it cost to go to college. All I know is that I reported to the office on the University of Oklahoma (OU) campus the first of each semester where men and women going to school on the GI Bill were to go; I signed my name, and that would be the end of it. I signed my name three or four times, and that was it. I had to buy books, but I found out where I could buy secondhand books, and I found they worked as well as new books. I didn't actually need to buy any books because I didn't read them.

I do not know how I was assigned to a professor who became my academic counselor who was a specialist in city government. When it was time to enroll in classes for a new semester, I would show this professor the courses I had picked out, and he would say, "No, you don't want to take those classes." I took the courses that he enrolled me in, and when I graduated, I was qualified to be a city manager. I didn't even know where the office was where I could find a job as a city manager. But I knew I was going to go into our family business as soon as I graduated, so I wasn't that concerned. It used to embarrass me to tell people what my degree was, but at 92 years of age, it takes more than that to embarrass me now.

When my Grandmother Cameron would come for a visit when I was a newborn, if one of my father's fraternity brothers was going to visit our house, my grandmother would pin my father's Sigma Nu Fraternity pin on my shirt. As a baby, I was indoctrinated about Sigma Nu Fraternity. I grew up with the thought that when I entered college, I would become a Sigma Nu. It was natural when I entered the university to become a pledge in the Norman Chapter of Sigma Nu. My dad had lived in the same fraternity house where I lived while I was at OU. The lady who came to clean the chapter house every morning had been there when my father was. If someone borrowed the cleaning lady's sweeper, she would stand at the top of the stairs and yell, "Mrs. Kirk wants her sweeper back." Most of us were quite prompt to return the sweeper.

One of the pledges' responsibilities was to check a list on the bulletin board with the names and times of the members who wanted to be awakened. It was a surprise to me that some who had put their names on the list would protest when I would wake them up. I assumed since they were adults that they would be prompt to pop out of bed, but some of them were not. They would protest saying they didn't actually need to get up, and sure enough if I would walk away, I would get a good chewing out for failing to get them out of bed and on their way to the shower.

I thoroughly enjoyed the times when the fraternity members would go to a sorority house and serenade the girls. The fraternity members would stand outside and sing, and the girls would hang out the windows and not only enjoy the singing but would join in with us. When serenading the girls, the boys who had girlfriends in the house would call out, "Throw out your bras!" Some of the girls would acquiesce to the requests, and bras came flying out the windows. The guys laughingly gathered their trophies; we left and went home.

My first attempt at skiing had been in Italy, however, I "majored" in skiing in college. I worked in a men's clothing store in Norman that had a shoe department, and I was able to buy some Bass ski boots there and rent skis in Colorado. Several of us from my fraternity on Thanksgiving, Christmas, and other holidays would go to Colorado and ski. I loved every minute of it.

I learned some marriage tips during my first attempt at skiing in Colorado. The place where we stayed, Bertherd Pass Inn, was owned and operated by a German couple who had come to the United States from Germany. The husband ran the bar, and the wife did everything else. She got up in the morning and fixed our breakfasts, and as soon as we left to ski, she cleaned up our rooms, and I had never seen anything like that in my life. They were a delightful couple that I truly liked and enjoyed. The husband had a special drink that he had concocted; he called it "Gersplitzin." I finally got the nerve to ask what that meant, and he said, "I don't know. I named it after all you guys who go out in the morning and ski and come in and are so sore you don't want to go out in the afternoon, so I fix you a Gersplitzin and you can go to the bar and drink." I learned that the drink had no alcohol at all. It was mostly ginger ale.

The men's clothing store where I worked was Leo Garner's Men's Shop on Campus Corner, and I almost broke even every month when my commission almost equaled how much I had bought in clothes. I found out that when neckties came in that I liked, I could sell those suckers like nobody's business — and shirts, sport coats, whatever if I liked them.

One time I was given a sales award from the owner of Garner's. The award was a case that held a fifth of whiskey and a bath mat with the outline of two women's breasts. The awards were given at a stag party. The rug was hung on the wall, and before the evening was over, both of the breasts had been cut off with pocket knives by cowboys in attendance and taken for souvenirs.

There was a well-appointed barber shop in the back of the store. One day while working at the store, a man came in looking for a haircut. I told him to go on back and have a seat and I would be back to take care of him. But there was no one to cut his hair. I finally had to go back there and tell him I was just teasing him and the shop was actually closed. It is a wonder he didn't sock me in the nose.

After traveling in Europe, I decided foreign language should be a part of my college course schedule. I had already decided previously, that French would be what I would study if I took a foreign language. On my first day of French class, I was delightfully surprised that my French teacher had recently come to the United States to teach here. Her name was Jeanine Corteone. During the second week of classes, I invited her to go with me to a performance at the Fine Arts Center at OU, and she accepted my invitation. It was a delightful evening, but when we left the performance, we found it was raining. She told me that her dress was made of paper. I was perplexed. I didn't have an automobile, and we had walked to the Fine Arts Center and had planned to walk home. We made it back to her house, and thankfully, her dress did not dissolve. I made a good grade that first semester in French, but she left the university to go to another university to teach. Her brother came from France to teach second semester. I must confess I did not make as good of a grade second semester as first. She gave me good grades because she liked me; he didn't particularly like me at all. Two semesters of French ended my foreign language pursuit.

I should be ashamed of myself, but I was a senior in college before I figured out what I was doing at OU. By the time I was a senior, I was inspired to volunteer to serve on different committees. However, committee chairmen would look at my records and say, "We don't need you now; you're leaving here right away. We don't have time to train you. We will find someone younger than you." I didn't make a single contribution to any committee at the University of Oklahoma before I graduated. That was a regretful state of affairs for me.

College for me was a true learning experience which sounds so silly to say since that's what I was supposed to do in college. But I didn't learn that until my senior year.

Beginning my Business Career

When I graduated in December, 1950, I immediately went to work in our family business, Bryan Office Supply and Furniture. I decided I was having too much fun in my job to go back to Norman to get a diploma with that huge crowd that always shows up at graduations, so I wrote a letter and said, "Why don't you just mail my diploma to me, and we'll call it even?" — and they did.

I found that selling office supplies was rather normal for me to do. I had been in and out of the business when I was growing up with odd jobs like sweeping out, dusting office furniture, and delivering merchandise — none of which encouraged me to go into business, but just before I graduated, my mom spent the summer in Lucerne, Switzerland, visiting with the family that I met when I was there in the military, and I worked for her while she was gone by calling on her customers. I think Mother's customers were all concerned, at least those who knew Mother well, that they needed to convince me to go into the family business, and they were successful. I never had so much fun in my life as calling on those people. My mother's customers had become her good friends, and because of those friendships, the customers encouraged me to like doing her job while she was gone. All of them were exceedingly kind to me hoping to influence me to go into the family business.

I remember a time when one woman needed a pair of hose, and she didn't have a way to get to the department store, but she gave Mother the money and asked if she would pick up a pair of hose for her. Mother was pleased to do it. Mother didn't have a car, but she walked to deliver the hose to her good friend and customer.

Mother started and conducted her business without the benefit of owning an automobile. It was after World War II that Mother bought her first car. When I graduated from college, Mother gave me a car. I was able to start business with an automobile and did not have to ride street cars, buses, and walk like my mother did when she began her business career.

I began building my own customer base, but it took years to accomplish. Friends and acquaintances recommended businesses and individuals that I might call on to establish a business relationship. That was the most successful way I found to add new customers. I also found that if I was enthusiastic about the products we had to sell when I called on a customer, I could talk about older or newer products that the customer was unaware of and convince them the product would help them conduct their businesses more profitably. I loved helping people in their businesses.

I also found that when I became a part of an association

related to our business, it helped me establish new friends and new customers. For example, one of the organizations I joined was called the Sales Executives Association. Everyone in it was selling something, and some of them could help me with issues I didn't know anything about, and I could help them by calling on their companies or others they might recommend. Another club I joined and enjoyed was called the Bachelors' Club. This was a group of single businessmen, and we held meetings and fun social activities.

I had been reared in Epworth Methodist Church. Over the years, I developed close friends who were for the most part older than I. They were interested in my wellbeing, and some would recommend that I call on their friends and business associates as well.

I joined and later became president of the district organization for office supplies, National Stationers Association, and as president, I recommended we have conferences at Western Hills Lodge.

All of my business experiences were invaluable and good training for me as a pastor. God had me on His chosen path for me.

My Sister, Marilyn, and Her Husband, Tom

During the course of my mother's life, she was married three times — outliving her three husbands, and my sister married once. Marilyn Rue Mason Black was my sister, and Tom Black was my brother-in-law, and he was a pistol. Tom was an excellent golfer. From the time he was a young boy, he and his dad won all of the Father and Son Golf Tournaments in Oklahoma City for years. Then Tom grew old enough that he won them for himself. While in the Navy, it was discovered what a good golfer he was, so he was assigned to the Admiral's Office Staff so he could play golf with anyone the Admiral wanted to entertain.

Toward the end of my mother's life, our lives became a little tense. Mother and Marilyn lived next door to each other, and Marilyn had an intercom. One day, Marilyn was at Mother's house cleaning ice off of Mother's front porch. She slipped, fell, and hurt her back. Tom called me on the telephone. All of the years when I would call Marilyn, he never said a word to me. He always answered the telephone, and when he knew it was me, he would say, "Marilyn, it's your brother." And that was the end of our conversation. But the night he called me, he said, "Your mother is dying, and my wife is worn out. Get your butt over here and look after your mother." I said, "Tom, I'm on my way." He spoke clearly about his feelings. He is the only man that I have ever seen in my life that when I would visit, he had a drink in his hand all the time. He would walk around the house and pass through the kitchen where he had a bottle of bourbon, and he would pour bourbon into a glass of beer and keep walking. I never saw him drunk, but he enjoyed his bourbon and beer.

Victor Hauser (from Switzerland) Visits Oklahoma City

When I was a single man and working in Oklahoma City, the only son, Victor Hauser, of the family that owned the Hotel Schweizerhof in Lucerne, Switzerland, came to Oklahoma City because his elder sister, Irene Chandler, lived there, and she had arranged for him to have a job for a year at the Skirvin Hotel for the experience. We made a family decision that Victor would live with me since I didn't have a roommate at that time. Victor was a good friend and an interesting person due to all of his European childhood and young adult experiences.

One evening after he had been in Oklahoma City for a while, Victor and I invited a handful of our friends to come to our house for cheese and bread fondue. Victor was a good cook; the fondue was excellent. Victor completed his commitment to the Skirvin and returned home. He had met a girl, named Wy, during his travels to Johannesburg, South Africa, and before my next trip to Switzerland, Wy and Victor had married. During subsequent trips to Switzerland, I met and got to know Wy, and we became good friends. Together they had three sons. Each one of their sons works at the Schweizerhof.

On my last trip to Lucerne in 2015 (with Adrian and Cameron), the two boys who are in management at the hotel were in Miami, Florida, on vacation; the other son (in charge of the landscaping and grounds) was there, and we had a good visit. Although we missed the other two boys and Victor, we had dinner with Wy. Victor had passed away May 1, 1999. One night he came home from work at the hotel and died.

The Billy Graham Crusade in Oklahoma City

By the time I entered seminary, I had graduated from college and had worked in the office supply and printing business for twelve years. The first five or six years of my business career, I was not a Christian. My Grandfather Cameron was a Methodist minister in Oklahoma; my mother was a Christian, and she surrounded me with people who loved me and who she wanted to have an influence on my life; they were all Christians. I knew all the words about salvation, but it wasn't in my heart. One night after work, my mother and a couple who were friends of mine, came by my house after work for a drink. We began talking about the Billy Graham Crusade that was in Oklahoma City at that time. The crusade was for an entire month. The Graham Crusades seldom ever lasted that long unless it was someplace like New York or London. But the four of us were so curious about our friends who were going night after night after night to the fairground to the crusade that we decided we would go. We went to the crusade, and that night, Billy Graham preached on the scripture about the wide road and the narrow road. That scripture is about Jesus talking to some people one day, and He said that life is like two roads. There is a wide road, and many people travel it; there is a wide gate, and those who go through the wide gate spend eternity in hell. But there is a narrow road, and not many people take it. At the end is a narrow gate, and not many go through, but for those who do, they spent eternity with God.

The Narrow and Wide Gates

13 Enter through the narrow gate. For wide is the gate and broad is the road that leads to destruction, and many enter through it.
14 But small is the gate and narrow the road that leads to life, and only a few find it. - Matthew 7:13-14 (NIV)

When Mom and my two friends went home after the crusade and I went to bed, my life passed before my mind's eye, and I could see that everything about my life as far as any sense of value was concerned was a part of the wide road. And for the first time in my early twenties, I did not want to spend eternity in hell.

Praying to Accept Jesus

As a bachelor and in my bed at home, I prayed and asked God to forgive me of my sins and to take away my bent for sinning. I turned over and went to sleep. The next day when I woke up, emotionally, I felt on top of the world. By the third day, all of the alcohol in my system had left my body. I felt like an athlete, and I was not one, but I felt strong physically, mentally, and emotionally.

Jesus Changes My Heart and Life

I was an outside salesman, and I spent every day calling on customers. I had a list of customers I called on Monday, on Tuesday, and so on. I found out that some of my friends had been going to the crusade, as quite a few of them had committed their lives to Christ sometime earlier in their lives. Every place I went, I heard talk about the Lord Jesus Christ and what He had done or was doing in the lives of people. I quickly realized I had support among my friends and grabbed hold of it. As time passed and I began to mature some, I wondered how these people had put up with me all the years that I had called on them and was not a Christian. I never did ask any of them because I wanted to start anew without discussing my past that they knew enough about.

I cannot say how important the next four years were in my life. Before Jesus became real to me, I was concerned about who was having the next party and if I were invited. Now, I became concerned about who was having Bible Studies in their homes at night. My friends realized a change had come in my life and they were supportive.

Much later in my life and during another crusade that Billy Graham was conducting, a friend of mine who knew Billy, arranged a time and place for me to meet him. We were to meet at a specific location in the large building where the crusade was being held. My friend took me to the place a few minutes early. Soon Billy Graham came by. We were introduced. I was surprised but touched that he remembered my name. I reminded him about the one evening during the last week of his Oklahoma City Crusade where he spoke on Jesus' story of the wide and narrow roads. He said, "Yes, I remember that." I told him it had a life-changing effect on me. He said, "Yes, our friend told me about your conversion experience." Billy has encountered a vast number of people whose lives were changed by a sermon he preached, and those individuals thusly entered the ministry. However, with all that he had going on, it was still gratifying that he knew my name and my story of conversion. He was dressed in a conservative business suit. He wanted people to remember the Lord Jesus Christ, who he presented and proclaimed, not Billy Graham.

Billy Graham continues to be a part of my life today by the work of other Christian groups that he has helped along the way. The Billy Graham Evangelistic Association is a vital and dynamic influence for Jesus Christ in our world. It is an arm of outreach that I support. Additionally, there are hundreds of Christian organizations that Billy Graham has been a part of and has influenced through these Christian efforts. I have never met but I follow the work of Billy's son, Franklin Graham. I am gratified that Franklin is always motivated to want to talk to people about Jesus Christ.

I believe that television will make Billy Graham immortal. For generations to come, people will be able to watch Billy Graham Crusades that were filmed forty to fifty years ago. I happened on to one of Billy's older crusades while flipping through channels on February 16, 2018, and I was blessed by the opportunity to hear Billy preach again.

Joe Blinco, was an English Methodist pastor. He was a part of the Graham Crusade Organization. One couple knew he was going to be coming through Oklahoma City, and they began to call their friends to come over, serve refreshments, and Joe Blinco would speak to us. Evening after evening was spent with groups of Christian people in Oklahoma City. Instead of serving alcohol, they served coffee and tea. I cannot begin to say how spending more evenings a week praying and studying scripture helped me grow in my newfound faith. Joe Blinco's personality and character were such that I responded affirmatively to his teaching. He was one of the outstanding Christian leaders who touched my life. When Jayne and I were newlyweds, Joe returned to Oklahoma City to speak in churches that had been active in the crusade. Jayne and I were hungry for time with Joe. His schedule was so full that coming to our home for breakfast one morning was the only way he could meet with us. The time we had with him that morning was one of the richer experiences we had with a Christian leader. Joe was born in England and told us he was from a poor home without God. His father was a miner. Joe told us that his mother had a conversion experience. Joe eventually became an associate evangelist with Billy Graham.

Meeting and Marrying Jayne

In 1958, I was 31 years old when I met and married Jayne Hazel. My mother had decided that I would be a bachelor forever and certainly have no children. She had sort of accepted that as her plight in life.

One day I was talking to Bill Flesher; Bill and I were both bachelors. We each had a hand in starting the Sooner Ski Club at OU which was about snow skiing and not water skiing. The purpose of that club was to bring groups of people together who wanted to go skiing, help make trip arrangements, and get them on their way. Between ski trips, we had parties and social events. I was talking to Bill one day and said, "Bill, who do you suggest I take to the ski party." He said, "Why don't you call Jayne Hazel." I said I thought that sounded like a good idea because I remembered hearing that Jayne and her husband, Bob Hazel, were considering a divorce. However, before Jayne and Bob Hazel got a divorce, I took it upon myself to go visit them. I had heard there were some marriage problems, and I don't know what in the world possessed me to do it, but I went by to see if I could help save their marriage. I can't believe I did that, but I was sincere about it; it was not a joke. Bob and I had grown up together in Epworth Methodist Church in Oklahoma City; we were in the same Sunday School Class from the time our mothers started carrying us until we went off to college. We were not best friends but friends nonetheless. When Bob and Jayne were married, they had Peggie. Bob's conduct was such that Jayne had pretty much made up her mind that she was going to get a divorce, but she didn't want to rear an only child. She knew that the marriage was not going to last, but she had Robin anyway. She proceeded with a divorce from Bob. When I started dating Jayne, Robin was about thirteen months old, and she was the cutest little girl I had ever seen in my life, and Peggie was a beauty at six years older.

Jayne and Bob had divorced, so I acted on Bill's idea to invite Jayne to the party. She accepted the invitation, and we had a good time. We were both 31 years old; she was born in

January and I was born in June; she was six months older than I. We started seeing each other every day. After work, I would call Jayne to see if I could come over. She always said, "Yes." The little girls were so well behaved and absolutely marvelous about going to bed at the reasonable hour of 8:30 p.m. Jayne and I would visit in the living room, and I stayed until about 10:00, then I would go home and go to bed. Driving home one evening, I realized this was kind of wearing me out, since we would talk until 10:00 p.m., then I would go home and not get to bed until about 11:00. One night when I got home, I called her and said, "What would you think about going steady?" She said, "I hadn't planned on dating anybody else." I was a salesman, and I thought I better ask for the order and not settle for going steady, and I said, "How 'bout let's get married?" She said, "I think that's a good idea." I went from late hours in her living room to being engaged in one fell swoop with a proposal over the telephone.

I asked Jayne after she agreed to marry me to not work outside the home anymore. She had taught school for one year, and she almost said, "Yes" before I could get it out of my mouth. She didn't like teaching school. I appreciated having her home with the two girls, and then nine months after we were married, we had our first son, Cameron.

Jayne and I came from different parentage. I came from an affectionate family; when we saw each other, it was hugs and kisses. When we said "goodbye" it was hugs and kisses. In Jayne's family, they shook hands; "How do you do; it's nice to see you." There was no hugging and kissing but instead, "Glad you could come, and we will see you again." I thought surely if we were married long enough Jayne would break down and be more demonstrative to me, but none of that ever happened. I didn't realize how much influence parents can have over their children.

We were married in Nichols Hills Methodist Church where Jayne was a member. Mother was a member of that church, but I was still a member of Epworth Methodist Church. I had accepted some volunteer jobs in the church that would carry over to the next year; Jayne transferred to Epworth, and we went to that church until I fulfilled my obligations; then we went to Nichols Hills Methodist Church. I never will forget the first time I visited Nichols Hills Methodist Church. The Sunday School Class that Jayne was a part of (she loved that class and the teacher) met in the basement. I walked in and I could barely see across the room for the cigarette smoke. That was a new experience for me — smoking in church. Over in the corner was this fellow named "Johnson" playing piano, and he could have made a living playing piano at a bar. I liked the music he was playing. I nudged Jayne and I said, "Tell me where we are." She looked at me and said, "What do you mean?" I said, "Is this a nightclub or a Sunday School Class?" Fortunately, she smiled.

Jayne and I Were Married

It was funny to me how we decided the date we wanted to get married. Years ago, the lodge at Fort Gibson Lake by Wagoner was fairly new, well known, and full all the time. I thought I would like to spend our honeymoon at Western Hills Lodge, and Jayne was in agreement since it was a popular place back then. I was able to get a reservation on a Wednesday, so that's why we were married on a Wednesday. Peggie was the flower girl and wore a pretty dress that made Peggie even more beautiful. The pastor married us, and Jayne's mother had a nice little reception for family members and close friends. We have some wonderful pictures of Robin and Peggie. Friends from the church decided not to take Robin to the church since she wouldn't know what was going on, so they had Robin take a nap during the wedding. After the wedding, we went to the house and Robin was so cute. Jayne's mother had Robin all dressed up in a little white frilly dress; her hair was nicely combed. Jayne's father had given both of the little girls a necklace. My sister, Marilyn, was Jayne's Matron of Honor, and my brother-in-law was my Best Man. I never did get that brother-in-law of mine to be cordial.

Jayne's Father, Bose McFarland

Our wedding reception was held at Jayne's parent's home. Jayne's father was Bose McFarland, and Jayne's mom was Mildred, and she talked all the time. She could talk while breathing in, and I had never met anyone who could do that. It was seldom that I ever heard Jayne's dad say a word. But one day he had the chance to talk, and he told about their honeymoon experience. They were married in Muskogee, Oklahoma, and after the ceremony, they went to someplace in southeastern Oklahoma. The hotel they stayed in was a two-story wooden structure, and the sheriff buttoned down the town when it was time to go to bed. On their honeymoon night, Mildred put on her gown, and Jayne's dad, Bose, was sitting on the window sill while looking intently out at the beautiful night through the window. Finally, Mildred said, "Bose, aren't you coming to bed?" He said, "Mildred, my mother told me that this is going to be the most beautiful night of my life, and I don't want to miss anything." I thought that was so funny that I began to tell it in every group we happened to find ourselves, and Bose loved to tell the story too.

Our Honeymoon

We arrived at Western Hills Lodge after the wedding for our honeymoon, and we had a wonderful time there. It indeed was a beautiful place. After we checked in and went up to our room, in fewer than ten minutes, there was a knock at the door. There stood a bellboy with a rollaway bed. He said, "Mr. Mason, I have a rollaway bed for you." I said, "I don't want a roll-away bed." "Well, Sir, this order says I am supposed to bring this to your room." I said, "I don't want a rollaway bed." I had never been married before, but I thought we were supposed to spend the first night together. I almost never convinced that fellow that I did not want a rollaway bed. In about another ten minutes there was another knock at the door, and I had left a suitcase down at the desk which was a legitimate interruption. About twenty minutes later, there was another knock at the door, and I told Jayne, "I'm not answering that door." I don't know what the person wanted, but they did not get a chance to talk about it. I suspected some of our friends were up to some tricks.

Vintage Jayne

We had occasion to return to Western Hills on several opportunities. One year when I was in the office supply, printing, and office furniture business and before I was called into the ministry, I was president of the National Stationers Association in the northeastern corner of Oklahoma, and we had a convention or conference at Western Hills Lodge. During a meeting, someone came rushing into the meeting room and said, "We can't get our car started; could some of you come out and help push us away from the curb?" Jayne and I went outside along with several others, and Jayne said, "I'll sit behind the wheel and steer, and you all push it out." We were pushing with all of our might, and the car was not budging. Finally, Jayne realized that when we started pushing, she was putting her foot firmly on the brake. We all had a good laugh. We finally convinced Jayne to keep her foot off the brake, and we got the car out.

Jayne also had an interesting method of crushing cookies or crackers when crushed cookies or crackers were called for in a recipe. She would put the cookies or crackers in a plastic bag, take it to the garage, and roll back and forth over the bag with the car. She called it the Radial Tire Method.

Back to Work

After our honeymoon, we went back to business. I leased my house to Neil and Pat Hill, friends of mine, and then eventually I leased it to my sister and her husband, but I had moved into Jayne's house where the family was established. We determined it was better to move one person than three. Eventually, I sold my house three years later.

For me our marriage with our two precious girls was like

a glorified, happy party. Mother was ecstatic not only to gain a daughter-in-law but these two little girls as well. Marilyn was happy, as she was married and had three children. Life and business were going well. During our first year of marriage, I learned we were expecting our first child together. When Jayne said we were having our first baby, I was elated. When William Cameron Mason II was born on May 19, 1959, I was incredibly happy to have a son and a brother for our two girls. Peggie and Robin were tickled to have a baby brother in the house. I loved taking care of Cameron when I got home from work and on the weekends. I loved helping with the laundry and holding Cameron. We didn't have a dryer when we were first married, so I loved hanging up the diapers and the clothes outside; it was pure pleasure for me. Both of the girls enjoyed it when I would hold, hug, and kiss them too; there was plenty of attention and affection. One day, Jayne called me at the office as I was heading home, and she began to tell me about a fourbedroom house that was on the market, and she would like me to look at it on my way home from work. There were two women who were partners in a real estate firm, and one of them was a close friend of Jayne's mother, and the other was a close friend of my mother's. When I arrived at the house, both women were there as well as Jayne. In my mind, I had decided there was no way we could afford that house, but I was pleasantly surprised how the real estate women had figured by selling my house and Jayne's, we would have more money than we needed for a down-payment. Wheels were set in motion that evening for a new home for the Mason family. I have few memories of moving to that house, but I have vivid memories from the time we left the house.

Life continued to be beautiful for the Masons. Married life was fun, and when planning social and family events, I learned to include Jayne in the discussions. Jayne initiated most of the social events, and we discussed and enjoyed planning the fun. As an illustration, Jayne suggested joining a dance club, and

I thoroughly enjoyed that. Jayne was a good ballroom dancer, and my mother had taught me to dance. Jayne and I loved dancing together. We didn't plan vacations when the children were young, but we loved being together where we were.

In late 1960, Jayne told me we were expecting another baby. William Randolph Mason was born May 27, 1961. Peggie was born in May of 1951; Robin was born in April of 1957; Cameron was born in May of 1959. There were two years between each of the last three children. My experience taught me that two years was the proper length of time between having children. Naturally, I was pleased to have another son, but I was concerned for Jayne because she had to spend the last three months of her pregnancy in bed with varicose veins. Thankfully, we had the help of our housekeeper, Xie (pronounced Ex-eee), to get us through those difficult three months, and Xie continued to help us every day until we left Oklahoma City. Jayne and I were incredibly busy with four young children even with the help of Xie.

My First Annual Conference as a Lay Delegate

We had a good experience at Epworth Methodist. Jayne's first husband's mother was a member at Epworth Methodist. As I mentioned, after my year of commitment at Epworth was completed, we transferred our memberships from Epworth Methodist Church to the Nichols Hills Methodist Church. Jayne's father sang in the church choir, and her mother was active in women's ministry.

My mother and my sister were both members of Nichols Hills, and by moving our memberships, the families became closer. There was a man named Dr. McBride at the church, and he was Jayne's first husband's grandfather, and Dr. McBride had been the lay delegate from Nichols Hills for about twenty years. Unbeknownst to me, our pastor said that Dr. McBride had spoken with him and suggested that I become the lay delegate for Nichols Hills for the next Annual Conference. The fact Dr. McBride would do this for me was a compliment. For the next three years, I served as the lay delegate for Nichols Hills Methodist Church. I learned how the Methodist church operates and that preachers like to talk. God's path for me was becoming clearer.

Our bishop, Angie Smith, had been the Bishop in Oklahoma for 25 years. He knew both pastors and local churches from firsthand experience. If he felt that a pastor had talked long enough during the Annual Conference, he did not hesitate to say, "You may be seated." The pastors did not like that, but they could not do anything about it. As a businessman, I appreciated the Bishop keeping the business rolling. I was favorably impressed with his method of conducting the conference.

Interestingly enough, there was a Bishop for China (not Communist China) that was a close friend of Bishop Smith and his wife. Bishop Smith (elected Bishop in 1930) would go to China about once a year to hold meetings. Bishop Smith was a dominant leader, and his wife was dominant as well. I found it interesting that the leader of free China, Shang Kai Sheck's wife was also a world-known presence standing by her husband. Bishop Smith coordinated with Shang Kai Sheck when in China. And while he was there, he had a favorite shirt tailor. He ordered six shirts to be sent to him every four months. Bishop Smith was no taller than I am and rather heavy. Tailor-made shirts were a blessing to him, but I never did understand how he could wear out that many shirts that quickly.

God Called Me to Ministry

Jayne had just had our fourth child, Randy, and I came home from work one afternoon and told Jayne that I had something I wanted to talk to her about. Jayne said, "All right." I told her that I felt God was calling me into full-time Christian service, and I wanted to leave business, go to seminary, then serve a church. Jayne said, "I just have one question. Are you sure that you couldn't be a full-time Christian as a businessman and continue what you are doing while serving the Lord? I said, "No." I explained to her that the call that I had and understood was to be in the ministry.

When I first felt God leading me in this direction, I immediately had three reasons that were excellent reasons that this was not a good idea. I thought, "How in the world can I earn enough money to send four children through college." And God said to me, "You remember your Grandfather Cameron sent six children through college." Grandfather Cameron, a Methodist pastor, never served a church that paid him a salary that came close to paying for six children to go to college. So that erased that objection. Another objection was my concern of who would succeed my uncle and my mother in the management of our business since I was the only male in the family. I can't remember the third objection, but that is the way God dealt with me. When I told Jayne that I definitely felt that God was calling me into full-time Christian ministry, she said, "Okay, we'll do it."

There were two goals I wanted to accomplish before I was ready to say publicly what we had decided to do. First, I needed to sell my interest in the business. I had no sense that I could continue to own my shares in the business and have my mother and my uncle running the business as senior stockholders. I called my aunt and uncle who had moved out on an acreage right outside of Yukon and told them I needed to talk to them. Jayne and I drove out there, and I had cooked up in my mind a fabrication if my uncle said he was not going to buy my interest in the business.

It was pitch black in their backyard; we talked about everything under the sun — or the moon — except about why we were there. Finally, my aunt suggested to Jayne that they go inside and fix some ice cream for us. While they were in the house, I thought, "This is it." I told my uncle the truth about why I felt called to the ministry and what I felt I wanted to do, and it seemed like he was silent forever. He spoke up and said, "Bill, your aunt and I will do everything we can to support you." He went on to tell me that he had felt called to the ministry as a young man, but he turned God down. He said, "I have never forgotten that, Bill." My uncle bought my interest in the business.

When Jayne was so agreeable about my desire to follow God's Will for our lives, I wanted to be as equally considerate of her as she was about to leave our home and business so I could attend seminary. The Methodist Church has eleven seminaries in the United States. I began to list all of the locations where seminaries were located, and the moment I said, "Perkins School of Theology at Southern Methodist University (SMU) in Dallas, Texas," Jayne said, "That's it!" Jayne had attended high school in Dallas, and for her it was like going home.

The second task I felt needed to be accomplished was where would a family of six live in Dallas, Texas? I knew that I needed to get busy finding a satisfactory location. My desire was that it would be a home located as close to the campus as possible. We decided on the nearest weekend that we could both be away, and we went to Dallas to look at houses. It was a strenuous experience, and we found nothing that I felt could accommodate a family of six that was within our budget. Discouraged, we returned to Oklahoma City on Sunday evening. On Monday, I went to work as usual. When I came back to our store at noon after making sales calls to write up the business I had produced that morning, I learned that there was a long-distance call from Dallas for me. When I returned the call, it turned out to be the secretary of the Dean of the Seminary. After a brief introduction, she began to tell me about a house, and I listened attentively as it sounded better and better as she described it. I thanked her and told her I would like for my wife to see the house and she could be there the next morning to which the secretary said, "The decision must be made today." I knew that Jayne was having lunch with some of her friends at a shopping mall near where we lived. I called the mall manager's office and asked for Jayne to be paged so I could tell her as soon as possible about this house. In the meantime, I had called Braniff International Airlines and made a reservation on the next flight to Dallas. Then I called Aunt Catherine to see if she could pick up Jayne at the airport, take her to see the house, and take her back to the airport. Jayne called me right away, and when I explained the call from Dallas about the house, her flight reservation, and Aunt Catherine was on standby, Jayne said, "I can't go today." My question was, "Why not?" to which she replied, "I have to take the cleaning lady to the bus" to which I replied, "I can do that."

Jayne went to the airport, Aunt Catherine met her, and Jayne leased the house for three years on the spot and we lived happily ever after in Dallas. By the way, Jayne was home in time to prepare our supper. Right away, Jayne said to me, "I would sure like to have a portable dishwasher and a disposal for that house in Dallas," to which I replied, "We are going to have a garage sale, and the proceeds of the sale can go towards those two items." Lo and behold the amount we made from the sale was the exact amount needed to buy the portable dishwasher and the disposal. We made the decision to move ourselves from Oklahoma City to Dallas which meant that Jayne's car and mine would be packed full including the top of Jayne's station wagon; my mother and stepfather said they would help as well as good friends, Roy and Mary Leggett. My good friend at work, Jim Pyle, was in charge of the truck delivery of merchandise we sold, and he said, I'll rent a truck and pack everything that won't go in all the cars in the truck." Imagine the shock of our new Dallas neighbors when all of these vehicles and a truck pulled up to the front of our new home. My stepfather, Howard Stephens, decided that he would set up the swing set in the backyard; the lawn had not been mowed in a couple of weeks, and he was eaten alive with chiggers. I felt terribly about that for him.

One of the features of this new home was a screened-in porch across the back of the house. My mother had purchased a nice wooden box from one of her customers. It had been built to transport the casket of a child. That beautiful and wellmade wooden box was placed on the screened-in porch and filled with our children's toys.

Beginning Seminary

The house was located two and a half blocks from the seminary. All of my classes were held in the two classroom buildings of the seminary, so each morning I had the choice of walking to class, riding my bicycle, or driving my Volkswagen. At that time, there was no public Kindergarten in the schools, so Cameron, our first boy, either rode on the back of my bicycle or in the Volkswagen since his school was right next door in the Highland Park Methodist Church. His Sunday school teacher was named Mr. Warnick. He loved little children, and he especially loved Cameron. Mrs. Warnick was the Perkins School of Theology librarian in charge of the Wesley Section. She helped me time and again to find the proper books when I was required to write a paper regarding John Wesley. She knew the books that were the favorites of the theology professors. She had read all of the books and knew exactly what I needed in my research. I remember one paper I submitted that was returned and looked like a chicken had red ink all over its feet and had hopped up and down all over my paper. There were spelling errors, grammar errors, and sentence structure problems. On the last page, the professor wrote, "The best part of your paper is the reference section."

Our new home was a three-bedroom house which was adequate for us. One bedroom was for the girls, one was for the boys, and number three was our bedroom. There was one bathroom.

Jayne was exceptionally good at making rules, and when the Cuban Crisis occurred, I came home from class one day, and Jayne said, "I'm out of money." I said, "Okay, but what did you spend it on." She said, "I have baked six dozen chocolate chip cookies, and I bought several containers of water." Silly me said, "Do you mind telling me why we have all of this water and all of these cookies?" She said, "Well, the Cubans are going to bomb us, and the fallout will reach Dallas." I said, "All right." I couldn't think of anything to say or do to counteract that, but we decided we better figure out some way to store all of this water. It occurred to me that if the portable dishwasher could hold water while it was washing dishes, why couldn't it store all of this water? We began filling that sucker with the water, and pretty soon we looked across the floor, and water was running all across the kitchen. I didn't think about the dishwasher having an overflow valve. So here we were on our hands and knees, mopping up water and laughing.

Our neighbors were both friendly and helpful. On one side of us was an older couple who had a daughter. Jayne and this daughter had gone to high school together in Dallas. This older couple filled the roles of our surrogate grandparents while we were in Dallas. They were kind, and we appreciated them. Across the street was a couple about our age, and he was a practicing attorney. They had two boys, and our children played together. We maintained that friendship for a number of years. I don't know what happened to Jim and Mary Ellen, but he was quite a successful attorney.

Chapel was a weekly occurrence in school. The faculty would take turns delivering the sermon in Chapel. I began to hear interpretations of scripture that I disagreed with, and of course I heard the same in lectures in classrooms that did not fit with my understanding of the Christian faith. At that time in the 1960s, professors were drawn to the teachings of German theologians. Some of these professors moved to Germany to complete doctoral degrees that were highly influenced by the German theologians. These professors then returned to the United States, found positions in Protestant seminaries, and taught the fashionable Rudolph Bultmann theology. If students had good academic backgrounds since the draft was still in force, some students with good academic backgrounds were interested in pursuing liberal theological degrees to avoid the draft by attending seminary. The rules were loose; if applicants had good academic backgrounds, that was a good way to avoid the draft.

I didn't buy into that liberal teaching. It was not that I was such a prodigious Bible scholar, but it did not seem right to me.

The first year in seminary, I thought every well-prepared Methodist pastor should have a command of Greek and Hebrew. My academic counselor told me that I did not have a language aptitude, but I thought I could handle Greek. I lasted two weeks in Greek Bible Study. I had to surrender because I was not doing anything but studying Greek. I was so grateful that Perkins allowed me to go the English language route. Some seminaries required that students take Greek and Hebrew, but at Perkins, we had a choice of taking Greek, Hebrew, or English Bible Study. The English option saved me a ton of grief.

One of the first people I met in seminary was Mike Clayton along with his wife, Ann. They had recently moved from Arkansas to Dallas and were living in a dormitory for married couples without children. Mike had graduated from the University of Arkansas with excellent grades and had been on the university's varsity football team. Mike's father was a Methodist pastor in Arkansas, and Ann's father owned a household furniture manufacturing business in Arkansas. Mike and I became friends, and he offered to help me learn how to study again since it had been a number of years since I had graduated from the University of Oklahoma. Mike was kind and patient with me and certainly was able to help me immeasurably in reading for retention and writing the papers seminary students were required to complete. Early on when we met, Mike told me one day that he had been given an academic scholarship for that school year. My interest was aroused and I asked him, "How did you do that?" He proceeded to tell me the name of one of the administrators responsible for scholarships. It was that administrator's job to discern who would be given scholarships, and he offered Mike a scholarship. The next day after learning this, I made an appointment to see the administrator. After I introduced myself and gave him a brief background of my business experience, call to ministry, and my wife and four children, I told him I had come to talk to him about applying for a scholarship to which he replied, "You have one." I left his office walking on air.

One of my first semester classes was New Testament. I knew that I needed that course, but I also felt like if I knew anything regarding subjects I would be taking, it would be New Testament. The instructor of the class that I was in was a Presbyterian minister who had been replaced at his church and did not have another church appointment to go to. It turned out he was employed by Perkins Seminary to teach New Testament. As the semester moved along, it was obvious that the instructor's method of teaching was by intimidation — making us feel like fools. As the semester continued, we learned his wife was expecting a baby, and there was tension at home. When I took the final exam, I flunked the exam and the class.

I was so shocked by that, I thought I might be sent home. Fortunately, I had a good visit with my counselor, and he convinced me that the next semester I should enroll in New Testament again but under a different teacher. I took his advice, and that semester I made a "B-." Students learned that the birth of the former instructor's baby was imminent. Our wives gathered up a good amount of infantwear and gave it to them several weeks before Christmas. That seemed to have a settling influence both on the instructor and the student body.

During my first year of seminary, I was assigned to do visitation evangelism. That was something I enjoyed, and I would have stories to tell Jayne about people I had visited. Most all of them were people who had visited Highland Park Methodist Church, and I was sent to call on them in their homes.

One of the activities we enjoyed most was a Sunday School class for those who taught Sunday School on Sundays. I wasn't a regular Sunday School teacher yet, but I did teach from time to time. Since I had been assigned to work for Highland Park Methodist Church, Jayne and I attended those Sunday School classes for Sunday School teachers. Usually the president of Southern Methodist University taught that class which began with dinner and continued on with his lesson. During that time, our children were wonderfully cared for with recreation and Bible stories. The children enjoyed going which was a blessing for Jayne and me.

I went to seminary thinking that everyone in seminary would be a born again, spirit-filled Christian. Wrong. I thought at least the faculty would be born again spiritually. Wrong again. I was in a class of about twelve students. We had a paper assigned to us, and we were to present our paper; the other students in the class would critique it. There was one student in that class who had come straight from college to seminary. It was his turn to critique my paper, and he said, "I hate your guts so badly that I couldn't say anything good about your paper." And I thought, "Where am I?" Jayne, as my counselor and confidante, got an earful when I went home and dumped on her for at least two hours. She graciously listened and said, "I love you," and we went on with life.

At the beginning of my second year, one of the associates at Highland Park, Don Benton, was assigned to Spring Valley Methodist Church in Richardson, Texas. He asked me to come with him and to continue doing visitation evangelism. I agreed. That brought into our lives the mother of the senior pastor's wife, Mrs. Benson. Occasionally, Jayne would have a Circle meeting in our home and Rosy Benton, Don's wife, would bring her mother, Mrs. Benson. The Benson family was quite well to do; they lived in the Valley in South Texas. Mrs. Benson would never embarrass anyone, but she loved to bring gifts to Jayne. I remember one time she gave Jayne a pair of gloves. When Jayne tried on the gloves, she found a generous money gift stuffed inside of the gloves. Another time she was in our home, the next morning, when I took the shaving cream out of the medicine cabinet, there was a large bill under my shaving can. Sometimes after church, Mrs. Benson would ask the head usher for the leftover bulletins. The usher asked her, "What do you do with these church bulletins?" She said, "When I fly home after my visits, I open my airplane window and throw out the bulletins when we are over the country club golf course."

One Christmas, I was taking part in the Christmas celebration, and two people in the front pews jumped out of their seats and came rushing toward the altar, and I thought they were coming after me. However, some of the flammable Christmas decorations on the altar had caught fire, and they were rushing up there to put out the fire. There was never a dull moment for me.

One night I was given some cards of people I should call on that evening. I went to one home and was warmly welcomed inside by the father of a family. We had a wonderful visit. He had visited Spring Valley Methodist Church, and he asked me questions about Methodism and Spring Valley Methodist Church. I thought I had struck gold and thought he was truly interested in becoming a member. He told me at the end of the visit that he was in charge of the Mormon congregation in the Spring Valley area. He wasn't interested in our church at all.

One of our church members was the manager of an automobile air conditioning plant, and he noticed I was driving a Volkswagen, and it was not air conditioned. This fellow said, "Bill, let me put an air conditioner in that Volkswagen for you." That was a wonderful gift for the Texas heat. When it was time to leave Dallas, I sold that Volkswagen to a church member. Then I went to AAA and ordered a Volkswagen convertible that we would pick up in Zürich, Switzerland, and we drove that Volkswagen almost 10,000 miles in Europe before we returned to the states.

My last semester in seminary, I needed one more grade

point, so I joined what was called the Seminary Singers which was a choir group. If I made all the rehearsals, I would make at least a "C," and that would be one more grade point. It turned out to be pure fun. I didn't make any of the trips with the choir since I did not have any business doing that with a wife and four children at home.

One of the girls in the choir fell in love with another New Testament professor named Victor Furnish, who was one of the liberals but a kind man. Someone in the choir wrote different words to a familiar hymn, "Blessed assurance, Victor is mine," and it went on like that saluting the fact that she had won his heart. She did not have to worry about getting a church appointment; she was going to be married to Victor.

There is at least one evangelical pastor on the staff of Perkins School of Theology, William (Billy) Abraham. He arrived at Perkins while I was a student there, and the last I knew, he was still there which I think is miraculous. I don't know why he would want to stay, but he expressed the desire to stay at Perkins so there would be an evangelical voice on the campus.

For me, seminary was both exhilarating and discouraging. I think I was most fortunate to have had years of business experience before seminary. My business experiences served me well not only in seminary but also as a local church pastor.

During my last semester in seminary, I found myself speculating about pursuing a doctorate, and the minute that would come into my mind, I would do anything to get it out of mind. My desire and ambition in going to seminary was to be qualified to serve people in a local church. I decided that I did not need to invest time and money in another degree to do that.

Graduating in December of 1963 meant that I would be available for an appointment to a local church in Oklahoma, but I did not want to commit myself to a six-month appointment. Methodist pastors are assigned each year to the churches they will serve beginning June 1; they serve to the end of May of the following year.

After Seminary, a Trip to Switzerland, Italy, Egypt, Israel, Greece, England, France, Germany, and Belgium

It became important to me to decide what I was going to do with my family for six months from January 1 to May 31. I finally decided, with Jayne's approval, that we would go to Switzerland. We would put our three younger children in boarding school in Unterägeri. We would travel to Switzerland in January of 1964 and return to the United States in about the middle of May so I could attend Annual Conference in Oklahoma to receive my first church appointment.

I wrote Aunt Elsa Hauser, a friend since my military days and owner of the Hotel Schweizerhof, to see if there were any houses available and any nurses — not medical nurses but nurses who took care of children. There were no houses available, but she told of a school in the mountains called Unterägeri — a kinderheim, owned and operated by the Bossard brothers, medical doctors who took care of young children. I wrote them, and they said they would be happy to look after our three youngest children.

My mother had told a fellow in Oklahoma City that I was going to take my family to Europe. He was in the business of three-quarter ton flatbed trucks and building high tension electric lines across the country. Before we left the country, he gave me his IBM tape recorder to take with me so I could record in the evenings all the events of each day. When I filled up the cylinders, I sent them to his secretary who typed up the contents of the recordings. When we returned, I was given the whole trip on letter-size paper, and I still have those pages. This man also gave me a business card and said, "When you are ready to come home, turn your car in at this address in Amsterdam, and your car will be shipped to Houston." That sounded good to me. This nice man had one of his employees pick up our Volkswagen in Houston and drive it to Oklahoma City when we returned to the states.

We gave away some of our furniture as we were leaving

Dallas after seminary and put the remainder of our furniture in a Dallas storage and took with us to Oklahoma City only what we would be taking to Europe. Having sold the Volkswagen to a church member in Dallas, we drove Jayne's Oldsmobile to Oklahoma City and stored it there. A few days later, we began our journey to Switzerland. We flew to New York City, then we had an overnight flight from New York City to Zürich, Switzerland. The children handled the flight fairly well exception the little boys were frightened when I would take them to the toilet.

Our approach to Zürich was breathtaking for me in that we were arriving before sun up and all I could see were the peaks of mountains sticking up through clouds. I was hopeful, to say the least, that the pilot knew how to navigate between the mountaintops and clouds for a safe landing. Obviously, the pilot knew where to penetrate the clouds as we arrived safely in Zürich. The transportation arm of the government in Switzerland had seen the wisdom of building a railroad track from the downtown train terminal to the airport. Having been forewarned of this, I made my way as soon as possible to the office where they sold tickets for the train. I told the ticket agent that I needed six tickets to Lucerne and wanted to leave as soon as possible. That was a mistake. The first train to leave the airport was what I would call a local which stopped at every town between Zürich and Lucerne. Our children were sleepy, worn out, and restless. Both boys fell asleep before we reached Lucerne. We were met at the train station by representatives from the Hotel Schweizerhof which was a big help. They escorted us to the hotel and quickly to our rooms. We put our clothing away and went downstairs for a meal. Our youngest son, Randy, couldn't stay awake long enough to tell us what he wanted for dinner. Cameron, the next youngest, stayed awake long enough to tell us what he would like for dinner, and Robin and Peggie stayed awake throughout the meal. I put Randy on the floor near our table, and then later placed Cameron there as well. When we finished our meal, we went back to our rooms, and everyone went to bed. Periodically,

I would go into the rooms of the children as well as Jayne to see if they were still alive as they all slept for twelve hours. After that long trip, I was truly concerned if they were dead or alive.

Graciously, the hotel provided storage space to store the clothing and luggage that we would not be taking on our first journey. When we would return from one of our planned journeys, we then took appropriate clothing to the area where we would be spending the next four to six weeks. The day after we arrived, Jayne and I took the train to Zürich to the Volkswagen dealership that was to deliver our car. When we arrived, we took a taxi to the dealership. The city of Zürich is built around a lake as are most cities in Switzerland. As the taxi driver began to search for the dealership, he learned he had gone around the wrong side of the lake. By the time he retraced our route, the dealership had closed for lunch which lasted from noon until 2:00 p.m. We sat in the lobby of the dealership able to see our car but not able to receive delivery until after 2:00 p.m. Once we had possession of our car, we returned to Lucerne, loaded the children and their clothing into the car, and drove to Unterägeri to get them established in their school for the next four months. A lovely young woman named "Kinga" was assigned to look after the three Mason children. We came to appreciate her as she watched carefully over our children from the time they woke up in the morning until she tucked them into bed each night. Each time we left the children, three or four times, they put on quite a show of crying and carrying on, but when we would return, we would watch them from a place where they could not see us, and they were having a wonderful time enjoying every minute. After Jayne and I returned to the hotel and went to bed, I developed uncomfortable stomach distress. I thought I had a 24-hour virus. But as it turned out, I repeated that each time we left Randy, Cameron, and Robin. I concluded that I was the only emotional twit among the Masons. Peggie and Jayne were as normal as they could be as were the little ones.

Kinga spoke good English. Each night on each of our journeys, I would write a postcard to the children telling them where we were and what we were doing. When the postcards arrived, Kinga gathered the children together and read the postcards to them and offered them candy. I am convinced that the children were more interested in the candy than the postcards.

The Swiss restaurants serve soup for lunch and supper, and one of my memories is standing where we could see the children but they didn't know we were there. The soup spoon was about the size of Randy's hand, and I loved watching him try to get that big spoon full of soup up to his mouth and swallowed. I vividly remember watching him to this day.

The children and their belongings were settled in the kinderheim in Unterägeri. Randy, Cameron, and Robin had their third, fifth, and seventh birthdays there. Peggie had her thirteenth birthday in Europe, and we took her with us on our journeys. We returned about every three to four weeks to see the children, get appropriate clothing, and head out again.

We had purchased and brought with us warm clothes for the children for the winter when snow was on the ground and lighter weight clothing when the snow melted. The owners of the kinderheim had purchased a little pony, and every day when there was snow on the ground, the children could ride in a carriage on skids pulled by the little pony. Also, when snow was on the ground, there were ice skates and they skated around the backyard. Each evening after the children were indoors, the caretakers would spray water on that area so there would be fresh, smooth ice for skating the next day.

When spring came, and the snow and ice melted, the skids on the little carriage were replaced by wheels, and the pony pulled them around the property. The children loved the carriage rides. When it became warm enough, the children could play out in the yard. Cameron had on a red sweater with gold-colored buttons one afternoon. He tried to be friendly with the pony, but the pony wanted to bite the button and bit

Cameron on the chin. Thankfully, the bite frightened Cameron more than it hurt him.

Our first journey was to the south mainly through Italy. When we reached a big mountain, as we were leaving Switzerland, we drove our car onto a flatbed railroad car. When it was ready to go, we stayed in our car on the flatbed that took us through the tunnel, and we came out on the other side in Italy. When we arrived in Rome, we checked into a hotel that was more expensive than I wanted. While we were in our room getting ready to unpack for several days, Father Bill Gothhofner, Roman Catholic priest from Oklahoma, knocked on our door and while visiting with us suggested a less expensive place to stay, and if it met with our approval, he would take us to the pensione, and I readily agreed. We repacked, checked out, and went on our way to the Foyer Unitas Pensione. This pensione was run by an Order of Dutch nuns. To work for Christian Unity was their mission and purpose. They were the most delightful group of women that I could ever imagine.

Each day, it was announced a certain nun would be taking pensione guests on a tour of significant Roman sites including the Colosseum and the Vatican. Toward the end of our stay in Rome, the Bishop in Oklahoma City had arranged for an audience with the Pope for the Masons, and one of the sisters agreed to ride with us in our car to the building this Papal Audience was to take place. When we arrived at the designated building, we learned that there were 5,000 Italian women present in that room in addition to the Masons and the sister. The fact that we were in the same building with these 5,000 women and the Pope was considered to be our audience. We were seated when Pope Paul VI was carried into the room in a big wooden chair. He passed by our row closely enough where Peggie could see the color of his eyes. The Pope addressed this large group of women in Italian, and he spoke in English the last three or four sentences. He was carried back out of the room, and that was the end of our audience with the Pope.

Each morning the sisters held mass before the day started, and one day they asked me to read the New Testament lesson. To me that was indicative of their commitment to Christian Unity.

Next, we boarded an airplane bound for Cairo, Egypt. The first day in Cairo, we were taken to a section of the city where there was one shop after the other on both sides of the street. The first item that they tried to sell us was perfume. They took us into a large room and seated us around the wall. They began to bring out bottles of perfume, and they sprayed it at us so we could smell the perfumes. We were not interested in buying perfumes.

The next place they took us was where they sold rugs. They were proficient at bringing out in rapid succession all different kinds of rugs, but we were not interested in rugs either. The next room they took us to, they managed to sell us a beautiful, ornate brass tray. I made arrangements right there to have it shipped to Oklahoma City where I eventually had legs made for the tray to make a beautiful coffee table.

I learned in Cairo what it means when traveling with prepaid reservations and tickets. One of my goals on this trip was not leaving any country with its money. We went to our hotel dining room to eat and were given menus; we ordered our meals. When it came time to pay the hotel bill, it was my understanding that everything was already paid for. However, I didn't know there were two menus; one was prepaid and one was not. When I went to pay the hotel bill, they told me an amount of money I owed for food, and I said I had prepaid our meals. They said, "You ordered from the other menu." I had to come up with Turkish money to make up the difference. I wasn't happy about that, but that was another lesson I learned along the way.

One of our days in Cairo, the guide took a group of us out to the edge of the city, and we were placed on camels that we rode until we arrived at the Great Pyramids of Egypt. Jayne was always afraid of horses, but she was determined to ride this camel. I looked over at Jayne and there she was holding onto the front and back of the saddle with white knuckles. There was a large horsefly that kept flying around her head, and she would only let go of that saddle long enough to swat at that fly each time it flew by her head. All the way while we were riding to the pyramids, the fellow leading our camels put verbal pressure on us for a generous tip saying that the owners of the camels didn't pay them much. When we finished the camelback tour, I gave him what I thought was a generous tip, but I found out I had given him Turkish money instead of American money. Needless to say, he was not very happy with me. Another lesson learned.

Next on our itinerary, was Jerusalem. No one flies to Jerusalem, but we flew to Jerusalem. The terminal in Jerusalem was a big metal barn. Jerusalem was not prepared for all of the tourists coming to their city. But we arrived in Jerusalem and spent a week there. We had our own guide, and we made trips around the city in an automobile rather than a tour bus. We enjoyed and preferred that method of travel. I could ask questions, and we could stop when we wanted without interfering with someone else's trip. At the end of the day, we returned to our hotel, and there were twenty-five or thirty tourists who all owned Coca Cola bottling companies around the United States. I learned that the father of a large family who had become a Coca Cola distributor eventually helped family members become owners of Coca Cola bottling facilities. This large group and others all met in the lobby of the hotel, and everyone would bring all of their gift shop purchases for the day to show what had been purchased and tell how much was paid for each item. It was fun seeing what everyone had bought.

Next on our itinerary showed that on a certain day we were to be met by a guide from Tel Aviv since the Jewish nation is separate from the Arab nations. This caused me anxiety. The day came when we were to be picked up and no one came to the hotel to get us. Even the time was specified, but the time came and went and no one showed up. Finally, out of a sense of desperation, I hired a taxi to take us to Tel Aviv. We then traveled to Athens, Greece.

We continued south on our journey to Naples. After spending the night there, next on our itinerary was a hotel near Sorrento. It was warm and beautiful, and we stayed five days instead of the planned three. Each day while in Sorrento, we took driving trips to see beautiful houses, office buildings, and apartments built on the sides of mountains. As we proceeded further south, one of my memories is that we were going to pass Mount Vesuvius, and Peggie was concerned to know if it was going to erupt as we passed by. I told her, "I certainly hope not." We drove up onto the edge of Vesuvius safe in the knowledge it had not erupted for decades. Peggie was relieved.

One day while still visiting Sorrento, we discovered a Volkswagen van with an American license tag (I believe it was a Michigan tag). We inquired and found out that a family was spending an entire year traveling. The parents were teaching their children day by day; they had a set of Encyclopedia Britannica to use. Instead of only reading about all of the beautiful and interesting sights and places in Europe, these children were experiencing all of these locations as well as learning about them. They would stay a few days in each location and then move on to new sights and more learning.

Highpoints of our days consisted of having lunches or evening meals in one of the beautiful resorts or hotels in the area. We returned after a week in Sorrento to Rome to see our friend, Father Gothhofner, again and to stay at the Foyer Unitas Pensione.

We then made our way to Florence and stayed with a woman in Florence who had been recommended to us by the nuns. This woman's husband had been an officer in the Italian Navy prior to World War II. She told us the story about when she was a girl and was taught how to knit. When a garment was considered sufficiently soiled, the owner of the dress would unravel the knitting, wash the yarn, and knit the dress again.

As I have mentioned earlier, Florence is well known for beautiful leatherwork by the leather craftsmen. The nun recommended one or two stores that we should visit and perhaps find some items we would like to have. That is where Jayne bought a dozen pair of leather gloves in 1964 in different lengths and colors that she never wore.

From Florence we drove to Venice. Our visit to Venice was less than outstanding. It was colder than a by gosh, and almost every building in Venice had ocean water running under it. That made it even more difficult to warm a room. The owner of the house where we stayed in Venice put Peggie, Jayne, and me in a large room, and we had three single beds. The proprietors gave us a device that looked like an aluminum football that was full of hot water and it was wrapped in a towel. Jayne would hold it under the cover until she thought she was getting warm. Then her conscience would bother her and she would hand it to Peggie, and Peggie would hold it until she was about warm, and then she would hand it to me. This went on all night long; the hot water bottle football went back and forth and around and around the room all through the night. That wasn't funny that night, but it has been funny ever since.

We went to a pizza place in Venice, and all of us were rather fascinated with the fellow who was making pizzas because he could speak English. He would love it when we would come because he could speak English instead of Italian. He had mushrooms and all kinds of ingredients for pizzas out in front of him with a big sharp knife that he used to chop with to his heart's content. While chopping, he would look around and talk to us, and I thought there was going to be a thumb in somebody's pizza since he wasn't paying a bit of attention to his chopping. He fixed a ham and egg pizza for another customer, and I had never seen one before or since. He cracked about three eggs on top of the pizza and put ham on it. When it came out of the oven, I wanted that pizza so badly, but I was stuffed and simply couldn't eat another bite. I had to watch this other customer eat that ham and egg pizza, and it looked delicious.

As we were sightseeing in Venice, Jayne complained about her hands being cold. I said again, "Why don't you wear one of your new pair of gloves," and Jayne said again, "Oh, I can't because they are new."

We were returning to Lucerne to visit the children at the kinderheim in the Swiss Alps, and I had planned on our return trip to include Austria, but I was so anxious to see the children that I told Jayne we would skip Austria. We enjoyed every minute with the children before our next journey north which was to include Germany, France, and Belgium. As the emotional one of our family and since we were leaving the next morning, I became ill again that night before we left.

England was the last country we visited on our trip. We took an overnight boat ride with our car to England after visiting the Scandinavian countries. We drove around England for two weeks seeing the sights. We visited a family friend, Oscar Hauser, while there. The morning we were to go back to the continent by way of the English Channel, our car was parked on the street, and we put our luggage into the car and started off. There was a man on the street in his car watching us, and when I made a wrong turn, he stopped us on the narrow street by angling his car in front of ours. He introduced himself to us and asked if we were catching the ferry back to the continent, and I said, "Yes." He said, "I am making a business trip in the direction you want to go, so if you would like to follow me, I will get you to the port where you will catch the ferry." I didn't want to do this since I thought I knew my directions well enough, but I didn't want to be rude, so I told him, "Yes," we would follow him. We got into our cars and off we went back to the ferry boat to cross the English Channel. In a little bit, he stopped his car and walked back to our car, and said, "I need to get some gasoline, so if you will follow me into the station while I fill my car, it won't take very long" — leaving me thinking, "This man is going to make us late and I don't like this stopping and starting." However, I wanted to be polite so we stopped at the gasoline station with him. Then we drove for about 30-40 minutes when he stopped again and explained to us that up the rode a short distance was a nice restaurant. He wanted us to stop there and have tea, and he wanted to tell us about all of the bombings and devastation he experienced during World War II. He added that he had some extra time and that he would drive us right to the port and we could simply drive onto the ferry and he would continue up the coast to his business appointment. Of course, I was concerned about the time, but we stopped at the restaurant, and his life story was absolutely fascinating. True to his word, he took us right to the port, and we were able to drive onto the ferry boat that would take us back to the continent, and he proceeded up the coast to his appointment.

My job now was to get us to Amsterdam where my friend, Nick Basanda, had given me his business card with the address of a company in Amsterdam that handled shipments of automobiles and trucks to various locations all over the world. Our instructions were to go to this office and to give them the title to the car, the keys, and answer any questions they might have. The company would be responsible for the car until it arrived in Houston. Jayne, Peggie, and I then made our way to the railroad station where I had every intention of buying the cheapest seats from Amsterdam to Lucerne. Much to my chagrin, I learned that only first-class seats were available, and if I wanted to ride that train, I had to buy first-class tickets. As it turned out, there were only three of us in the compartment, and we were able to move around in our compartment so that we could clearly see what we were passing by, and it turned out to be a beautiful trip of castles built into the side of the mountains that we could see from either side of the train. The following day when we were back in Lucerne, the Hausers let me borrow one of their cars for Jayne, Peggie, and me to drive to Unterägeri to pick up Robin, Cameron, and Randy. This was a happy day for the Masons. The little ones understood that we were going back to the Schweizerhof, then we would be on our way to the United States.

We were in our hotel in Lucerne, and Jayne told me that if I would take all four children away from the hotel for the whole day that she would pack, and it was no small task. There were five or six barracks bags full of clothes, plus all of us had suitcases, and it was a pretty hefty job to do that much packing. I decided the best way for me to keep the children entertained was to go part of the way up Mount Pilatus and walk down. It was a sunshiny, beautiful day, and the mountain was full of people walking everywhere. Randy was three, Cameron was five, and Robin was seven. We started down that mountain, and I ended up having to carry Randy because he kept falling down the mountain; pretty soon I had to hold Cameron's hand. Peggie had a hold of Robin's hand, and she said, "Daddy, if you get those boys down, I'll try to get Robin down," and we finally made it. I prayed almost continuously going down that mountain. Once we got down the mountain, we would be able to get on a city bus, and the bus would take us back to the hotel. We finally made it down the mountain and to the hotel, and Jayne had us all packed; we were ready to return to the United States.

At the time we were there, it was far enough back in time that the airport authorities permitted our driver who took us from Lucerne to Zürich Airport to drive the car right up to the airplane with our luggage. We dumped all of those bags and suitcases out, and they put them on the airplane. We showed them our tickets, and they let us get on the airplane. That would never be allowed today.

Our trip home from Zürich to New York to Oklahoma City was more comfortable since we were well-traveled by this time. That meant that the boys would finally use the airplane facilities. Most of the trip was at night, and we slept most of the way. When we got back to the United States, we were in New York City. Here I was with four children, Jayne, and all of this luggage. I thought that the inspector man was pulling my leg but

I wasn't sure. He saw all of this luggage, and he said, "Where did you get all of that?" I said, "I have six people in my party." He said, "Well, I don't believe it. I want to see those six people." And I was not taking his harassment warmly. I went over where Jayne was with the children and brought them to where the guy was, and he died laughing. He finally let us go through, and we were able to get on an airplane and fly back home.

Jayne's parents and my parents all lived in Oklahoma City, so for the few days we were there, major visiting happened. We drove Jayne's Oldsmobile station wagon since our Volkswagen was en route from Holland.

We were so busy seeing friends, going places, and preparing for Annual Conference, there was little time to reflect on the outstanding experiences of our beautiful trip to Europe and the Middle East.

The Methodist Church

In the Methodist church, the smallest unit in our organizational system is called the district, and Asbury Church used to be in the Tulsa District, and there was a District Superintendent. There were twelve District Superintendents in Oklahoma, and those twelve District Superintendents worked under the supervision of the Bishop. The Bishop would meet with these twelve District Superintendents on a regular basis, and one of their tasks was to decide who was going to serve in the various churches in the Tulsa District. This is true today for the United States churches as well as our other United Methodist churches for other countries. As I mentioned before, the Bishop who was in charge when I came into the conference was a man named Angie Smith. He was the Bishop of the Oklahoma Annual Conference for so long that the General Conference passed a rule that a Bishop could not stay but for eight years, and then the Bishop had to move. Nevertheless, I came in under the supervision of Bishop Smith. He was not only the Bishop of Oklahoma but of New Mexico, the Indian Missionary

Conference, and he had something to do with the Conference in Taiwan. He was a colorful individual.

My First Appointment

When Jayne and I reported to our first Annual Conference at Boston Avenue Methodist Church in downtown Tulsa, we found a parking place right up close to the door. Jayne and I thought how fortunate we were, and we got out of the car and headed into the building. Someone came along and said, "I think you better move your car; that's the Bishop's reserved parking place." That kind soul surely did save me some embarrassment.

The rule, way back yonder, was that at the end of the conference session, the Bishop would read the appointments. I knew from being a lay delegate that it was Bishop Smith's custom to wait until the last hour of the Annual Conference to read the appointments announcing which pastor was to go to which church. I grew up with that understanding, so it didn't bother me one bit to wait. However, someone came to me the second day of conference and asked if I wanted to know where I was going to be assigned, and I said, "I'll find out the last day of conference." The minister said, "Oh, I can tell you now." I followed him to the lobby, and he told me I would be going to Asbury Methodist Church in Tulsa. I was offended at this fellow changing the tradition; that guy was cutting across the practice, but it turned out that I was the naïve, goofy individual who didn't know come here from sic 'em. I didn't know any better because I had never served another church.

I was pleased to know where we would be living the next year. David Thomas and I came out of seminary about the same time, and the Bishop read, "David Thomas; Tulsa District, Aldersgate Methodist Church; Bill Mason, Tulsa District; Asbury Methodist Church. I didn't know what David knew about Aldersgate at that time, but I knew zero about Asbury. Another one of my brilliant thoughts about being assigned to Tulsa was it was close to Arkansas, and we would be able to go over there all the time and drive through the hills of Arkansas and enjoy the beauty. I bet we didn't go to Arkansas three times in the 29 years I was pastor at Asbury, and one of those times was for a funeral.

That's how I got the job of a lifetime, pastor of Asbury Methodist Church, Tulsa, Oklahoma.

Every year, pastors are eligible to be moved to somewhere else, but every year we were reappointed to Asbury. The District Superintendent made up an annual form and gave it to the Staff Parish Relations Committee, and they gave one to the pastor. Printed on the form was, "Do you want to move, stay, or it doesn't make any different." The form had about 15 other questions. The local church committee would make recommendations to the District Superintendent, and he would report to the Bishop, "Asbury wants to move this sucker out of here" or not, but fortunately for 29 years, the Asbury committee kept saying, "Send him back to Asbury." I certainly didn't want to move, so I always put, "I want to stay." And that worked out. I stayed 29 years as Senior Pastor which is a bit unusual.

Becoming a Bishop

In today's Methodist church, ministers can make up their minds ahead of time that they want to be a Bishop, and they begin to talk to their friends and lobby to the extent now that there are now conferences in Oklahoma City where the delegates that local churches have elected can go and hear different preachers who want to be Bishops present their cases. That's not meant negatively at all; that's how it is done. One pastor (while I was still an active pastor) was at a large church in another city, and he requested and received permission to take a leave of absence for three months or so to go around and visit with all the elected delegates in the jurisdictional conference in addition to going to Oklahoma City and being interviewed. It is my understanding that he was given an advance list of questions in order to be prepared to answer those questions.

A Good Lesson

I did learn a good lesson. At one point in my ministry, we had a Bishop who I went to with what I thought was some sage advice, but he reminded me that he was Bishop and I was the pastor and to mind my own business. I didn't speak much to Bishops after that. I would say, "Hello," but I never again asked a question or offered information.

Bishop Hardt

We had one Bishop in Oklahoma that I related to and got along with beautifully.

John Wesley Hardt was his name. When he retired, he moved to Dallas, and became Professor Emeritus on the staff of the Perkins School of Theology. Bishop Hardt was open with me, and I shall always be grateful for him. He told someone when he came back to Oklahoma for a visit that he had been in a faculty/staff meeting at Perkins — I had been out of the seminary for ten years when this happened — and someone got up at the staff meeting and said, "You know, we had Bill Mason in here at Perkins for three years, and we never changed him one bit. That was not supposed to be a compliment even though I considered it a compliment. That was such a liberal seminary that half of my efforts while there would be warding off the liberal professors so I wouldn't have to get in a debate with them.

I was now on the path that God had chosen for me.

Part III
The Masons Arrive in Tulsa

It was in June, 1964, right around my birthday, when I reported for duty at Asbury Methodist Church. The day we arrived in Tulsa, the movers had not yet loaded the family that the Masons were to follow, so we sat on the curb at 6090 East 56th Street.

Nobody was out of sorts; it was kind of like a big party. As people came to say "goodbye" to the Holstons, we were able to meet these people, and our children got a head start in becoming acquainted in the neighborhood. We joined the Sungate Pool right away, and our children met almost all of their classmates over the summer which helped make the new school experience a good one.

Down the street from the parsonage was Key Elementary School. One of the district level church employees had made arrangements for members of Asbury to meet in Key Elementary School. There had been two pastors prior to our coming to Asbury. The first pastor was J. O. Whitworth and his wife Wilma; they had a home by the Tulsa Country Club, and every day during the week they would drive over to south Tulsa and go down the streets knocking on doors, and when they would find a Methodist family, they asked if family members would be willing to help start a new congregation in south Tulsa. They were able to find about twelve families willing to help start a church. After a year and a half of making these calls close to Key Elementary,

J.O. Whitworth left, and a man by the name of James Holston was appointed to be the pastor at Asbury. He had been serving in Mississippi and transferred from there to Asbury. He stayed for a year then went to Moore, Oklahoma, and from Moore he went to St. Luke's located in Oklahoma City. Jim's children were a bit older than our children. They were cordial to my family, and we enjoyed meeting them.

On moving day, it was fun getting to meet neighborhood families and young people before we moved into the parsonage, but finally the Holstons were out, and we moved in.

It was a happy day as we moved into the lovely parsonage. The reason why such a small congregation could afford such a nice home for the parsonage was that it was owned by members of the church. The man was vice president of an aircraft company, and this man and his wife were being transferred to Washington, D.C.; they needed to sell the house. Carol LeDoux, a charter member of Asbury and close friend of the people who wanted to sell this house, found this out and somehow or other the congregation got enough money together to buy the parsonage. This worked out well for us as the house was quite adequate for our family.

Something funny I remember about the house on East 56th street is that in addition to a nice double car garage, it had water pipes across the front yard that would occasionally break. Sometimes I would look out to the front, and water was shooting up in the air. After one or two of these experiences, I knew who to call immediately to fix those pipes.

The house had three bedrooms — one bedroom for the two girls and one bedroom for the two boys. Jayne and I got the third bedroom. The house had a small dining room that I used for an office. We had a family room that was comfortable for our family, and the living room was used for a choir rehearsal room until we moved into our first building. We had about ten or twelve choir members, and they came to the parsonage every Wednesday evening to rehearse. We were fortunate to have a piano and a pianist for choir rehearsals before Sunday services.

Excerpt from personal letter to Bill Mason, dated September 18, 2018 from Harry O. McLeod. Jr.,

We officially joined Asbury as members 81 and 82. We started a choir in your living room with [my wife] Sandra as director.

You counseled and prayed with me and mentioned a potential job with the Dowell Division of the Dow Chemical Company. I interviewed with Dowell and accepted a position from them. I was able to complete my Ph.D. dissertation and graduates from the University of Oklahoma in Engineering Sciences.

We began meeting on Wednesday mornings with other laymen. You were there early and cooked eggs and bacon for us, and we talked and prayed before work.

Our years with you enabled us to grow in discovery and experience in the church. You were always understanding and encouraging in our walk. You and Jayne bore with my inattention to grilling and ate most of the steak I burnt when you had dinner with us. We so enjoyed Christmas Caroling with you and Jayne and others.

You and Jayne were always a steady and faithful presence in our lives. You have always been a strong and faithful witness to Christ and we continue to praise God for you and Jayne and are forever grateful for your grace and love in our lives.

Sincerely yours,
Harry

We were meeting at Key Elementary School along with the Church of Christ that was formerly located on 51st Street, west of Sheridan. The Church of Christ met first for church at 9:00, and we came at the same time and met for Sunday School at

9:00; then we flipped, and we had church, and they had Sunday School. It worked out beautifully; the preacher and I became good friends. He said, "You know Bill, the only complaint I have is that you Methodists have coffee, and my people smell that coffee percolating and they all want some too." I think he was joking.

Two New Members on My First Sunday at Asbury

The first Sunday I was in the Asbury pulpit, Jayne and Peggie joined the church which swelled the church membership to 120. I was proud to have them as members. The church maintains the records of who joined in early days at Asbury, and I'm sure we will maintain those records until Jesus calls us home.

Meeting New Lifelong Friends

Among the Methodist gathering on my first Sunday morning was the Gerald Himes family: Jerry, Johnna, Jan, Jamie, and Joe. The Himes family members were active church members, and I remember meeting them like it was yesterday. Johnna soon became the church secretary and served the church until nine months after I retired in 1993.

Sandy Wagner wrote about Johnna Himes in The Tidings, April 25, 2003, that Johnna "and her husband, Jerry, joined the church in 1962 when it was meeting in Key Elementary and Rev. Whitworth was the pastor. A dynamic young man named Bill Mason came as pastor in 1964, and soon they were moving into the first church building at 58th and Sheridan." Johnna told Wagner, "It has been quite a ride." Johnna "later became church secretary, after giving time as one of five women who volunteered one morning a week to keep the church office manned." Johnna explained to Wagner that at first Bill Mason did everything out of his home. Choir practice was even held at his house. Dr. Mason is a remarkable person, and I think that is true because he truly did seek what God wanted him to do. He was and is wonderful with people. He literally spent hours visiting individuals, knocking on doors, and getting acquainted with people.

Johnna told Wagner that "In the early days, she and Dr. Mason did almost everything from setting up tables, and if need be, cleaning. One time a truck came to deliver a load of grapefruit for the youth to sell. Dr. Mason and Johnna unloaded the entire shipment while the truck driver watched." Johnna laughingly admitted to Wagner that her time at Asbury "has been a ball." Johnna explained to Wagner that each time changes were made in the buildings [at the Sheridan location], "it wasn't a month before they were out of room again." Johnna said it was a testament to the vital ministry taking place at Asbury.

Johnna described working with Dr. Mason as "such a delight." She described herself as a detail person and said, "He could care less about details." Johnna recalls that for many years the two of them were the only staff. Her husband, Jerry, an accountant, was Asbury's first treasurer, a job he faithfully fulfilled for years. Johnna added that her son and a friend mowed the lawn (with the Himes' mower). Eventually Bill and Johnna were joined by Bernice Stewart who became the membership secretary, and her late husband, Bud, posted the financial giving records for years. Johnna remembered, "We also had lots of fun. Bill had trouble staying awake during meetings. He got up at 4:00 a.m. every morning to have his time with the Lord before going to the hospitals. His drowsiness became a standing joke around the church. Anytime during counseling or during a board meeting, he could drift off."

Johnna also remembers Jayne Mason as remarkably gracious and equally enjoyable, saying, "I remember when Jayne once came into the office waving a butcher knife. She had been trying to put on some false eyelashes and her thumb and finger had stuck together. She wanted me to cut them apart."

There were many funny and exciting times in the church; there were hard times as well. The grief and illness that came to members were personal to Johnna. However, Johnna told Wagner that it's been a trip she would not have missed.

When Dr. Mason retired, Johnna worked for Dr. Tom Harrison for nine months then retired. Johnna told Wagner that she "sees not only great respect between the two men but similarity in their demeanor and their biblically-based sermons. Johnna said, "They are both so open, so out there for all to see. They have differences too, but they are wonderful men. There was absolutely no jealousy between them. Tom had the insight to know what a value Bill was to the church. And Bill respects Tom as senior minister."

During My First Year in 1964 . . .

During my first year in 1964, we spent that period of time at the church conducting worship, Sunday School, and Vacation Bible School — everything we were supposed to do. Additionally, we had a functioning building committee that spent its time in the architectural planning of the new building. Members had driven around Tulsa looking at existing buildings to decide what our church should look like. The District Board of Missions and Church Extension had already purchased the land where Asbury was to be built. And as far as I knew, everyone in our congregation thought it was a wonderful idea. I had nothing to do with it since it occurred before I came.

I was exceedingly grateful the members of the building committee had looked at an Episcopal Church on Atlanta across the street from Dan and Margaret Slagle. I was glad they chose that style of architecture because I liked it. The committee chose the architect and responsibly raised the money to construct the new facility by selling bonds; ground was broken, and construction began.

Electric Fans Appreciated by All

Key Elementary School was not air conditioned at that time, so right away, we took up an offering to buy some window fans to stir up the air to be bearable during the summer months for Sunday School and Church. We were successful in doing that, and the Disciples of Christ congregation was pleased that we agreed to leave those fans at Key Elementary

School when we were ready to move into our first building since it was air conditioned — Praise be to God!

Completion of the First Phase
of Church Construction

When our first phase of construction was completed for the new church building, we were happy to move in. We held worship services in the Fellowship Hall. We had a raised platform for our choir loft, and Jayne built our altar out of three tall North American Van Line packing boxes. She covered them with a clean bed sheet and changed it when it became soiled.

We brought the two Communion rails from Key that a fine couple had paid for. We had the rails built into the Fellowship Hall for worship. The man who bought these for the church had a carpenter make the two Communion rails, and they were beautiful. One Sunday we were going to have Communion, and I thought why not involve the youth, so I asked four of our youth (two for each side) to serve the elements. After the service was over, the wife of the man who had the Communion rails built said to me, "It is not appropriate to have young people serving Communion, and I want you to know that, and I also want you to know that I am leaving the church as long as teenagers are serving Communion and until you read from the real version of the Bible (King James) rather than the Revised Standard." The next month I invited her and three other godly women to serve Communion, and I was back in the good graces of that family. They didn't teach me about that in seminary, but I quickly learned under fire. I'm not the smartest one on the block, but sometimes I did quickly figure out what I needed to do.

At the beginning of our second year at Asbury, we were under construction with the first building which consisted of our Fellowship Hall which doubled as our worship area. It had a kitchen attached to it, a few offices, and one education building where all of our Sunday School classes met. It was built for the young children, but the adults squeezed into the chairs that Boston Avenue Methodist had graciously given to us. The Boston Avenue Methodist pastor called us one day and asked if we needed chairs with arms on them, and I said that we needed any kind of chair. He said that we could have fifty chairs, but we would have to get them the next day. One of my main responsibilities was to find volunteers who would get chores and tasks done. We were able to find some pickup trucks and some happy volunteers to pick up those chairs. I stored them in the parsonage garage; the garage on our house had high ceilings, and we stacked them high, and they remained there until the building was ready to be occupied. Meanwhile, the men in the congregation began to pick up the chairs, take them home, and take them apart, clean, fill cracks, and paint them. They were remarkably handsome chairs when the men finished.

I have no words to explain what a joy it was to be in our own building. However, I do have to say that meeting at Key Elementary School was the easiest job I ever had.

All I had to do was show up on Sunday morning, visit some of the Sunday School classes then preach at 11:00. It was not quite that easy when we had our own building. I was the only employee and the one to turn on the air conditioning or the heat early of a morning, the lights, and whatever else needed to be turned on and to empty the wastebaskets and keep everything clean and ship shape. Although I did not learn this at Perkins, I had enough sense early in the game to ask for volunteers.

From Gary and Ruth Beatie: Since years and years have passed, all I can remember is meeting Brother Bill when Ruth and I joined Asbury shortly after moving to Tulsa in 1969. Bill swore us in on the Sunday we joined. I call him "Brother" because we are Brothers in the Masonic Lodge Organization; Bill is a 33 Degree Mason and I am a 32nd Degree Mason. I do not know when Brother Bill became a Mason, and I cannot remember when or how I discovered Brother Bill was a Mason, but I remember Bill asking me to serve on the Board of Directors of the church while we were still on Sheridan.

I also well remember, shortly after we joined Asbury, one Sunday Bill was preaching about not partaking of alcohol but he said, "I know probably everyone in this church has the best stocked shelves of alcohol in Tulsa." That brought heaps of laughter from the congregation. Bill asked me to run the sound system, which I was happy to do for a few years until I joined the choir under Marvin Reecher. Asbury Church is like home, and Bill Mason is a fantastic minister, brother, father, and grandfather, and everyone loves Brother Bill. And he loves us. Our family would go many, many extra miles for Bill because we love and respect him deeply.

God bless you Brother Bill,
Gary and Ruth Beatie

Life and Times of the Mason Bridge Club
by John Westervelt

It was about 1967 when three-table bridge began among several Asbury members. The original members included Bill and Jayne Mason, Harry and Sandy McLeod, Ed and Marilyn Gastineau, Otto and Ellen Cantrell, Dick and Jeanette Dupuy, Hugh and Lorraine Atchison, Jim and Betty Bentz, Don and Pat Chandler, Wallace and Barbara Westervelt, Ed and Geri Voorhees, Jim Grice, and my wife, Nelda, and me. In 1987, when my wife, Nelda, died, Jim Grice became my partner. Jim died in 2011, and when Jayne Mason died in 2014, the Mason Bridge Club ceased. The week's hostess revolved among all six women, and the hostess fixed the desserts. Jim Grice brought dessert when playing at my house. Something funny happened every time, and it was usually due to Jayne's effortless humor.

Making of the Order of Worship

When we met at Key, I wrote up the Order of Worship, and I made the copies for Sunday mornings since I had a mimeograph machine in our utility room. This was not my favorite activity. In my business, I sold mimeograph machines, but I never did learn how to operate them well. When the new building on Sheridan was completed, it was still necessary to conduct three worship services. We were growing and the first building phase did not include a sanctuary.

In anticipation of conducting worship in our new building, I contemplated, prayed, and then made changes to our regular Order of Worship. One of the changes I made was to sing before the pastoral prayer. I sang, Turn Your Eyes Upon Jesus and He Is Lord. I believed that the words and the melodies of these two praise songs would prepare the hearts and minds of those who had gathered to worship. Those songs always calmed my spirit when I heard them or sang them. My singing seemed to be well received, so I sang every Sunday throughout my time as Senior Pastor at Asbury.

I have been asked to sing those two songs and another song, In This Very Room, at weddings and Celebrations of Life clear up until this very day. I was largely influenced by Larry Dalton, pianist, composer, and arranger, who played In This Very Room on many occasions, and the song always touched me. I still sense the spirit of God and I am touched when I sing those songs. I am gratified that a change I thought would quiet and calm the spirits of those worshipping has remained important in my ministry.

Norma Helen Hampton was the church organist at that time, and she accompanied me when I sang. I have had several accompanists over my years at Asbury; Rosanna Corrales and Barbara Graves have accompanied me for years, and it is comforting to be with those two talented musicians since they know what I'm going to do before I do. All of my accompanists have been exceedingly kind and patient.

I was quite happy when the time came that I was able to relinquish the task of mimeographing the bulletins for Sunday worship.

Dewey and Oralene Sherbon told me this story. *For so many years the words "Asbury" and "Bill Mason" were synonymous to the Sherbon family. On Sunday morning, our spirits were attuned to worship by Bill singing Turn Your Eyes Upon Jesus and He Is Lord. When we first attended Asbury, Bill did not sing during the worship service. But as years passed, we wondered if it was Hart Morris who convinced him to sing! Maybe not, but whatever the reason, we were so glad he began singing each Sunday morning.*

Bill's sermons were always meaningful and delivered in a straightforward manner without verbal sophistications that we "plain" folks might have trouble comprehending. One sermon that was so timely for us was about the fact that Jesus at thirty-three years old was single; Christians did not have to be married to do the Lord's work and spread the gospel. Our youngest child was in his early thirties at the time; we believed that Bill's words were comforting and empowering for our son.

Bill performed the weddings for both of our daughters. Our younger daughter decided the male attendants should wear brown suits and cowboyboots. As we recall, Bill said he did not own cowboy boots and could not comply; we suspected the real reason was "Sooner fans don't do cowboy!"

We always felt that Bill's words in the wedding ceremony provided a foundation for the joy of long-lasting unions blessed by the Lord; likewise, Bill's messages at funerals provided the "Going Home" peace for those mourning the loss of a loved one. We fondly recall Bill's statement made at the end of one memorial service we attended: "If people want me to do their funeral service, they need to hurry up and die! I'm already eighty-five and do not know how many more services I'll be able to do!"

Every church banquet we attended concluded for us with the remembrance of Bill Mason picking up dirty plates, cups, and silverware from the many tables and carrying them to the kitchen or designated receptacles prior to the washing up. After many small group evening meetings where Bill was also, we frequently left with the cherished image of Bill Mason nodding off; everyone understood this because we all knew that he had been awake since 4:00 a.m. each morning in order to pray for his entire congregation.

We once participated in a study group which met in Bill and Jayne's home — a most gracious setting which was perfect for large groups. Those of us in the group took turns bringing the filled crockpot, and Bill always looked forward to the contents of the pot. Jayne also hosted an afternoon Bible study, and we were often blessed with Bill's presence. No one could pray and open a meeting like Bill. Like the words in the song, those of us in that group felt "Surely the presence of the Lord is in this place!"

God bless Bill Mason!
Dewey and Oralene Sherbon

Barbie Paige shared this story with me: Dear Bill, A favorite memory of you is hearing you sing In This Very Room every Sunday. It always touched my heart deeply and focused my mind completely on our precious Lord. What a sweet, sweet memory to me. I imagine you have had a lot of people tell you that, but I wanted to as well.

I also wanted to tell you a memory I have which might seem a little odd to you. My wonderful father died in 1990, when he was only 61. (I was 34.) He had been terminal for a year and yet when we lost him, it came as a bit of a surprise to me. The very next time I saw you after losing Dad, you smiled and chatted with me in the foyer of Asbury. I was stunned to see my dad in your eyes. It really caught my breath. Somehow your eyes, so warm and loving, looked exactly like his. It was a huge comfort to me. What a lovely gift from the Lord.

Thank you for your lifelong gift of serving the Lord in big ways, as a Godly loving pastor to your congregation and in small ways, by comforting one of us by simply smiling with your eyes. Glad you're writing a book! What a GREAT idea!

Hugs,
Barbie Paige

Nancy Smith shared this story: *Dr. Mason, In the summer of 1999, my husband, Stephen, and I, and our two grown sons visited Asbury at the Sheridan Avenue location. Our family had not been attending church but felt a need to do so. At that time, I didn't have a personal relationship with Jesus. On one Sunday, you were preaching the sermon, and at the end of that, you asked us all to close our eyes, and you sang to us, In this Very Room. It was at that moment that I knew, for the very first time, that Jesus was there among us, and I felt He was standing right next to me as you sang. His presence was so strong that it seemed as if I opened my eyes, I would have seen Him standing there. That moment made me know that Jesus cared about me, was real to me, and that I would love Him every day of my life from that moment on. I have always thought of you as the person who showed me the caring and loving Jesus.*

Thank you, Dr. Mason.
Nancy Smith,
Asbury member since September 9, 1999

Ellen and Rick Boothe sent this story to me: *Pastor Bill, We're thrilled you're writing this book! A few memories: When Asbury was at the Sheridan location, we looked forward to hearing you sing (solo) EVERY Sunday morning In This Very Room. I would cry sometimes as it touched my heart so much. When my dad was in his last days at the nursing center, I continually played your CD which had this song and other hymns, and the nursing staff that attended* *my dad remarked how much your music blessed them. And I know it blessed my dad too. It comforted me greatly. Thank you for taking the time to record your singing of those time-less beautiful hymns. Many years ago, I was awaiting sur-gery at St. Francis at o-dark-thirty. Rick and I had prayed about it, and others had with me but I was still scared. At the perfect time just minutes before they wheeled me away, you appeared from nowhere, held my hand, smiled sweetly at me, and said the most wonderful comforting prayer. I'll nev-er forget it. I had no idea how you even knew I was there! I was so grateful. And the surgery went perfectly well!*

The new church on Mingo was near completion, and Asbury folks took a prayer-walk from 58th & Sheridan to 67th & Mingo. The icing on the cake was to see Bill and Jayne Mason leading the procession in a bright red VW convertible! Talk about two people looking like they were having the best time! I understand this was a throwback to your early pastoring days when you visited people in your red bug. They must have loved to see you coming!

We sincerely look forward to reading your book!
Ellen and Rick Boothe

Rose Hill

I suppose all new congregations like Asbury have at least one family that has always been Methodist. And every time we had a church meeting to talk about doing something or not doing something, this particular man would always say, "But at Rose Hill, this is the way we did it." By Christmas, I had genuinely grown weary of hearing that, but I never did mention to the fellow. This man's wife is the one who got after me for asking teenagers to serve Communion.

Rocks on My Head

At the parsonage, there was a sewer line that connected at the back-property line to the city's sewer. Our sewer line collapsed. As a layman looking at the hole the workers had dug, I could see that they had to dig a deep hole. When they finished the job and were refilling that deep trench, there was quite a bit of dirt that didn't fit into the hole. The ground was some kind of clay that had hardened when it was on the surface. One afternoon, I was sitting on the porch looking at that mess, and I knew at the church location we were putting in sprinkler system lines. The front-end loader that they used to put the dirt back into the church trenches looked like something I could drive to our house that was only a few blocks away. I contacted one of the men in the church who had trucks and reasoned with him that if he would park one of his trucks in front of our house, I could scoop up my excess dirt with the front-end loader, put it in a truck of his, and he could haul it off. On one of my trips, there was one operation step with that front-end loader that I forgot to do. I scooped up and filled the front end with dirt and raised it so I could drive the loader to the truck, however, when I raised the front end loaded with dirt, I was supposed to tip the front end down a little bit. I didn't tip it down, so I dumped the whole load of dirt on my head. That dirt was actually hardened clay, and it was like a bunch of rocks dumped on my head. I got off the tractor and grabbed the garden hose and started spraying my bleeding head. Those rocks knocked off my glasses but didn't break them. Jayne came out on the porch and saw what had happened and began to lecture me about, "I told you not to do that." The man who delivered the truck to our house for the dirt saw what happened and said, "Reverend Mason, if you will promise not to do that anymore, I will promise not to preach." I didn't load anymore trucks with dirt, but the kind owner of the truck sent a man out to finish the job I had started.

"Just Preach It, Brother."

As a new pastor at Asbury, I remember one responsibility that used to give me headaches. I was convinced that a good minister should have his sermon in manuscript form by

Thursday night. Making my own deadline gave me trouble in the form of a headache, and I was weary of having headaches every Thursday night.

When I became a minister, my mother had given me a black minister's robe, and when I was preaching one Sunday, my sermon manuscript was on the pulpit, and I made a sweeping gesture. The cuff of the arm of that robe caught that stack of papers and they went shooting out and flying everywhere. In that instant I didn't know what I was going to do, but I got down and began to gather up my papers. Someone yelled out, "Just preach it, Brother." That made a vivid impression on me, and I began to pray asking God to free me from having a manuscript sermon by Thursday nights. In the matter of a week or so, I could write my sermon out on some note cards and not have a manuscript. I never enjoyed preaching a sermon to that point like I did afterwards by getting rid of that manuscript. Praise the Lord!

The Wonderful People of Asbury

The wonderful people of Asbury were more than willing to pitch in and see that jobs were assigned, accepted, and done. Upon moving into the new building, several women agreed to assume responsibilities as church secretary. Among the volunteers was Johnna Himes who I had met for the first time at Key Elementary School. After helping out as part-time church secretary, Johnna saw the need for a full-time secretary and she volunteered (with no pay).

From the beginning, Johnna did all that was needed (that I was not doing). She not only did all that was necessary, she did each job perfectly. Johnna had worked for her father, an orthopedic surgeon in Edmond, so she had multiple skills for a well-run office and was a quick learner for jobs she had not done before in our church office. For example, upon coming to my office one morning, I found she had labeled each drawer of my two file cabinets as "Sacred" and "Top Sacred." As employees came on board, Johnna trained each one as to what they would be doing. As new equipment was acquired, Johnna always learned the machine then trained the whole staff.

Johnna's skills in dealing with members, new members, non-members, strangers off the street, or vendors on the telephone and in person were outstanding. If either Johnna or I had to be away from the church for a period of time, it was always far better for me to be gone and Johnna remain to steady the ship.

A Couple of Difficult People

These folks are long since deceased and shall remain nameless, but the parents of a woman in our church started attending Asbury. They had been members of one of the downtown churches. When our service was over, I would go to the back of the Fellowship Hall and there was a narrowing of the hallway where I could greet folks and thank them for coming. This couple lined up along the wall across from me so the flow of members came by them at the same time. The man would introduce himself to each one who passed by and tell where his office was located downtown. He told our Sunday morning worshippers that he was an attorney, and if they were ever tired and wanted to rest a bit when downtown, they were welcome to come by his office to rest in his lobby in his comfortable chairs until they were ready to go. I knew before I attended Perkins that two plus two equaled four, and what this guy was doing was not appropriate to be hustling customers right there in front of God and everybody. If new members passed by him, he went after them extra hard. Finally, I had to address the situation and explained that they must not do that anymore. They stopped.

One other interesting experience I had with that couple was after we had been at Asbury for three or so years, we had been able to acquire our own postage machine which was the hot tomato back in those days. I don't know if they still are or not. It sure did help us process mail more quickly. I learned that the postage meter could be programmed to write a passage of scripture or whatever we wanted to print alongside the stamp. I thought that was a brilliant idea, and we used that feature of the postage machine. This guy interpreted that as me sending a message directly to him, and he did not appreciate it. He thought I was trying to get to him through my message from the postage meter. I could not believe someone could possibly ever think that.

Learned the Hard Way

On a subsequent trip to Dallas for Minister's Week at Perkins Theological Seminary, Jayne and I went to Cokesbury Bookstore, and without permission, I ordered offering plates, Communion supplies, and candelabra. When they arrived, we put them on the altar Jayne had built, and they looked quite handsome. At the next board meeting, I was scolded for spending money without permission. Carol LeDoux spoke up and said, "I will raise the money to pay for them." That ended the conversation, but there it was: a new pastor's failure to get permission before spending money.

I Needed a Pulpit

When I attended a District Ministers' meeting in Tulsa, I mentioned to several pastors that I was in need of a pulpit. John Keefe, pastor of Epworth Methodist Church in Oklahoma City, informed me that there was a pulpit in the basement of the abandoned Epworth Methodist Church (a highway was to be built through the property). John gave me a key, and Ken Maltby and another man whose name I cannot recall drove to Epworth Methodist in Oklahoma City to pick up the pulpit. It was so big that Ken, the other man, and I had to remove door facings to get the pulpit from the basement to the back of my station wagon. We took the pulpit to Ken's garage, and he repaired and resurfaced the pulpit. Then we brought it into the Fellowship Hall. That pulpit currently serves as the pulpit in the classroom where the Joy Class meets in our Mingo location.

Another Building Program is Underway

The beauty of Asbury's architecture and exterior Arkansas Ledge Stone was all decided by a committee before I was assigned to Asbury. When we moved to our first church building, Asbury experienced rapid growth. Each time we completed a new building phase, we experienced rapid growth. The Fellowship Hall was unable to handle the attendance, so we added a second worship service. Another building program was underway when we built more Sunday School rooms; the Parlor was added to handle the United Methodist Women and wedding receptions. As the church continued to grow, we began plans to build our sanctuary.

Finding Jayne

When the sanctuary was built and we moved in, I found that until I could locate where Jayne was sitting, I couldn't settle down and tend to the business. One Sunday when I failed to ask at the right point in the service for the ushers to come forward to receive the offering, one of the ushers went to Jayne and said, "Bill forgot to take the offering; what should we do?" Jayne said to him, "Tell all the ushers to gather in the center aisle with the offering plates, and Bill will see you, then he'll ask for the offering." Sure enough they did and I did. Jayne was the perfect partner in ministry for me.

The church continued to grow, so eventually it was necessary to expand the sanctuary. That was quite an undertaking, but it was a good addition to our space problem. The last building program at the South Sheridan location was the construction of the Mason Center which included a gymnasium and multiple large Sunday School rooms. There was a full basement under the gymnasium for our high schoolers to use.

We continued to have three Sunday worship services, however, there was absolutely no more room for expansion. The church faced the necessity of relocating.

Dr. Loerke to the Rescue

One Sunday morning, a lady was asked to sing a solo. When it came time for her to sing, she fainted. I turned toward the choir loft when I heard her go down, but then I turned back to the congregation and said, "Don't worry, I see Dr. Loerke, and he will take care of the situation." She fainted three or four more times before realizing that singing solo was not good for her, but Dr. Jim Loerke (a member of the choir) always came to her rescue.

One of My Bright Ideas and Peggy George

As a new pastor at Asbury in the early days, I will never forget this lesson. I got an idea to make a list of volunteer positions, and when the list was finished, I asked all of the members to pick three of those positions that they would be willing to do. On Monday morning, Peggy George appeared at my office door, and she had that paper in her hand. She said, "Bill, I've gone over this list, and I'm doing 25 of these 25 jobs; which ones do you want me to quit doing?" I told Peggy that this was not how I had intended for this to turn out. I didn't come up with bright ideas like that again.

Another Misstep

In my early days at Asbury, I took our Volkswagen and our two boys every Sunday afternoon to deliver church bulletins. I could remember who was in church that Sunday and who wasn't, so we put bulletins in the mailboxes of the people who weren't there. I thought that was fun. One day I got a telephone call from the post office, and a lady said, "Reverend Mason, we need to let you know that someone in the church is breaking the law." She explained that it is against the law for anyone to put anything in a mailbox that doesn't have a stamp on it. I said that I would certainly tell the person who was doing that to not do that anymore — and I didn't do it again.

And Again

One time we needed some folding chairs for our Fellowship Hall, and because I had been in that business, I had them drop shipped from the manufacturer to Asbury. We wound up with a whole lot of cardboard shipping boxes. I was trying to decide what to do with those boxes, and in my wisdom, I was aware that the west parking lot was gravel and not yet paved. I thought, "Gravel doesn't burn, so I'll get out there one day after work and burn these boxes and be done with it." One of our wonderful members said, "I'll come help you." It was dark when we were burning those boxes and huge flames were shooting upwards. We heard a fire truck. At this time, except for the Texaco Station, there wasn't anything at the 61st and Sheridan intersection. The firetruck was going around and around and around trying to find the fire, and finally they spotted us and came over. When they pulled into the parking lot, my partner disappeared. I stayed to face the music. The firemen were very kind as they explained that burning open fires was against an ordinance in Tulsa and would I please not burn anymore boxes or anything else? I assured them that I would not burn anymore boxes, and I didn't. It was kind of scary when they pulled into the parking lot because I had no idea what they might do to me, but they were very polite and it worked out well for Mason.

The Beautiful Church Chimes

I will never forget being so surprised at receiving a telephone call one day from a lady who complained about our new beautiful electronic chimes that played a hymn of our choice on the hour. I could not imagine the chimes being offensive to anyone.

After I heard the woman's complaint, I got nowhere in convincing her to enjoy the beauty of the chimes. I hung up and decided to go by and see her at her home. She welcomed me into her home, and I began again to explain the beauty of the musical chimes. She said, "You don't understand! Each and every time the chimes play, it shocks me so that I throw whatever is in my hands in the air which creates a terrible mess to be cleaned up." I was certainly surprised by that response. We talked a bit longer, and I was getting nowhere in changing her mind. I left her house with her threat that if I "did not stop playing the chimes," she would report me to the police. A police officer came out and listened from his patrol car to the beautiful chimes. He left telling me, "Don't worry about it. We won't arrest you; the music is beautiful." Thankfully, I never did hear from that woman again.

Wasted Money

At some point during the midpoint of my time as Senior Pastor, I became concerned about the doors on staff offices. Most of the doors did not have windows, and I began to think how vulnerable that made that staff person and me as pastor, so I got a carpenter in there to cut holes in the doors and insert panes of glass in each door. Anyone who wanted to look in, could stop and see what was going on. The result of my concern and considerable expense was that ninety-nine percent of the staff cut out pieces of cardboard and stuck them in the windows. I didn't ask the right questions or I wouldn't have spent that money on that.

Wooden Chests for Pledge Sunday

The only times I ever got in trouble was saying something from the pulpit that I should have kept my mouth shut about. But one day after seeing a beautiful chest made of wood, I thought it would be perfect to have a beautiful wooden chest up front when we had Pledge Sunday. Newer members of Asbury may not recall those times, but folks would come on Pledge Sunday and put their financial pledges to the church on the Communion rail. When I mentioned offhandedly about the value of a wooden chest, three different men had built chests but didn't tell me about them until they were finished. At the time I remember my mind raced with "What in the world am I going to do with three handsome wooden chests that have been built by members of the church?" We did use the chests for Pledge Sundays, but I don't remember what became of them after I retired. I remember thinking at the time how blessed and fortunate Asbury was to have such talented and generous members.

Another Generous Member

Stuart Gibbs was an early member of Asbury who was gracious and generous enough to assume responsibility when once again we ran out of Sunday School classrooms. Stuart said, "I'll fix that." He ordered a big prefabricated room and had it sent to the church and parked it close to a door; instantly we had a new classroom. I don't remember what became of that prefab building, but it let us continue growing our Sunday School classes. Much later in the life of the church, Stuart's company built and installed all of the beautiful metal railings in our Mingo sanctuary, in the balcony, along the beautiful main foyer staircase that ascends to the balcony, as well as other places in the building. The company gave us a good price which made for a significant contribution to the church.

Naming Names

As Asbury grew at the Sheridan location, we put names on various items in the church with plaques that were fastened onto the pews and other places in the other buildings, but when we moved to Mingo, that was stopped. The only places that I know of that have names are the Mason Chapel and a bench that is dedicated to Jim and Debbie Mizell's daughter, Amber Rogers, who was shot and killed in a bank robbery in 2004. The guilty man was sentenced to life without parole.

Reverend William David Clark

Bill first became involved at Asbury in the youth program. The youth leader invited Bill to come in and help, and it turned out Bill was a tremendous help with the youth. When it was time for Bill to go to college, Bill chose to go to the University of Oklahoma. As tall as Bill is, he did not show any interest in going out for basketball.

Bill was good about coming home on the weekends to be a part of the youth programs at the church. I began to notice that he was unusually mature for a young man his age. I learned that when an occasion arose which prevented me from hospital visitation, I asked Bill if he would do it, and he said he would be glad to. Upon my return, Bill gave me a thorough and intelligent report on the result of his visits with our members.

As Bill was approaching his junior year at OU, he began to think about a seminary education, and after a good deal of prayer and study on Bill's part, he chose Fuller Theological Seminary in California which meant that he was in Tulsa less frequently. Nevertheless, every time he was in Tulsa, he was present with our youth.

As Bill proceeded through his seminary studies, after much consideration he made the decision to be ordained in the United Methodist Church. While Bill was in seminary, I wanted him to be as active as possible in his home church. He finished his work at Fuller, was received into the Oklahoma Annual Conference, and he was appointed to serve at Asbury United Methodist Church. Bill served the Lord and Asbury Church exceedingly in every single area that a pastor has responsibilities, and he welcomed the opportunity to gain experience.

In a few years, Bill came to me one day, and said he would like to run for the Oklahoma State House of Representatives, and he wanted my approval to do so. After much prayer, I decided that if I said, "No," we would likely lose him altogether, and if I said, "Yes," at least we would have him half-time. I supported his decision and told him that I would appreciate him staying on our staff giving us half of his time.

In the meantime, Bill had met and married Laurie, who is a doctor. Bill was an excellent preacher, pastor, and highly regarded as an Oklahoma state legislator.

Again, Bill came to me and said the Methodist church had become too theologically liberal for him. His decision was to leave the Methodist Church and be received into the Covenant Church. His first assignment was to start a new Covenant Church in Tulsa. The new church met for a year or so in a Jenks public school building, then property was purchased, and the first of several buildings was built. Several years later, Bill was asked by his denomination to leave the pastorate and become a moneyraiser for two hospitals in Africa. This meant that Bill would do a good bit of traveling in the United States — calling on Covenant Churches and other donors.

After several years, Bill shared with me that it had reached a point where ministers were not returning his calls because they knew that he was a fundraiser. After several years of raising funds for the hospitals, Bill was invited to join the staff of a Covenant Church in Sacramento, California, to be the pastor to the twenty-six pastors on staff. My admiration for his wife was heightened when I learned that she accepted a position in a clinic in Sacramento and most of her patients were Russian immigrants. From Sacramento, Bill accepted a position as an associate pastor in the Chicago area at another Covenant Church. From there he accepted a position at Redeemer Covenant Church in Tulsa — the church he had started. At the writing of this book, Bill was still Senior Pastor of Redeemer Covenant, but Bill announced that he would retire at the end of 2020. Bill and Laurie became grandparents in 2019 to their granddaughter, Maisie Tyler Clark.

Bill and I have maintained our friendship over all these years. We talk on the telephone now more than we see each other, but I cherish our time together. I love and admire Bill Clark.

Reverend Bill Clark wrote this story: *One of the unique features of Bill Mason was his work ethic. Even when I was a young pastor, I couldn't keep up with him. Most pastors of large churches tend to do the "big things" and leave the rest of the work to other staff. Not Bill Mason. As an example,* *every Sunday, after preaching three services, followed by a quick lunch, Bill would lead a 1:30 p.m. service at Skyline Terrace Nursing Home at 61st and Sheridan. There he would lead the singing, preach for a while, and then greet as many of the residents as possible before he left. Most preachers are exhausted after Sunday morning.*

There is a draining quality to preaching and greeting hundreds of people on a Sunday morning. Bill was different in that way – it all seemed to energize him. Anyway, back to Skyline Terrace…

On the few Sundays that Bill wasn't in town, he would ask me to replace him at Skyline Terrace. The first time I did so I walked into the community room and told the group who I was and that I would be replacing Bill Mason for that afternoon's service. As soon as I said that, I heard their collective groan by the attendees. "What, no Bill Mason!" "Is he OK?!" "Will he be here next week?!" And on it went… Finally, I got the crowd calmed down and attempted first to lead the singing, as Bill would do. I don't have the good singing voice of Bill Mason, but I got through a couple of hymns, prayed, and proceeded to preach.

My voice is soft, and the room's amplification was modest at best, so several times people asked me to speak up. Being relatively new to this, I felt at best deficient for this kind of ministry. Finally, it was time to close. After I finished the sermon, I announced that Bill Mason would be back the next Sunday. A cheer arose from the assembled voices and applause broke out. People were turning toward each other exclaiming, "Bill Mason will be here next week!" Finally, after all got quiet, one dear woman on the front row shouted out, "Who in the heck is Bill Mason?!" Frankly, it just was the comic relief I needed!

The point of this story is not that Bill was beloved by so many people, though he certainly was and is. The point is that Bill had no sense of entitlement as the leader of a large and growing congregation. Most pastors I know go home on Sunday afternoon, watch football, take a nap, or both. There are usually Sunday evening obligations to attend to – and a rest is almost required to keep going. God gifted Bill with energy, but I think it was Bill's deep love of Jesus and of all people that gave him energy. Bill preached love, lived love, and taught love. I'm convinced that Asbury "succeeded" in amazing ways primarily because of the love and the grace that was a hallmark of the church – modeled by Bill Mason in large and small ways. Great churches are built by the sovereign work of God, but they must be led by people of vision, energy, and a certain kind of fire in their souls. Bill had all that not only for the congregation of a large and beautiful church but also in a place where people needed encouragement in a challenging season of their lives. No wonder those good people loved Bill – he loved them!

A Trip to Hawaii

After our son, Randy, graduated from high school and was a student at Oklahoma State University, representatives of American Airlines management were on campus recruiting young men and women who would consider taking training to become cabin attendants. The proposition was that if the cabin attendants went on strike, the trainees would be given jobs as cabin attendants. If they did not go on strike, American Airlines would give each of the trainees two roundtrip passes to anywhere American Airlines flew. Jayne and I gave our permission for Randy to take the training at American Airlines in Dallas/Fort Worth. The cabin attendants did not go on strike, so Randy was given two round trip passes. In discussing this with his mother and me, a decision was reached that Randy and his mother would use the two airline passes; I would buy my own seat, and we would go to Hawaii for vacation.

In the meantime, conversation was going on with the girl

Randy was dating about going to Hawaii for their honeymoon. As it happened, Randy and Hilde were married at Asbury, and I conducted the ceremony. The bride and groom used the passes to go to Hawaii. Jayne and I bought our own tickets. Peggie and Gary as well as Gary's mother, Juanita, also joined the group heading to Hawaii. I had leased a house from an American Airlines' employee, and we all stayed together in that house. Jayne, being the "manager" that she was with concern for equity in everyone's enjoyment of the rooms and the views, determined that the couples and Juanita (by herself) would be assigned a bedroom, and after two nights, everyone had to move. Apparently, that did not sit well with the bride and groom. They rented a car and drove to a community where they stayed in a hotel the rest of the time. The house had one second-floor bedroom which was a room with a view of the ocean. When Randy and Hilde had to move from that room, that's when they decided to move to a hotel. The rest of us played the game that Jayne had designed: spend two nights in one room then move to a new room.

I chose not to go to the beach every day like everyone else did, but one day I decided to go. Jayne and Juanita chose a location for their beach chairs as far from the water's edge as practical. All of us left our cameras, glasses, and other items that we did not want to get wet with Jayne and Juanita. I found myself standing ankle deep in the surf having introduced myself to a couple from Kansas. In the midst of our conversation, a powerful wave came in knocking the three of us head over heels. My sunglasses were knocked from my head, but fortunately I found them before they were washed away. After regaining our composure, we carried on our conversation only to be hit by a second more powerful wave that knocked the three of us down again. I didn't find my sunglasses this time. As I was trying to get back on my feet, I noticed the bathing suit top of the woman in our threesome was gone. In trying to decide the proper thing for a gentleman to do, I also noticed my bathing suit was around my ankles. I quickly determined my need was greater than hers, and I pulled up my trunks, then I assisted her in looking for her top. That same wave went clear up to where Jayne and Juanita were sitting. It turned them upside down, soaking everything they had. That was the end of my visits to the beach.

The house where we were living was not air conditioned, and it was rather warm. Jayne and I made a trip to JC Penney's and purchased a box fan for each bedroom. The only embarrassment regarding the fans was at the airport; I had decided to take the fans back home. When I went through Customs, the Customs agent asked me, "Do they not sell box fans in Oklahoma?" We brought these fans back to Tulsa, and they sat in the garage for years.

Nancy Durham Baxter

When Nancy came to Asbury with her family, she was a teenager. Her parents were Dave and Maxine Durham, and Nancy had a brother. The family had transferred to Tulsa and bought a home in the Asbury area. They visited the church and made it their church home, and as a family, they became active in the life of the church. Dave assumed leadership roles, and Maxine was active in the Women's Ministry. It wasn't long until Nancy was off to Norman to begin her college studies. During the summer months, the young man in charge of youth ministry invited Nancy to work with him during the summer months. She responded enthusiastically to the opportunity to spend time with the younger people. It was during her sophomore or junior year that she met a Tulsa boy on the campus at Norman named Phil Baxter. It was not long before they were dating steadily. Not long after they met, Phil visited Asbury with Nancy, and he became a member of the church and participated in the youth ministry with Nancy.

Nancy is a warm and affectionate person, and young people were drawn to her and she generously shared her love. Phil and Nancy were married at Asbury, and it was my pleasure to conduct the ceremony. Phil progressed rapidly in the corporation he worked for and became a great provider for his family. Phil and Nancy had two children — a son who became an architect and a beautiful daughter. Both children live in Jackson Hole, Wyoming, where Phil and Nancy have another home.

Recently, Nancy teased me about three families living in Jackson Hole as the reason there is so little crime. Plus there is only one way into town and one way out making it easy to catch would-be thieves or robbers. All three families are happy to be living in that beautiful town with its magnificent surroundings.

Both Phil and Nancy have continued their activities through Asbury and their church in Jackson Hole as well as reaching out to other Christian organizations.

During Nancy's teenage years, she demonstrated her God-given ability for teaching, and she has developed that to a higher degree. She is one of the most outstanding women lay leaders and teachers I have ever known.

Jayne and I visited Phil and Nancy at their Jackson Hole home one summer. One night we met the horse whisperer at their church. Phil and Nancy bought a video tape which introduced us to the life and activity of the horse whisperer. He is quite well known in Wyoming and perhaps across the United States for his unusual profession.

Nancy loves to talk about her five grandchildren. She reads scripture to them and not just a few verses. She told me recently that she and her five-year-old granddaughter read the granddaughter's Bible in five days.

Nancy, Phil, and I remain friends. We enjoy seeing each other and having lunch as we can.

Nancy Baxter wrote this story: *We have known Bill for many years. My family came to Asbury the same year Bill and Jayne and their children arrived in 1964. I was 16 and we were meeting in Key School. There were 4 people in the choir; Rex Smith Sr. was one of them. We moved into the "new building" in June of 1965. Two families joined Asbury that first Sunday, Glenn and Jean Hack-*

ler with children Vicki and Kelly and my family, Dave and Maxine Durham, along with me and my brother George.

Bill did everything in those days. He was our youth leader. Peggie Mason, Charles Ryser, and I were part of the group and names still recognized at Asbury today. Bill made and delivered the Sunday morning bulletin to our mailboxes in the red Volkswagen when we weren't in church.

I remember Bill preaching from neatly typed notes and reading them word for word in the early days. It was a joy watching him become more comfortable in the pulpit. With his servant's heart, I have seen Bill leave the pulpit while preaching to pick up a bulletin that someone dropped on the floor in the first row and return it to them. It was not unusual for him to stop a sermon and pray when sirens were heard passing the church. Bill is down to earth and relates well with all people. I remember a sermon in the early 70's when he was preaching about coming to Christ as Lord and Savior. He said, "You could bring your beer can and come along; Jesus would take you just as you are!" Everyone loved having a pastor who could sing. So many wanted Bill to sing "Turn Your Eyes Upon Jesus" at their weddings and funerals because it was so dear to them! In the 70's, Bill was a big supporter of the Bill Gothard Seminar. He attended multiple years and encouraged the church to attend which many of us did. They were excellent! Bill also brought a Lay Witness Mission to Asbury in the 70's. That was the weekend my mom, Maxine, came to the Lord after being in church her whole life; one of the lay testimonies opened her eyes to His grace not works! When Jayne arrived in Tulsa, she said she didn't want to have to pray out loud. She made it for several years until the World Action Singers from Oral Roberts University came to sing at Asbury one Sunday morning along with Oral and Evelyn Roberts. The Roberts invited Bill and Jayne to Southern Hills for lunch where Oral asked Jayne to bless the meal — her first prayer out loud.

One morning Jayne found a paper bag in the cul de sac in front of their home. She said she thought it might be a kitten, but it was a six pack of beer. She brought it in the house and placed it in the garage fridge. She said she could rinse her hair with it. That afternoon a veteran from the Vietnam War came to the house for counseling with Bill. Jayne offered him tea, Coke, or water which he refused. Then she said, how about a beer which he gladly received! Eighth Grade Camp at Camp Egan was a priority for Bill. He was camp director for many years because the youth group was a big priority to Bill. In 1971, Bill hired me to be the first full-time Youth Director at Asbury. There were only three full-time staff then: Bill, Johnna Himes, and me. The church had a lot of teens and Bill cared! He decided we needed a bus for youth activities. Jerry Himes and I bought a used Tulsa School bus for $150. Bill had it painted white with Asbury written on the side for $300.00. We were in business!

Our family story with Bill Mason is just one story of so, so many. My parents, Dave and Maxine Durham, left Asbury in 1970, moving to Houston. Bill maintained a relationship with them until their deaths. He even flew to Houston to perform my Mother's funeral in 2000. He telephoned my dad two or three times a year until his death in 2015.

In 1968, Bill baptized my husband, Phil, on a Sunday morning shortly after Phil's conversion. He married us in 1970 at Asbury in our old Fellowship Hall. He baptized both of our children, Chris and Becca. He performed Becca's and Ryan Block's wedding, one of the last in the old Asbury location. Bill read scripture at our son's wedding to Jennifer Wallace in Oklahoma City.

Bill performed the funerals for Phil's parents, Jake and Edna Baxter. They both became Christians in Bill and Jayne's home in the early 80's. Bill also performed the funeral for Phil's grandmother, Maggie Baxter. Bill has visited us, sat with us, prayed for us through multiple hospital stays and surgeries. No one truly knows Bill until they spend time with him in the hospital receiving his prayers, love, and compassion.

People often comment on Bill's sleepy times. How I wish we would all rise at the very early hour before dawn that he does every morning to pray for so many. He has a prayer list that is amazing for one prayer warrior! Our family has been so very blessed by God through Bill's prayers. Bill always spoke so fondly of the Mason family trip to Europe after his seminary education. Cameron and his wife traveled with him a few years ago to revisit some of the highlights.

Bill has served so many — even the lady swimming in the ocean in Hawaii who lost her swimsuit top to a wave; Bill tried to come to her aid and help her recover the top on their family vacation!

If you wanted to find Bill and Jayne on Saturdays a trip to Coney I-Lander for lunch would do the trick!

The best way to describe Bill, "True Servant of the Lord!" We dearly love him and count ourselves most blessed to have shared life together with Bill Mason and his family!

In Jesus,
Nancy

Bob and Hilda Bynum, Lecture Series, and Francis Asbury Statue

When Bob and Hilda Bynum joined the church, we became friends. As time passed, Hilda began to need assistance with her care. One day each week, Bob and I would go to lunch at the Cedar Ridge Country Club where they belonged, and then we would go visit Hilda, who by this time needed more care than Bob could provide at home.

Bob was Chief Financial Officer for Parker Drilling Company and was well liked by the employees. Bob and I visited about all kinds of topics over lunch, but primarily we discussed Hilda and their two children, Beverly Bynum Hanby of Arkan-

sas, and their son, who was a professor. The older congregation members of Asbury will remember that the Bynums made
it possible for us to have the Bynum Lecture Series, which became a selection of outstanding speakers in the United States.
A speaker would come to Asbury and be with us for the better
part of a week delivering outstanding messages each night.
The church was full during the Bynum Lecture Series.

Bob gifted to the church a full-size statue of Francis Asbury
on horseback; Asbury Church was named after Francis Asbury.
The horse, when located on Sheridan, faced southwest. David
Willets, the pastor of Parkview Baptist Church, across the street
from our Sheridan location at that time, and I enjoyed ribbing
each other on occasion. One day, he called me on the telephone
and said he was sure disappointed after the statue had been put
in that place because when he looked out his study, he looked at
the rear end of the horse. We had a good laugh about that.

As we were removing the covering from the statue the
day of the dedication of the statue, a little girl standing beside me said, "Reverend Mason, what is the horse's name?" I
didn't know it, but I told her I would find out. I tried to find the
name of his horse for her, but I never did. Google research
now indicates that "Little Jane" and "Little Fox" were two of his
horses. Francis Asbury was known far and wide in the 1700s.
He came from England at the behest of John Wesley's call for
missionaries. Asbury rode thousands of miles by horseback
visiting Methodist churches. We were able to move the statue
to the Mingo location from South Sheridan, and it was placed
in the front of the new church sanctuary.

Hilda preceded Bob in death. Bob and I spent more time
together as I realized he had time on his hands without Hilda. Bob joined our Monday afternoon Bible Study in the parsonage and quickly became a special addition to our special
group. When it was Bob's time to go to Heaven, I stayed with
him until his daughter, Beverly, arrived. Bob had a peaceful
and calm homegoing.

Worship

I decided for Sunday sermons, I would use my book that had listings of suggested scriptures for each Sunday of the year. That listing of scriptures for each Sunday contained a scripture from the Old Testament, the New Testament, and a scripture from Psalms. I always found among those scriptures at least one that spoke to me that inspired my message to bring to worship every Sunday. I read other scriptures that those scriptures referred to, and I included life experiences that I thought were relevant at the time. From all of that, eventually my Sunday sermons were developed. Sometimes I would begin sermons weeks ahead, and sometimes I would start the Monday before Sunday. Most ministers read abundantly, and in my reading, I always found topics that I would underline and keep that were relevant to develop into sermons at the right time.

I always concluded my sermons by inviting Christians and non-Christians who had been touched by God's presence to come forward. When Christians would come forward during my altar call, they often asked me to pray for them. Non-Christians would ask how to receive Christ as their Lord and Savior. When the Asbury Room was in place at the Sheridan location, non-Christians were invited to go there to start the process of becoming a Christian and a member of Asbury. When we didn't have the Asbury Room, lay people were available.

We included in our church bulletin and at the end of my service, "To all who sin and need a savior, to all who mourn and seek comfort, to all who are weary and need rest, to whosoever will come, this church opens wide her doors and her heart in the name of Jesus and bids you welcome."

The choir concluded our worship services with:

The Irish Blessing
May the road rise to meet you,
May the wind be always at your back.
May the sun shine warm upon your face,
The rains fall soft upon your fields.

And until we meet again,
May God hold you in the palm of his hand.

We tried to find out who wrote both the Irish Blessing as well as "To all who need a savior," but we were unsuccessful.

As the organist played the recessional, if I didn't need to talk to someone right at that moment, I enjoyed going to one of our exits and greeting the people who had come to worship.

After Sunday Services

After Sunday services, Jayne and I would gather our children, and we would go out for Sunday dinner. Afterwards, I would go to Skyline Terrace Nursing Home to bring the message to the residents. I loved those dear people. My family went home after Sunday dinner, changed from their Sunday clothes, and relaxed together. After preaching, singing, praying, and visiting at Skyline, I would go home to relax with my family. God's path for me was beautiful with abundant blessings.

It was fairly common that someone would bring news on any given day that a member had been admitted to the hospital. I would go as quickly as I could to the hospital to be with that person.

When a pastor serves only one church as I did for twenty-nine years, rather than moving from place to place, a relationship develops between the pastor and the congregation that is warm, loving, and trusting — like a family. As a consequence, I was more likely to know from a concerned member about needs, illnesses, loss of employment, and all kinds of unexpected events that happen. A neighbor or a member might know about an occurrence and would call me or come to our house to make sure I knew.

This deep relationship with my congregation was fulfilling, satisfying, and helpful to me since I was able to respond to needs sooner than later. By and large, our loving church relationship was satisfying and supportive to all concerned.

There was one lady who was a member that I remember would hide from me at the hospital when she would see me coming. She was there for cancer treatment. Sometimes I could sneak up on her though, and she didn't get a chance to hide, and then I would get to pray with her.

Janie Hedrick shared this story: *Bill, Your image of following my John and me into St. Francis hospital at 6:00 am for his surgery is forever imbedded in my mind. Also seeing you, Ken Myers, Bud Mathis and Daryl McRight standing at the door of the ER as I approached that fateful night in October 1992 was a HUGE comfort to me.*

You also fully supported Mary Randolph when she started the VERY successful singles programs at Asbury not long before I became active.

I recall numerous nuggets of wisdom from your sermons, including when you said, "We all know God is with us to the end, but it's those meantimes and inbetween times that get us bogged down." So many people love and respect you, including me.

Hugs and love,
Janie Hedrick

Pastor Versus Office Furniture/Supply Salesman

The greatest advantage my business experiences provided to me as a pastor was first of all, I had made a living calling on people every day in their offices, sometimes at lunch. I found that it was equally appropriate and important as a pastor to call on and visit both members and prospective members of the congregation.

Secondly, spending thirteen years in business prepared me in the overall supervision of the business of the church — financial accountability and personnel supervision. My business experience helped me to easily conduct the business of the church inside and outside the congregation. God's path for me to spend time working in my family's business served me well.

Jayne and the Fourth of July Parades

Jayne thought it would be a good activity to draw the neighbors together. Jayne led a group of women who planned Fourth of July parades for the neighborhood children. In anticipation of the next Fourth of July, Jayne started an advertising campaign. She made signs to take to local merchants to put in their windows which they all did. At the given time on the Fourth of July morning, we were to meet at the Key Elementary School. The children were the main attraction of the event. The regulations were few but very precise. There could be no animals in the parade, no motorized vehicles, and the children were to be the ones to ride in decorated wagons, tricycles, and bicycles. We began by raising the flag. Jayne found a number of students who agreed to come and play the National Anthem on their instruments as the flag was raised on the pole at the school. David Hughes is in Asbury's orchestra now and as a young lad, he played the trumpet. I don't think David will ever forget playing the National Anthem for our Fourth of July parades. The musicians led the way playing drums and a few instruments. We would walk from Key Elementary to the parking lot of the Asbury location on Sheridan.

When we arrived at the Asbury location parking lot, Jayne had arranged games for the children and a watermelon seed spitting contest which Marvin Reecher, Minister of Music, won the first year. The year that we first held our parade, I contacted the man who owned the two McDonalds in town to see if he would bring his machinery that produced cold lemonade for drinks for the children. He did this for several years in a row. The generous man died on a trip to Mexico. There were problems getting his body back to Oklahoma, but I conducted his funeral service at Ninde's Funeral Home. He was generous to our Asbury children on the Fourth of July.

One year, one of the radio stations called Jayne to interview her about the Asbury Fourth of July parade, and when they played the interview on air, we were all sitting around the breakfast room table listening to Jayne, and we thought she sounded just like Lady Bird Johnson. Jayne said, "I'm never going to let anyone interview me again."

My sister, Marilyn, dressed up her three children and drove from Oklahoma City for her children to be a part of our Fourth of July celebration.

Just as Jayne felt led to start the Fourth of July events, she also felt led to stop. Two or three laymen in the church decided they would continue the tradition. It lasted a few more years. Over the years, a large number of people have mentioned to me how much those celebrations and parades meant to their families. It was a ministry Jayne started and is fondly remembered for.

After the first parade, I was contacted by the police department by telephone, and the spokesperson informed me that people who desire to have parades in the city limits must seek permission. I assured them that we would try to follow all the rules from that point forward, and we did.

David Hughes shared this story: *My first memory of Bill was around 1964 when mom, dad and I first began to come to Asbury when our church met at Key Elementary School. He drove his bright red Volkswagen convertible and kept on the move constantly. Jayne asked mom if she could get me to play my trumpet for the raising of the American flag at her Fourth of July parade, and there's not much telling how it sounded but I did my best.*

When we moved into the new church on Sheridan, mom was one of four ladies who volunteered answering the phone during the week.

I always remember Bill singing Turn Your Eyes Upon Jesus on Sunday morning and saying, "To all who sin and need a Savior this church opens wide her doors and her heart and bids you welcome." The calming of his voice on those Sunday mornings and his message of the gospel always set the week on a good path forward for me.

Then as my teenage years approached something terrible began to happen in our home that had a deep impact on me, an only child. My parent's marriage took a turn for the worse, and at the same time Mom was having health issues. As I began to react negatively in rebellion, Mom found herself losing both dad and me. Bill would come to visit her at Miss Jackson's where she was cosmetics manager and support her through her emotional distress. Of course, as he did with all of us in our congregation, when mom went to the hospital, Bill was there, as early as she was, waiting with her and praying. As I got to college, my rebellion got me to the breaking point and I wound up in the hospital myself, in a coma for eight days and then the psychiatric ward for eight weeks. Bill was one of the only ones allowed in to see me during those dark times, and he was there on a regular basis. I was so out of touch with reality that for a time I thought that I was Jesus Christ. I must say that with my pastor, Bill Mason, there with me, it was a little difficult to keep thinking that way! He ministered to my parents the entire time I was hospitalized, caring for them thoroughly.

Seven years and many experiences after all of that, I met my Leslie, we married, and had our first son. I had been living a wild life, playing rugby, drinking, and was not the husband and father Leslie wanted me to be. She was sad, and I thought we should try going back to my old church, Asbury. We brought our son, David, to Bill for Baptism, and Bill charged us with the question that went something like this, "Will you so live your lives before this child that he will learn the gospel, giving reverent attendance to the worship of God?" Through Bill's words at that sacred moment, the Holy Spirit convicted me of just how far away I was from fellowship with Him. I left David's Baptism deep in thought. It may have been the next Sunday that Bill mentioned the Men's Prayer Breakfast, and I figured that I had better try that. Through the message from E. Stanley Jones, presented by pastor Charley Ryser, I was convicted, with the two scriptures I had probably heard from Bill's sermons: Revelations 3:20 " Here I am! I stand at the door and knock. If anyone hears my voice and opens the door, I will come in and eat with that person, and they with me," spoken by LORD Jesus. On February 18, 1983, early in the morning at my breakfast table at home by myself I asked Jesus to take control of my life and forgive my sins. He is always faithful, so of course He did just that. Leslie saw a change in me within 24 hours and asked what happened to me. I told her. She asked how, and I told her how she could do the same. She asked the LORD to come into her life, and her life was forever changed.

When my mom passed away seven years ago, Bill presided over her service. As he and I sat planning the service, Bill told me that I should play my trumpet for her memorial service. Mom had always loved to hear me play, and I couldn't figure out how Bill thought I was going to do that at such a time. But just like always, he was right. I played "Softly and Tenderly Jesus Is Calling" and it helped to begin to heal my broken heart.

Bill went on to baptize Mike and then later Hillary. And then much later he stood before our congregation with our two grandsons, Hunter and Jamison, at about age three and baptized them. One of those little boys said a big "AMEN!" giving the whole congregation some entertainment!

These days I have the privilege of picking Bill up from Montereau on the fourth Wednesday of every month and taking him to Men's Prayer Breakfast. There is no better time in my week than that time we spend together. He is like a father to me; I love him so much. When we get back to his place, we just sit in the car and talk, sometimes for a long time, and I get to hear stories. There is so much wisdom inside him that it reminds me of all of the early morning hours he spends just sitting with Jesus. I often tell people who know Bill that if I can't be with Jesus right here on earth in the flesh, then I've got Bill Mason.

I love you, Bill!
David Hughes

A Surprise Visitor

We had a little dining room that I converted into my office in the 56th street parsonage, and when we built our first building, I had an office at the church. I kept the church telephone installed at home, and when it rang after hours, I could take the call. One evening it rang, and I picked it up, but before I could say, "Hello," I could hear a conversation already in progress. After briefly listening, I figured out that someone was in my office even though the church was supposed to be locked up. It sounded like a teenaged boy talking to his girlfriend. From the conversation, I could tell that he had bought some fried chicken, and he had pulled out the leaf on my desk to use for his supper table. I hung up my telephone, and I called the police. Since I lived only a couple of blocks away, I went to the church. About the time I got there, the police arrived, and I explained who I was and that I was going to go in and see who was in my office. The officer said, "Sir, we strongly advise that you leave the inside work to the police department." It turned out it was indeed a teenaged boy. I had a tape recorder on my desk, and he took it. Believe it or not, that tape recorder was returned to me about ten years later. I was stunned when it was returned, but by the time I got it back, it was so old that it was of no use. I never did know who took it.

Cameron's Goose Egg

We had an all-church celebration that included different activities, but I can't recall what we were celebrating. The boys were out on the corner of the church property playing baseball. Somebody hit Cameron in the head with a baseball bat. I had always heard about goose eggs, and he sure had one. I learned that as long as those goose eggs come out rather than go in, the patient would be all right. It sure did hurt Cameron, but since it bulged outwards, he was okay in a day or so.

The Mission Society for United Methodists

Fairly early in my ministry, I attended an organizational meeting in St. Louis, representing Asbury Church, and from that meeting was borne The Mission Society for United Methodists. A plea was made for individuals and churches to make significant pledges in order to establish an office and to employ a secretary who would be the coordinator as we attempted to bring together other United Methodist Churches that would be interested in establishing The Mission Society. I made a pledge of $10,000 at the meeting not knowing where I would get $10,000. Upon returning to Tulsa and back to work at the church, the Asbury person responsible for Missions, Mary Ann Smith, came to my office and said that $10,000 had become available, and she was in my office to find out where I wanted it spent. I quickly said a prayer thanking God for those funds, because I had no idea where they would come from. Asbury Church produced the amount of money that I had pledged at the meeting. The Missions Society grew into a worldwide organization and is still operating faithfully today.

Mary Ann Smith sent this note to me: *Dear Bill, I thank God every day for your influence in my life through Asbury. You have been a constant encouragement, mentor, and example for our feeble attempts at living out the Christian life. Thank you for being such a blessing to so many people over the years and truly helping others follow Jesus!*

In His love,
Mary Ann

From Paula Rinehart: *Dear Bill, Tim Durie is on my husband's board now and he mentioned you were still in Oklahoma and very much alive! You probably won't remember my husband and me, Stacy and Paula Rinehart, but we served with The Navigators at OSU in the late seventies (78-82). I remember you as a pastor in Tulsa who supported and validated what we were doing on a college campus. It meant a lot. Stacy is 71 now, directing a leader development work called Mentorlink. I've spent the last twenty years counseling others. We have two grown children and five grandchildren. Whenever I hear the song, Turn Your Eyes Upon Jesus, I think of Asbury and thank God for your ministry.*

> *God bless you,*
> *Paula Rinehart*

John Collier, Bruce Olsson, and Oral Roberts

The first year we were in Tulsa, the construction of Oral Roberts University (ORU) was far enough along that a dedication was held. Billy Graham was the principal speaker, and it was held outdoors. Jayne and I attended and marveled at the experience. There was limited seating available; Jayne and I sat on the hood of our car. Billy was well received in Tulsa. When he conducted the first crusade in Oklahoma City, he traveled to Tulsa to speak at an engagement and then returned to Oklahoma City to the crusade. We were so pleased to be able to attend Billy Graham's dedication of Oral Roberts University.

After Oral Roberts and I became acquainted, I was invited to his office. I found Oral to be open and a warm conversationalist. His office was quite large, and his desk was on a raised platform. Having been in the office furniture business, his office was an impressive place for me to see and experience. We discussed all manner of ideas, and I always enjoyed spending time with Oral.

John Collier served on Asbury's staff for three years. John

had responsibility for Singles Ministry and as a consultant to me. I admired John for a number of reasons but one reason in particular: he went to Asbury Seminary his first two years of seminary and then transferred to Perkins School of Theology at Southern Methodist University for his last year. I asked John, "Why in the world would you do that?" He said he wanted to prove to himself that he could uphold the evangelical standard in that hot bed of liberal professors.

I had come to know John when he was the Director of the Wesley Foundation at the University of Tulsa. I served on his board for most of the time he was at the foundation. I became acquainted with him as I watched and listened to his leadership ability of that group of people. He had made the decision to leave the Wesley Foundation and move to Houston to pursue a Ph.D. at Rice University. I persuaded him to delay the move to Houston and come serve with me at Asbury in Tulsa. He agreed.

One day, John told me about a young missionary from Minnesota who felt called to serve as a missionary in South America for the Montilone people. John said that I should invite Bruce Olsson to Asbury to speak.

I did invite Bruce and he came. He stayed with Jayne and me, and he was with us for one week. That connection to Bruce Olsson lasted the entire time I was Senior Pastor at Asbury. He made periodic visits at our invitations to return, and the people at Asbury grew to love Bruce and look forward to his visits. His time was scheduled from the moment he arrived until he departed — teaching and sharing in his selfless manner about the progress of the Montilone people. When Bruce first made contact with the Montilones, they did not have a written language. Bruce developed a language for them, established schools in the jungle where children were taught the Montilone alphabet and language. He also was knowledgeable enough about medicine that he was able to introduce treatments for jungle diseases that were previously only doctored by the Medicine Man. Staying with Jayne and me in our home provided times for us to have lighthearted and serious conversations that impacted our lives.

At one point, Bruce was held prisoner by a rebel group in Colombia for over six months. They threatened to kill him if he did not join their group. They believed that if Bruce were a member, the people of Venezuela would think more of the rebel group. However, Bruce had his reasons for not wanting to be associated with any of these groups. The day came that they said they were going to kill him. They tied him to a tree and had about six tribal people there who Bruce had reached for Jesus Christ. One of them whispered in Bruce's ear, "If we don't shoot you, they will shoot us." The time came and the signal was given to shoot Bruce. It turned out that the leaders had placed blank bullets in the young men's rifles, and when they pulled the triggers, the guns made loud noises, but Bruce was not shot. Bruce later told friends that his reaction to the blank bullets made him angry. He had prepared himself to die, but they pulled this silly trick on him. When the word reached us in the United States that they had not assassinated Bruce but had released him to the Colombian government authorities (since that was closer to the Colombian border), there was a group of us meeting at Lake Junaluska in North Carolina, and as if someone had given us a signal (which no one had done), we all stood up and sang the Doxology. It was a highly emotional experience.

Some years earlier, Bruce had met and was planning to marry a young woman doctor. Bruce was in the United States, fulfilling speaking engagements, when he learned that she had been killed in an automobile accident in Venezuela.

Years later, Bruce was enjoying sending email messages on the computer he built in the jungle, and one day he received a message from a Ph.D./M.D. inquiring how to make coffee from Colombian coffee beans. Bruce responded to the lady's request with instructions. The lady had a follow-up questions about the coffee. Emails were exchanged back and forth, and eventually Bruce said, "Why don't you just come to Bogota (Colombia), and I will teach you how to make Colombian coffee." She went to Bogota, and eventually they were married.

As a result of Oral's interest in Bruce and his work, Oral and I became better friends. Soon, Oral wanted to travel to the jungle to film Bruce's life and ministry. Bruce knew what a monumental task that would be to accommodate Oral, his people, and a big film crew. No one was accustomed to living in jungle conditions, so Bruce declined Oral's request; Evelyn Roberts continued to support Bruce's ministry.

When Oral would learn that Bruce was in Tulsa to speak at Asbury, Oral would contact me about having Bruce come to ORU and speak at Chapel services and to the students in Spanish classes.

The relationship with Oral and Evelyn Roberts continued to grow. Jayne invited Oral and Evelyn to have dinner with us when Bruce Olsson was in Tulsa. Jayne always prepared a banquet, and we enjoyed entertaining them in our home. Bruce would speak at ORU as his time permitted, and without fail, two or three young women would become infatuated with Bruce and would want to marry him and go to the jungle. Bruce would ask me to talk to the women for him since it embarrassed him to talk to women who thought they had fallen in love with him. I don't think I ever saw any of those girls face to face, but I would talk to them on the telephone and was able to dissuade them from thoughts of marriage and ministry in the jungle.

Our friendship eventually led Oral to preach at Asbury on occasion. When Oral would speak at our church, at least half of the attendees would be enthusiastic followers of Oral and there would be exuberant participation from the congregation that I was unaccustomed to. Those were interesting and happy experiences in the life of our church.

Due to this fondness of Bruce by both Oral and Evelyn, Jayne and I were invited to dinners with them. One night at a dinner at Southern Hills Country Club, Evelyn said, "Jayne, Bill and Oral pray all the time. Would you pray for our meal?" Jayne told me later that she had white knuckles and was scared to death as she offered that prayer in front of Oral Roberts.

In Bruce's most recent newsletter, he writes, "The indigenous peoples among whom I am associated (14 different linguistic groups) love the message that God took on human flesh, born Jesus, 'to walk our trails of life's experiences.' He is redeemer and involved in all our lives. The Gospel does not challenge nor destroy the authenticity of traditional tribal values but enables their goals to know their Creator in a personal way; His Spirit can live in each individual's life!" (November/December, 2019)

From Bruce Olsson: *Bill, you introduced me to the Asbury Congregation in the 1960's when a few Methodists were brought together by you and you were meeting in a local school. (I had just finished an engagement at the Native People's Permanent Commission at the United Nations in New York, and was returning to Colombia.) Ever since that meeting, you and Asbury became a faithful supporter as we pioneered to share the Gospel among isolated tribes of NE Colombia.*

I have been living among the Bari (Motilones) since 1960, perhaps the most primitive of South American tribes (according to the Smithsonian Handbook of SA Indians.) My objective was to share the Gospel through the Bari cultural expression and language, respecting God's sovereignty as Creator. They had no contact with the Western world other than conflict, had no barter system, much less a numbering system, and had refused any contact with the "outside" world.

Today, their language is written, and members of the Bari people are composing their legends and histories vindicating their place in Colombian history. Besides their creative literature, we have the translation of the New Testament which is the anchor for the Christian confession within the tribe. Over the past fifty-five years, we

*have sponsored more than four hundred students for ad-
ditional education, besides the basic jungle school preparations, graduating medical physicians, nurses, tropical
agronomists, lawyers, accountants, architects, educators
and the like. Not one of the four hundred tribal students
abandoned their jungles for preference of city life, and all
serve respective communities in the areas of specialized
training. Education is not an end to itself, but is a tool to
better serve the tribes and a means by which the tribes
can forge their own future into the 21st Century.*

*The technical Bari personnel and spiritual members
are sharing the Gospel among nineteen different tribal
communities speaking as many different languages! Bill,
you and Asbury shared resources and life in the compassion of Jesus Christ with the Bari, and they respond in like
manner to assist other isolated peoples. You and Jayne
made an indelible touch on my life and have been so generous to the cause of the Gospel advancement among
the primitive and isolated tribes of NE and SE Colombia.*

Good News Organization

I began to hear about this organization that wanted to return the United Methodist Church to Scriptural Christianity. I
became involved because I contacted the man who was the
executive director of Good News, and he sensed a sincere
interest on my part to become a part of the Board.

I served as Chairman of the Good News Board which was
comprised of men and women from all over the United States
who shared a deep concern about where the church was
headed and what they could do about it. I met some wonderful
people while serving on the Good News Board. Some of them
have served for twenty years or longer and certainly have en-
hanced the ability of this working body because of their experiences and wisdom.

Asbury Church was a young, enthusiastic, growing body

of Christ. Most of the members were born again, spirit-filled Christians and were also concerned about the theological liberalism within Methodism. Dr. James V. Heidinger II soon became the Executive Director and served in that capacity for twenty-eight years. His most recent book on this matter, The Rise of Theological Liberalism and The Decline of American Methodism, published in 2017, is an excellent review of liberalism making its way into the leadership of the mainline denominations in the United States and from there into local pastors and employees of boards and agencies of those denominations. Heidinger is now retired from his position as President and Publisher of Good News and retired as a United Methodist minister. Rob Renfroe is now President of the Good News Organization and Publisher of the Good News Magazine. I haven't met Rob yet, but I have read his theology, and I am enthusiastic about his conservative theological stance.

Every four years prior to the meeting of the General Conference of the United Methodist Church, Good News has had a Legislative Strategy Task Force, made up of both lay persons and clergy, present at General Conference to follow the development of legislation as it was being dealt with in some twelve legislative committees. Thus, Good News would publicize the progress of legislation from the committees and help delegates be better informed and assist them in supporting conservative social and theological positions. This means that at General Conference, there are members of the Good News team working through the night to reproduce information that is then distributed early the next morning to delegates. It is an arduous task. Prior to General Conference, Good News sends appropriate papers to the delegates to inform them about the conservative position regarding proposed legislation. During my administration at Asbury Church, it was not unusual for conference committees to call on Good News to provide the conservative or evangelical point of view for matters being considered at the various Annual Conferences. The latest information on controversial, strategic, and sensitive church matters can be found in the Good News Magazine.

Jayne and I sent monthly financial support to the Good News Organization, and I still support the organization to this very day. I have subscribed to that publication for some forty years and still look forward to every single issue.

Tulsa Faith Leaders

At some point during my middle years at Asbury, I became involved in an Evangelical Crusade in Tulsa. A relative of Billy Graham's was to be the speaker of the crusade. Oral saw to it that I became involved at a level more than I was accustomed. The week's crusade was held downtown at the Tulsa Civic Center; it was attended by thousands and deemed a grand success. I was impressed and pleased by the acceptance and appreciation of Tulsans of the crusade.

When the City of Faith was built then opened, I was named to the Board of the City of Faith Clinic; Evelyn and Richard Roberts were both on the board as well. I continued to enjoy my relationship with Evelyn. It was my only association with Richard Roberts.

The First Presbyterian Church pastor, Dr. Jim Miller, was another outstanding Christian leader in our community. Jim was a warm, caring man with national responsibilities for the Presbyterian church. When meeting Jim, it becomes readily apparent why he was an outstanding faith leader, and I enjoyed my association with him.

When David Willets was pastor of Parkview Baptist Church, located across the street from the Sheridan location of Asbury, we had a friendly relationship and took turns sharing each other's pulpits on Thanksgiving Eve. Both congregations would attend, and David would bring the message at Asbury; the next year I would bring the message at Parkview. We did that for a number of years.

Billy Joe Daugherty, founder and pastor of Victory Christian Center, told me one day in conversation that when he graduated from Oral Roberts University, he came to my office looking for a job. I had no recollection of that meeting or conversation at the time he told me about it. Billy Joe went on to start the Victory Christian School, Victory Bible Institute, and Victory World Missions Training Center.

I have known First United Methodist Church, Tulsa, Senior Pastor Jessica Moffat for years. She also came to Asbury when she graduated from seminary seeking a job. Jayne asked me if I hired her, and when I said that I had not, Jayne wisely said, "You missed your chance." In addition to being a wonderful United Methodist Pastor, Jessica is highly skilled and trained in opera. I wish I could remember all of her many achievements.

Campus Crusade and Don and Sue Myers

During my tenure at Asbury, I always supported Campus Crusade for Christ; I understand the organization has undergone a name change to "Cru" and one of the Sunday School class that I attend, the Joy Class, sends monthly support to a couple who works with college students in Colorado with Cru.

Don and Sue Myers worked with Campus Crusade for Christ, but Sue and Don have died. Before joining Campus Crusade, Don was a manufacturer's representative for a company, and our family office supply and furniture business in Oklahoma City was a customer of Don's company. Don knew my mother before he and I ever met. On one of his trips to Tulsa, Don looked me up, and from that first acquaintance, we became fast friends. Don left business to join and work for Campus Crusade full-time. Don and Sue spent years in Kenya, London, and American locations, but they always kept in touch by mail. When returning to Tulsa, which was their home, they would let us know they were coming, and we would always make time to visit and catch up on their activities.

Don and Sue had children when they joined Campus Crusade, and I remember the stories they would tell about the children's experiences in Kenya. Never having traveled to any African nation, I knew nothing about the country nor customs other than what friends would tell me. Each time the Myers would tell me about activities or programs the children were involved in, I read the details with keen interest. This included an ongoing story about one of their little boys who was bitten by an insect which has left him with pain throughout his body for all of his adult life. He lives with this pain with help from God, prayer, and faith.

Honorary Doctor of Humane Letters Degree from Oklahoma City University

I served on the Board of Trustees of Oklahoma City University for a number of years, and on May 15, 1982, I was asked to attend commencement and was awarded an Honorary Doctor of Humane Letters Degree from Oklahoma City University. Jayne and I attended with my mother. It is heartening to me to this day to continue to receive communications from the university highlighting students' success in Broadway careers.

Boards and Associations

Due to Asbury's growth, I was asked to serve on more and more boards and associations. Some of the associations that I served are: Alumni Association of the University of Oklahoma, Governor's Committee on Ethics in Government, Board of Trustees for Oklahoma City University, and the Alcoholism Advisory Council of State Department Board of Mental Health.

My Tulsa community involvement included being a member for over twenty-five years of the Southeast Rotary Club of Tulsa. I served as Secretary-Treasurer, and Asbury member and physician, Dr. Jim Mizell, was the general chairman of the bell ringing crew, and the whole group of us served as bell ringers for the Salvation Army at Southroads Mall at 41st and Yale. I served as a bell ringer for over twenty years, and every year I was a bell ringer, I caught a bad cold. It was fun speaking to and watching all of the people as they would come and go. I served as president of the Southeast Rotary Club of Tulsa from 1981 through 1982.

I was also a Member of the Board of the American Red Cross of Tulsa. When I was overseas in the Army, I heard criticism of American Red Cross workers, and I wanted to learn if the employed workers of the American Red Cross were negligent or committed to their jobs. I was pleased to find they were responsible and hard workers.

Additionally, I am a past member of the Mayor's Council on Alcoholism of Tulsa; I was chairman of this board at one time. Part of our responsibility was when those organizations sought financing for their organization and approached our board for assistance, we were responsible for studying the activities of that organization and making decisions whether or not to support them financially. My motivation to serve on this board stemmed from firsthand experience with alcohol. With those individuals who experienced alcoholism, I was able to deal with the alcoholics and their problems. One of the important facts I learned was that alcoholics are generally liars. They would tell a lie rather than the truth in order to acquire that next drink; knowing the behavior of an alcoholic saves considerable time and untold resources that would otherwise be consumed following their lies and stories. I have dealt considerably with alcoholics I met while on the board and within my own congregation.

At one point a member asked to start an Alcoholics Anonymous (AA) group at Asbury, and I knew there was an active group at St. Francis Hospital. I received approval from Asbury to begin a group; I called the hospital to find out if they still had the group, and I learned the group was being discontinued. I told the director to send anyone interested for help to Asbury UMC since we were beginning an AA group at our church. The group was well served by several church members who were committed to the AA program.

I also served on the Board of Tulsans for Community Values. Johnna Himes was responsible for me being named a "Point of Light" recipient on December 7, 2001.

"Points of Light are the soul of America. They are ordinary people who reach beyond themselves to the lives of those in need, bringing hope and opportunity, care and friendship." – President George H. W. Bush

I was incredibly touched that Johnna, who I met in 1964 at Key Elementary School, would go to so much effort for that award.

My Mother Was One to Help Out

I tell this story since my mother loved Harry Denman, and I received the Harry Denman Award for Evangelism from the Oklahoma Annual Conference of the United Methodist Church (UMC). Harry Denman never married but gave his life to promoting evangelism in local churches. He had a living room/bedroom in his office in Washington, DC since he traveled so much. My mother enjoyed listening to him preach, and at an event at Pennsylvania United Methodist Church in Oklahoma City where a dinner was served, Harry dropped food on his clothes during the dinner. My mother took Harry's shirt, tie, and suit to the cleaners and returned it to him promptly. Mother loved good Methodist preachers (her daddy was a Methodist preacher); she even offered to pay for lessons for this poor Methodist preacher that he might improve and become a good Methodist preacher.

One time, Mom was visiting her sister in Dallas, and they attended her sister, Catherine's church. Catherine's Sunday School class met in a large room and they sat in circle. Catherine and my mom were sitting on one side of the circle, and there was a woman across from them with a mink stole who wouldn't keep her knees together. Mother got up and walked around the circle and took the ladies' mink stole from her shoulders and draped it over her lap. The teacher continued.

David Thomas

During United Methodist Church district meetings, I reconnected with David Thomas. I had met David when he was commuting to Perkins School of Theology at Southern Methodist University in Dallas, Texas. We did not have classes together since he was a year ahead of me. We became acquainted, but he was from Tulsa, and I was from Oklahoma City, with no idea where I would be appointed. David was serving churches while in seminary, and his wife, Patty, stayed in the parsonage in Tulsa as he commuted each week. He was appointed to Aldersgate Methodist Church in Tulsa before I came to Tulsa. When I graduated from seminary and was appointed to Asbury in Tulsa, David had been serving Aldersgate a full year before I arrived. I looked upon David as an experienced pastor. Anytime an issue would arise that I didn't know what to do, I would quickly pick up the telephone and explain my dilemma and ask for help. David was always generous with his time and his obvious desire to help me. David served several Oklahoma Methodist churches before retiring and coming to Asbury. Tom Harrison hired David to serve as pastor. I was delighted David was at Asbury, and we have enjoyed working together and enjoying our lifelong friendship.

From Pastor David Thomas: *I'm grateful for my relationship with Bill Mason through the years. Patty and I first met Bill and Jayne in the early sixties while we were attending Perkins School of Theology at Southern Methodist University in Dallas, Texas. We were both in school together. We both graduated, but I think that Perkins just gave up on us and let us go. I came to Aldersgate Methodist Church in Tulsa in 1963, and Bill came to Asbury in 1964. Both of those churches were new congregations. I watched Bill as he drove his red Volkswagen around and poured himself into that small congregation as he visited every home in his area, taking the Gospel of Christ to* *lead a number of people to come to know the Lord Jesus Christ for the first time.*

Bill did it right as he developed Asbury into a strong, vibrant congregation of over 5,000 members. I do not know of another pastor that I have admired more than Bill, and I praise God that we can blend our lives together in our retiring years at Asbury. My wife, Patty, and Jayne both died from brain cancer only two months apart. What an inspiration and comfort it was to go through the Grief-Share program at Asbury with Bill.

I am honored to call him my friend,
David Thomas

Little Blue Books

At some point in time, someone gave me a little blue prayer booklet that had meaningful scripture references for people who were ill. I thought the booklet would be useful for Asburians, and the church made them available to anyone who wanted one. Two dynamic women, Sarah Bailey and Mary Ellen Bridwell, took that booklet and amplified it by adding to it. One of the women received some money from someone who had been ill and passed away and did not ask me for money to reproduce the booklet. The women published it and provided it to members, but they wanted no attention nor did they put their names in the booklet.

Barbara Engler provided me with her story about the use of that Little Blue Book. *Bill Mason had a blue prayer booklet available to members of the church to commemorate the lives of two personal friends, Ronald Mermoud and Donald Plant, who were two faithful servants of the Lord. I carried one of the booklets in my purse for years for the purpose to bring my husband to the Lord. Ronald Engler was raised a Christian, but as a young boy, he saw people in church act differently when* *they were in town. He decided he wanted nothing to do with that Christian thing. We married in 1973, and at that time we both were not following Jesus. I accepted Christ with some direction from the Holy Spirit thru Bill Elliott, my Sunday school teacher in 1978. My childhood was very dysfunctional, with my father beating my mother so badly, that she died nine months later in the hospital. About this same time, 1978, in our marriage, Ronald begin to have heart attacks, strokes, and I realized that I did not want to be alone again, as I was the oldest in my family, and took the blunt of the family troubles. My husband battled the heart problems for twenty years with no complaints, but refused to hear any talk about Jesus from me. At last, he was a patient in Hillcrest Hospital (we had been in all Tulsa hospitals the twenty years he fought the disease) where he had a particular dangerous episode and I was called by the hospital from my job (which just happened to be across the street, Parkside Mental Hospital). When I walked into his hospital room in September, 2000, he said "Tell me about Jesus." I was really ready with the Mason blue prayer booklet and begin our discussion for many days, until he went to be with Jesus on December 11, 2000, at our home. The Hounds of Heaven prevailed,*

Praise the Lord,
Barbara Engler

Miracle of Seed Faith

Thinking about books, Oral Roberts would send me books from time to time. One book he sent me, I ordered to provide to Asburians. One book was *Miracle of Seed Faith* by Oral Roberts.

Susie Barrett provided this story of how Oral's book influenced her life. *When Jim and I first joined Asbury in 1971, Bill sent us (and other families) a copy* *of Oral Roberts' book, Miracle of Seed Faith. We first thought the book was asking for money, but this was totally about giving and receiving. When we put our faith in God's hands like a seed we planted, we are giving God something to work with. Give a smile, receive a smile; do a good deed, one will come to you. This was a big turning point for me to see that it was not just about money but love. I do thank and love Bill for all he has done for Jim and me over all these wonderful years,*

Susie Barrett

Dick McKee

In my latter middle years as Senior Pastor, Dick McKee joined our staff. He is the nearest person to a brother that I ever had. I love that man, dearly. Dick introduced a twist to our evangelism program that I had not had an experience with, but I trusted him. In the sanctuary, there were double doors on the north side of the sanctuary adjacent to the choir loft. Those doors led to Goodwin Hall, but Dick thought we should create the Asbury Room on the other side of those doors. When I gave an invitation for salvation and church membership at the end of the sermon, as I always did, those interested were to go into the Asbury Room at the front of the church rather than come to me to receive them into the church. Lay men and women were in that room who had been trained and were prepared to ask those who answered my invitation, "If you were to die tonight, do you know where you would spend eternity?" The plan of salvation was given to anyone asking to be saved. The change in how we handled those who answered the invitation for salvation and interest in church membership had a tremendous impact on the growth of Asbury. Only one couple interested in church membership when asked about salvation was incensed to be asked, "If you were to die tonight, do you know where you would spend eternity?" as they had been Methodists for a number of years, and they announced that they would not be returning. However, the responses I received from the lay persons who manned the Asbury Room and those who began their membership process in that way were cooperative and pleased with the Asbury Room. Before leaving the Asbury Room, an appointment was made for each person to visit with one of the staff pastors in the coming week to talk about a relationship with Jesus Christ and the desire to make a public profession of faith. I was heartened to see church membership growing again and souls being saved. When the board and I closed the Asbury Room, our new member numbers began to decline.

On a day that I was not in the office, Johnna answered the telephone, and it was one of the laymen in the church. Although I wasn't there for him to talk to, he was hot enough that he was going to talk to someone, and he chewed Johnna out about the Asbury Room blocking his ability to go straight from the sanctuary to Goodwin Hall. Most anyone can chew me out from now until next Sunday, and I can handle it, but I did not want our employees to be chewed out. The fellow was totally inappropriate. I returned his call and got him out of a meeting. I said, "I'm calling you about the way you treated Johnna on the telephone, and I don't want you to ever do that again. If you aren't happy about something, you wait until you can get me on the telephone." I always tried to be reasonable; I always listened because I knew I was not perfect, and I could learn from other people. But I was not going to stand for Johnna to be treated that way. That is a memory that will not leave me, but fortunately I have very few of those.

Johnna Himes

Johnna and I worked together with God for twenty-eight years, and she must be equally credited for Asbury's progress. Everything about Johnna was letter perfect. We remain good friends to this day. Jerry and Johnna live in the same building where I live at Montereau. They were bringing me to church every Sunday morning until their recent health issues, and they were picking me up just before noon on Saturdays to have hot dogs together at Coney I-Lander. They are both still God's blessings to me and to the Asbury Church family.

Monday Afternoon Bible Study

At some point in our ministry in order for our members to know scripture better, Jayne and I began a Monday afternoon Bible Study in our home. The Bible Study was well attended, and Edie Washburn was the teacher. The Bible Study continued on into our retirement. I became the teacher after Edie "retired."

A Sweet and Sorrowful Fact

As I have mentioned, I had earned a living in the office supply business for several years by calling on customers. I had developed a schedule whereby I would visit my customers on certain days of the week. I called on prospective customers as time permitted. On Sundays in the church, I seized the opportunity when we had Sunday morning visitors. Through the week as time permitted, I would always visit the visitors in their homes. If they indicated they wanted to join the church or were interested, I could answer any question they had when I visited. I made sure I visited every person before they joined Asbury.

I remember feeling hurt the first time that a family joined the church that I had not had an opportunity to visit first at home. I truly felt like it was my responsibility to visit in the visitors' homes, and when that first family joined without a visit from me, it felt like they cut me off at the pass by not getting to visit them in their home. The fact of the matter was, the growth of the church had become such that I could not visit everyone before they joined. It was a sweet and a sorrowful fact of helping God grow Asbury United Methodist Church.

Still, after writing this book, I do not know what I want to say about helping God grow Asbury's Church membership from 118 to over 5,200 members. However, I do know that each and every morning I asked God to lead me in His path He had set before me, and I trusted His leading throughout every single day. I still ask God every morning to lead me, and I trust and obey.

We received new members who moved to Tulsa with Amoco. Hundreds of employees were transferred to Tulsa from Casper, Wyoming; Chicago, Illinois — four or five different places. When a family or individual would buy a lot or a house, the news was shared with Amoco friends about the location of the lot or house, and people began to move hand over fist into the area where Asbury was located. Several of the new people were Methodists, and Asbury was close. Many Methodists and new Methodists joined Asbury after visiting.

I will be forever grateful that Asbury was a welcoming and pleasing church to so many wonderful people. God's path for me was oftentimes hard to imagine.

Jim and Beth Goodwin

One family, Jim and Beth Goodwin, joined Asbury in that Amoco stampede. They had two daughters and twin boys, and every Saturday morning, Jim would get those two boys and bring them to the church. Jim made it his business to find out how every Sunday School teacher wanted the classrooms arranged, and Jim and the boys would go to every one of the rooms and arrange the furniture in the classrooms as he knew the teachers wanted it. He was better than a paid employee. He was dependable and insistent, and I don't know how he got those boys to come to the church every Saturday morning, but he did. Jim devoted endless hours working at the church after his work day ended at Amoco. Beth was active in teaching little children and worked in our weekday preschool. We named one building of our church, "Goodwin Hall." I don't remember how many years the Goodwins were in Tulsa, but eventually

Amoco moved them to another location. They returned to Tulsa for visits with their remaining daughter and always attended church at Asbury on Sunday. I stayed in touch with Jim and Beth until each of them died. Jim was highly committed to the Lord Jesus Christ and to serving the church. Beth Goodwin had an endless supply of love that was shared willingly with the children she spent time with every week.

Five Building Programs

During the time I was Senior Pastor at the Asbury Church at Sheridan location, we had five building programs, and we financed every program by selling church bonds. I had never sold church bonds, but I found the key to success was that whatever the savings and loan companies were paying in interest, we paid an additional one percent. We paid more than the savings and loans, so people could take their money out of their savings accounts and buy Asbury Church bonds and tell their friends, family, and neighbors about it. I became so weary of selling church bonds, but I cherish the memories of all of our precious church members who worked so hard to sell those bonds.

I was about to give up one day during our fifth bond program. That fifth program seemed to be the toughest of them all. We had sold all but $55,000 of the church bonds, and I did not have any idea of who to contact or where to go to sell the rest of those bonds. As I sat working in my office one day, in walked Wayne Rogers. He said, "Bill, I just retired from Sun Oil, and I took cash for my retirement money, and I want to invest it to pay for my children's educations. I've got $55,000 I would like to invest." And with that one statement, that put us out of the bond business. I have only fainted once in my life, but that was a close second. We lived happily ever after. Praise the Lord!

We could not get any banker interested in talking to us about financing any of our building projects, so that is why we sold church bonds. As soon as Asbury's current Senior Pastor, Tom Harrison, came to Asbury and we decided to build on

Mingo, bankers lined up to talk to Tom to lend us the money we needed for the enormous building project.

Fair Haven

We lived in our first Asbury parsonage on the 56th street almost ten years, and the children were ten years older. Sharing bedrooms was still a necessity, but it was no longer a popular necessity with our younger generation. I began to talk to the trustees about building a parsonage. About that time, Never Fail, who was a member of the church and a real estate developer, bought a piece of property behind The Kirk (formerly Kirk of the Hills Presbyterian Church). Never Fail said, "Bill, why don't you and Jayne come over, and if the trustees approve it, I'll build a new parsonage up here, and you can choose your own lot." That piece of property sloped from 61st to maybe 66th; we picked a lot that was at the highest point of the land. We could see all of downtown Tulsa. There was obviously a good bit of cutting and filling that was going to have to take place except on the top of this hill, so we thought that would be the place for our home. Never Fail and the trustees got together, and Never agreed to build the parsonage for money realized from selling the original parsonage on 56th street, and I am here to tell you that the price of the 56th house and the cost of the house on Sandusky was not close. Never paid a good bit of his own money for the house to finish it. Jayne did the floorplan of the new house, and when Jayne went to Heaven, I sold it and moved to Montereau. We loved Fair Haven so very much.

Honorary Doctor of Divinity Degree from Oral Roberts University, May 1, 1977

Oral Roberts called me one day on the telephone and asked if I would be willing to accept an Honorary Doctorate of Divinity Degree from Oral Roberts University. I was genuinely surprised, and I told him that I would. The night before this honor was bestowed upon me, Cameron went to a Memorial High School class party. He and his friend were body builder enthusiasts, and at this party, the boys pulled up shrubberies to show who was the strongest. Memorial security took a dim view of that and suggested calling the police. The boys did not think that was necessary. The physical layout of the party's location had a way for the boys to get away by dropping down from the security level into the swimming pool area. When Cameron dropped, he hit his chin on the pool's edge causing damage to his mouth and teeth. Friends took him to a friend's house whose parents weren't home to make sure he didn't die. In the meantime, I was receiving telephone calls late at night from people asking if I knew where Cameron was. I said he was at a class party. Finally, some people came by our house late at night to tell me that Cameron was not at the party; he had been injured. I began calling hospital emergency rooms, and I could not locate Cameron. Eventually, Cameron called me, and I told him to come home immediately, and he did. I called Dr. Rex Smith (an Asbury member and dentist) and told him what had happened. He said to bring Cameron to his office the next morning for an examination. Although Cameron made impact with the cement with his chin, his chin wasn't cut but some of his teeth were broken. The next morning the Mason family went to ORU for the presentation of the Honorary Degree, and Cameron sat behind Jayne and me suffering in silence while I received this high honor.

A Hard Lesson

A dear woman came to Tulsa with her husband who worked for Amoco, and from day one, I argued verbally with her, as she didn't hesitate to tell me how she felt about anything I said. This went on for thirteen, fourteen years. One day I was praying, and the Lord said, "Bill, do you think your attitude toward this woman is Christian?" And I said, "No, Lord, I don't." He said, "You need to get to work on your attitude." I continued to pray about that, and this dear woman and I are now the best of friends. She tolerates me and seldom does she criticize me unless I start talking about gambling, and she says, "Now Bill, farmers are gamblers." I'll go to my grave hearing her say that, but I wasn't about to argue or debate with her whether or not farmers are gamblers. God changed my attitude, and I love that woman now.

Trips to Israel

After our first trip to Israel in 1964 after seminary, we made six more trips to Israel. I thoroughly enjoyed going to Israel, and I looked forward to going each and every time. However, as our Asbury Israel groups continued to grow, the trips became more and more demanding and exhausting. However, with each trip, I became better acquainted with the guide I always requested who was with the tour company. He had an amazing knowledge of both the Old and New Testaments and was always able to answer any questions that anyone in our groups had regarding where we were or what we were seeing. Since he gave scriptural references to those kinds of questions, it was hard for me to believe that he wasn't a Christian although I knew he wasn't. We always stayed in nice hotels and received wonderful service for meals and good care of our rooms; we were always on time for departures for our day trips.

There were always people ready to suggest that it would not be wise to be making trips to Israel because of dangers. I concluded after the second trip that there will never be a time in history other than ancient times when anybody could say with any certainty that safety could be assured. The guides were briefed each morning before taking their groups out about the places that were hotspots at that particular time and best to avoid. They didn't mention that to tourists, but if necessary, they would always substitute a different sight for us to enjoy visiting.

There is nothing I have experienced in life that made scripture come alive like walking in places where Jesus walked, seeing prisons where Christians had been persecuted, and I've never had anyone say to me that the trip to Israel was a big disappointment.

We always visited the Dead Sea. From my notes I made when we visited Israel the first time, I wrote on Sunday evening, February 23, 1964, "From Jericho we drove to the River Jordan where tradition says John the Baptist baptized Jesus. I was surprised to see the entire area showing the signs of a most recent flood. Our guide told us that the river had flooded three times this year. At the point we were looking, the river was at least 50 feet wide and about 18 feet deep with the water coursing down. This river empties into the Dead Sea. This river is the cause of much unrest between Arabs and Jews in that the Jews say they are going to divert it all into Israel. The Jordanians and Arab Republic states say that they will fight. The animosity toward the Jew is quite real here. From the River Jordan we went to the shore of the Dead Sea. This was somewhat interesting to see. The Jordan people say that the River Jordan will dry up in 100 years if the Jews cut off the water supply.

It was fascinating to me to see the place where the Dead Sea Scrolls were found. Some shepherd boys were eating their lunches and saw a small cave, went inside, and found them. Those scrolls have been put on temporary display in exhibitions at museums and public venues. One museum close to the Dead Sea where the scrolls are displayed is of particular interest to me since it is a rich part of our Christian history.

The Kibbutz communities (agricultural) in Israel that started in 1909 were also of interest to me. They had a series of years where they did not receive much rainfall. The Sea of Galilee became smaller and smaller until it revealed a wooden boat stuck in the mud. They carefully dug all around the exterior of the boat, excavated it, and placed it on dry land in a building where they could control the moisture so the wood would not dry out and rot. The people who ran this place were knowledgeable about the Sea of Galilee. No one claimed the boat was the one that Jesus rode in when he quieted the storm, but it was a large boat that existed at the time that Jesus would have been at the Sea of Galilee, and that was most impressive to me.

On one of our trips to Israel, my mother and her mother, Rue Mother, joined us.

Mother bought Rue Mother (my grandmother) a campstool, and each time we stopped on the walking tour for a lecture, Rue Mother would sit on the campstool and enjoy the lecture and the rest. They didn't miss one day of the entire trip to Israel.

Revisiting Switzerland and Israel with our Older Children

Jayne and I wanted to take Robin, Cameron, and Randy to Switzerland and Israel when they were older since they had been tots when we were there in 1964, but of course we wouldn't leave Peggie behind. We traveled to Switzerland, stayed at the Schweizerhof, and made day trips to several beautiful places. One memorable place that Peggie and Robin planned for us to visit was to a glacier on the side of a mountain. We started out on a bus ride and encountered a farmer who was herding his cattle down the highway, and our bus driver stopped to let the farmer and his herd pass through. Farmers were able to buy the hay up in the mountains, and the way they gathered the hay was by securing a long, long cable stretched from the valley into the mountains where the hay was cabled down to the farm. They cut swatches of hay to fasten to the cable, and the hay would slide down the mountain on the cable to then be fastened to a vertical pole in the ground on the farmer's property. As the pile of hay grew, it resembled the shape of a Christmas tree. The farmer would start at the bottom and slice a chuck of hay to feed the cattle, and the shape of the tree would then change to a pole shape. The process fascinated all of us.

We left the bus and boarded a cog railway that took us further into the mountains until we came to the entrance of the tunnel that had been dug so that people could walk through the tunnel to see the world through the ice glacier which was beautiful. At the top was a restaurant with a beautiful view where we enjoyed lunch.

At one point in this trip, we headed to Israel. The children were older, so it was a wonderful, enjoyable trip and experience.

Having gone the number of times I have gone and with different groups, it was always interesting to me to see the reaction of people in the groups as to what they saw, heard, and experienced. Frequently, fresh ideas and questions arose which had not happened in previous groups. The guides frequently made comments in talking about sites and places and added what scripture had to say. Interesting observations were made about how those sites and places had affected society to the present time. For example, when we would have a layover at an airport, the people in our groups would want to walk around and look at places. They were cautioned by airport personnel not to put down pieces of carry-on luggage or briefcases they were carrying and expecting to pick them up when returning. Those who did leave briefcases or purses would find them gone, but they got their items back after showing their identification papers substantiating the items were their belongings. The government's intent was that no one would leave a briefcase with a concealed bomb.

One of my visits to Israel included part of a cruise. The ship docked in Tel Aviv, and we indicated where we would like to visit that day. We all boarded appropriately labeled buses and scurried off to see our places of interest. It was dark by the time we started back to the ship in our bus. A woman got on the bus while the driver was waiting for us to return to visit with the bus driver. As we traveled back to the port, I became sleepy as did most everyone. Suddenly the bus came to a halt; the lights turned on in the bus; the driver held up a purse asking, "Is this your purse?" No one identified it. The driver left the bus to open the purse to inspect the contents. There was nothing to threaten damage to the bus or people in the purse, so he announced that was the case, turned off the lights, and off we went to the port. We learned that a lady had come to visit the bus driver, and she had left her purse on the bus. I was no longer sleepy after that.

When driving around the country of Israel maybe every quarter mile off to the side of the road, there was a hole big enough for a refrigerator. Finally, out of curiosity, I asked what the holes were for. The guide explained that if people discovered bombs in their vehicles, they could dispose of them in one of these holes.

Hart and Marty Morris

At a Staff Parish Relations Committee meeting, the decision was made to begin the search for a new Minister of Music for Asbury. There is an organization that communicates with Ministers of Music throughout the United States, and the Staff Parish Relations Committee notified the organization of our desire. We received more than 24 applications for the position. Asbury's committee divided the applications, studied them carefully, and came up with a half dozen prospects. The entire committee went over the six finalists and made a decision: Hart and Marty Morris. We extended an invitation for them to come to Asbury for an interview. They interviewed us, and we interviewed them. At the time we invited them, they were serving a Presbyterian church in Texas. Between the time they accepted the invitation and their actual arrival, I attended a seminar. The Senior Pastor of the Presbyterian church where they were serving was at that seminar, and I had an opportunity to talk to him at length about Hart and Marty Morris. The Senior Pastor knew that the Morrises had applied for our position. Marty's parents lived in the Tulsa area.

Jayne and I drove to the Tulsa airport to pick them up then we drove them to the church. I was not aware of this, but Hart's background was Southern Baptist, and there is a practice in the Southern Baptist church that when a Senior Pastor leaves a church to go to another, the leadership (which would include the Minister of Music) was expected to submit a resignation. While walking to our car after meeting them at the airport, among other things, I wanted them to know I would be retiring the following June which left Hart trying to figure out, "Why are we here interviewing for this job when I will have to resign in fewer than six months?" Later in the process when I found out about the Southern Baptist tradition, we both had a good laugh.

The Morrises made the decision to accept our offer, and they set about finding a place to live and making preparation to move.

Both Hart and Marty are Christians, and they practice their Christianity in their daily living. They are both exceptional people as well as musicians. They served Asbury for twenty years and one week. They stayed an extra week since the interim music director couldn't start until the next week.

Hart and Marty had outstanding relationships with the congregation, choir, and orchestra members. It was only after Hart had a health incident that he and Marty felt the best decision was for them to retire. They bought a farm in Coweta and have lived there happily raising horses and vegetables (as Marty is a vegetarian) and participating in a Baptist church in Muskogee, Oklahoma, where their daughter and her young family are members.

Senior Pastor Tom Harrison and the Morrises also developed a friendship of respect and Christian love that endures to this day.

Hart and Marty are invited to fill-in when needed at Asbury and graciously accept and carry on their tradition of music, Christian love, and excellence. They continue to be loved by all. The multitude of musical programs that Hart and Marty have produced (in addition to regular Sunday services) have been stellar and will long be remembered by Asbury United Methodist Church and by me.

Weddings

One year, I looked back on the number of weddings I had conducted the previous year, and considering all the time spent in pre-marital counseling, rehearsals, rehearsal dinners, the weddings, and the receptions, the time added up to one-third of the year — just in weddings. At the time, it didn't seem that consuming, but when I looked at the facts, there they were. My judgment is that the pre-marital counseling was as important as anything else I did. I believe it is vitally important for the bride, groom, and pastor to have opportunities to sit and talk. Hopefully as the pastor, I sensed areas of the relationship that might not be as strong as it could be or might not exist at all within the people I counseled. Pre-marital counseling for me was not merely saying, "This is some good advice I would like to suggest to you." It was more than that. I wanted to help them look seriously and honestly at personal convictions. I believed that the pattern that I had developed regarding a Christian marriage might not be definitive but would come close. A successful marriage begins in the heart and mind of a man and woman that Jesus Christ is Lord, Master, and Savior of their lives and that they will promise God if they have not already done so that they will see to it that they continue to grow in their love for Jesus and their commitment to Him. That can best be done by faithful attendance to Sunday School and Worship and not merely hit and miss experiences for their lives.

I felt that if I was going to conduct the wedding that this was important enough to be brought up in pre-marital counseling then spending enough time as necessary in two, three, or four more meetings regarding their marriage.

There is one area that was difficult for me and that was to realize how time was changing attitudes of individuals and large segments of society regarding pre-marital sex or living together before marriage. And my deficiency was my reluctance to bring up the subject.

As Senior Pastor and then Pastor Emeritus of Asbury United Methodist Church in Tulsa for over 56 years, I have had the rare opportunity to see individuals and couples I had conducted the weddings for return to Asbury to visit. It has become a meaningful and wonderful blessing for me to hear them say, "We are still married."

Barbi Davis reminded me of a story I had forgotten: *Hi Bill, When Adam and I were engaged and about to marry at Asbury, we went through pre-marital counseling with you. This included meeting several times. We talked about the upcoming wedding service and what it takes to have a successful marriage. During the time we spent with you, you told us a story that has stuck with us to this day. You said, "There is no such thing as the underwear fairy." Adam and I looked at each other and didn't quite know what to say. You then said, "If you have fresh-folded underwear in your drawer, always thank the person who put it there." Bill was telling us in his sweet way that we should never take even the smallest kindness for granted and to always say, "Thank you." To this day, no matter who has folded and put away laundry at our house, we always say to each other, "Thank you, Underwear Fairy." We've been married over 23 years with two girls who you baptized.*

> *We love you, Bill,*
> *Barbi, Adam, Lila Jayne, and Kate Davis*

Basil James reminded me about two James' Family Weddings: *On June 17, 1979, my son, Dan, and his bride, Debbie, married in our living room, and Bill Mason performed the ceremony. On May 30, 2005, Gay and I married in the living room of Dan and Debbie James, and Bill Mason performed the ceremony.*

> *Basil*

Basil James

Basil was born in Wagoner, Oklahoma. He had known his first wife, Barbara, since elementary school. I met Basil on the tennis court behind my grandfather's church in Wagoner when Basil was a kid, and I was almost a teenager. The tennis court was a dirt court, and Basil and Barbara would come to the tennis court to play tennis when they weren't in school or working to have fun with other teenagers. Then they would be in church for the youth group on Sundays and for worship.

When Basil and Barbara were young people and when they started dating, they attended my grandfather, Papa Cameron's church. Papa was their pastor as they were growing up. Papa and Rue Mother were going to retire in Wagoner, and announced to the church that they would remain active in the life of the church, but Papa would no longer be able to perform weddings, funerals, and Baptisms. Basil and Barbara were going to marry at some point but not in time for Papa to perform the wedding. Basil and Barbara did get married in Muskogee, and Papa and Rue Mother were able to attend.

At one point, Basil and Barbara were members of Memorial Drive United Methodist Church in Tulsa. They discovered along the way that I was the pastor at Asbury. When they heard that I was coming to Tulsa to serve at Asbury, and they realized I was Papa's Cameron's grandson, they joined Asbury, and it was like finding family. I love Basil and Barbara, and I enjoyed my relationship with Barbara until she went to Heaven. I had the privilege of performing the wedding of Basil and Barbara's, son, Dan, and his wife, Debbie. And then I had the pleasure of performing the wedding of Basil and Gay.

Basil is one of the men who picks me up on Wednesdays to attend the Men's Prayer Breakfast at the church. Basil takes me to get my hair cut, and he is a dear and faithful friend. The only time I have ever been squirrel hunting was when Basil lined us up to hunt in the Choskee Bottoms (the river) closer to Muskogee than Wagoner. I shot at one squirrel, and it sailed down to the ground. I thought I had shot it until he got up and ran off. It was flying squirrel which I had never heard of.

Baptisms

Baptisms for the most part were generally extraordinarily enjoyable occasions for me and for the families. To illustrate what I mean, Barbara and Adam Davis named their first baby girl after my wife, Jayne: Lila Jayne Davis. When Barbi and Adam were going to have Lila Jayne baptized, in 2007, I thought it would be fun to have Jayne participate in the Baptism. Jayne was excited to do her first Baptism, and she did a good job of holding the water vessel; I remembered my lines; Lila Jayne was good as gold, and the parents, grandmother, great-grandfather, and friends all looked on lovingly and adoringly. Lo and behold the church bulletin indicated Lila Jayne was being baptized as Lila Jayne "Mason" not "Davis." We all had a big laugh over it and another laugh when Victoria Williamson said she had typed Jayne Mason's name so many times in her years at Asbury, that she typed "Lila Jayne Mason" without giving it a thought. Barbi said I would always have to claim Lila Jayne which I am happy to do. Sometimes Lila Jayne and her sister, Kate, come to the Joy Class dinners on Tuesdays with their grandmother, and I get to see how they are growing up. It was definitely my pleasure to write letters of recommendation for them to be admitted to a private Christian school. I took one course on preaching at Perkins, and I remember one lesson about it. The professor said, "If you are going to baptize men and women in a flowing stream, always put the women's heads upstream when you put them under the water." We all looked at one another and caught on quickly, because if you put their heads downstream, their skirts or garments would wash up over their heads, and that would distract from the holiness of the occasion. I baptized some folks in the Jordan River in Israel, but that's the only time I ever baptized someone in a flowing stream. But I remembered the lesson I had learned at Perkins.

I learned over the years the difference in baptizing infants and adults. One family, after they married, went off to Alaska for the husband's employment. After a period of time, they had a little baby and decided they wanted to wait to have the baby baptized in the bride's home church. I took the baby from the mother and was holding the baby in such a way that her sweet little face was right toward me. I proceeded with the service, and all of a sudden, the baby spit up and it all landed all over my robe. After I got over the shock, I got tickled, and the bride's mother was handing me a diaper to wipe the burp off my robe and we completed the service. That sweet mother reminds me of that from time to time now that they have returned to Tulsa and are a part of the life of the church. From that time on, I always held their faces toward their families.

An adult friend of mine named, Jack, a sheet metal worker at one of the airplane plants at our airport came to me one day and said to me that he had been baptized as an infant, but he thought he should be baptized as an adult. He specified that he wanted to be baptized by immersion. That was no problem since my Baptist minister friend across the street from the Sheridan location of the church, David Willets, was willing for me to baptize anyone at any time in their immersion facility. The day came and Jack, his family, my wife, and I showed up at Parkview Baptist Church. The pastor had provided the water boots and other regalia necessary for me so that my street clothes did not get wet. My friend, Jack, simply had on a white gown suitable for the water. It was time to start, and I walked down into the steps into the water. With all of the clothes I had on, I didn't feel the temperature of the water, but Jack did not have temperature-proof clothing on as I did. As he stepped down into the water, I saw him shudder, and I thought we might not be able to get this done. The pastor had forgotten to turn on the heater to warm up the water. Naturally since he had forgotten, he didn't mention it. Jack toughed it out, and he was baptized by immersion in very cold water but nearly froze to death. We all had a laugh after it was over and he could dry off.

Carl and Sue Richards Remember an Ice-Covered Baptism: *On or about Christmas Day, 1987, Tulsa suffered one of the city's worse ice storms. As transformers blew and ice-covered lines came down, a good part of Tulsa was without power, including Asbury UMC — at least part of it. The church did not have power to heat the facility, but the lights in Mason Center glowed at about 50* *percent. Bill Mason decided that would be just enough to have church service on Sunday, two days after Christmas.*

A faithful few, in warm coats, gathered that morning to sing Christmas carols. As Bill began the service, he announced that on this special day, three infant Baptisms were scheduled, but only one little girl showed up – our fiveweek- old Ashley Richards from Anchorage, Alaska. (What's a little ice when you live in Alaska?) Her parents, Scott and Megan Richards, had attended Asbury while growing up, were married by Bill, and they wanted him to baptize Ashley while they were home for Christmas. Bill said that it was the first and only time he had ever conducted a Baptism while wearing an overcoat.

Fast forward three years, and Scott and Megan, who by that time were living in Carrollton, Texas, brought their second daughter, Melanie, to Tulsa for Baptism by Bill. The family all gathered in front of the altar rail for the ritual. Bill took Melanie, as was his custom, and walked back up on the Chancel area to show her to the choir. Three-year old Ashley, not understanding the process, said, in a voice loud enough to be heard for several pews back, "Where's that man taking my baby sister?" After the choir quit laughing, Bill sprinkled Melanie, and her family celebrated a second memorable Baptism.

Love,
Carl and Sue Richards

One afternoon in 2018, I went for a medical test, and a very big fellow in the waiting room recognized me. He came up to me and told me that I had baptized him long ago. His grandmother, Alma Robson, had attended Asbury for years and then lived at Montereau until her passing. Her oldest son, Ed, asked me to baptize his first son (Alma's first grandchild), and this was the man who recognized me. I told him it was a good thing that I baptized him when he was a baby since I surely couldn't hold him now. It is always a true pleasure for me to see those whose lives have been a part of mine. I am grateful to him for speaking to me. (I wish I could remember his name.)

Funerals

Funerals are special times in my life as a pastor and also times when close family members and friends are aware of the brevity and end of life, and hopefully they understand the importance of our destiny after we die.

Funerals or Celebrations of Life were times that I felt most appropriate to offer the simple, loving plan of salvation for all people and the opportunity that exists for each one in the congregation who has never professed faith in Jesus Christ. The time made available for the pastor and families to meet to discuss the service is important. Since retirement, I have learned that Tom Harrison, Asbury's Senior Pastor, has excellent computer skills, and family members meet with him in his office. He can feed into his computer the questions and discussions that transpire. Tom is able to reproduce all that was said and following the funeral service, he gives to the widow or widower a copy of the conversation in his study. I never developed that kind of skill on the computer, and as a consequence, I don't recall all that was shared, and I often left out details that I wish I had shared.

I followed the conventional Order of Worship for funeral services that included the opening of the casket following the service, and guests and family members could pass by the casket seeing the deceased. On one occasion, the widow came to see me several months after her husband's funeral and said, "Pastor, I am unable to come to worship anymore because when I do, all I see is my husband's casket with his body inside." We had prayer together, and she left.

I thought and prayed a good bit about that and made a decision that is still in effect at Asbury that neither the casket nor the body are brought into the church at all. We go to the cemetery first and conduct a graveside committal service, and then we proceed to the church where a memorial service or Celebration of Life is conducted. Following the service, there is a reception for coffee, tea, cookies, and time to visit with family and friends.

One day the owner of a funeral home asked me if I would conduct the funeral for a man who was a horse trainer and cattleman. Because of our relationship, I said I would do it. I called a rancher friend of mine to see if he could help me find out anything about this man. The next day, he called me and said he had talked to five people from that area and could not find out anything good about him. The man's exwife called and made an appointment to come in to visit with me, and her parting remark after we talked was, "I would like to ask you not to mention in the service that I was a good wife." The day of the service, I arrived at the funeral home, parked, and entered by a back door. There was a room available for pastors to pray and study their notes to prepare for the service. While there in that room, one of the funeral directors came to me and asked me if I had seen the bouncers at the front door to which I replied, "Are you serious?" And he said, "Yes." I began to pray and think about what in the world should I say or could I say at this man's service. After some time of prayer, I came to the conclusion that I would offer some opening scriptures; offer the plan of salvation; I would then pray for the committal of this man's spirit to God; pronounce a benediction, and hightail it. I later learned that the man had moved out the ex-wife, then moved in a new wife who shot him to death. Several weeks passed before I saw my funeral owner friend, and I told him when I saw him, "You owe me," and we both had a good laugh.

Donovan Collins sent this story. *Dear Pastor Mason, I have met you once yet feel like I have known you a long time. My friend, Charlie Bonner, had a deep love for you as a person. My business was next to him for many years, and I became quite fond of him; in a wonderful way he was the grandfather I never had. When I would help him deliver furniture, sometimes he would be playing a cassette tape of you singing. He thought the world of you. I knew this* *when he told me he wanted you to preside over his funeral. I will never forget the story of him hanging drapes and his pants falling down while the women were playing bridge. This is one of many stories he had, and I was fortunate to be part of some funny ones with him as well.*

Thank you for baptizing his grandson. Charlie would have been really proud that it was you presiding over that wonderful occasion, and my family is thankful for what you have done for Asbury Methodist.

All the best,
Donovan Collins

From Sheila Bays: *Hi Bill, Our dear friend, Sue Freeman, had been urging us to come to Asbury. "You will love Bill Mason," she said. I had found out the pastor of the church we were attending believed in abortion. The next Sunday we visited Asbury. Bill's sermon was wonderful, and he spoke out against abortion. Ken and I decided to join Asbury — a decision that changed our lives.*

One day not long after we joined, we saw Bill outside the church, and he called out, "Hi, Ken and Sheila." We were stunned. He remembered our names after one conversation we had before joining Asbury. During the following years, Bill and Jayne became our dear friends. When Ken had his difficult cancer surgery in 2003, he informed me that he didn't want any hospital visitors except Bill Mason. When Ken passed on in 2007, Bill was dealing with painful shingles. When I called Bill about Ken's service, I said, "Bill will you be able to do Ken's memorial service? I don't care if you sit down the whole time." He said, "I am able," and the service was wonderful. When I moved to Colorado to be closer to my family, Bill and Jayne gave me a beautiful music box that plays Amazing Grace. We had that sung at our wedding, and my son-in-law sang it at Ken's service. That music box is one of my treasures.

Bill always signed his letter in the church newspaper, "I love you with the love of the Lord." That was always so comforting to me, and that is the way he signed the note in my music box. When dear Sue told us we would love Bill Mason, I never dreamed he would love us too as he loved all the people of Asbury.

I could go on and on, because as I said, Bill changed our lives by leading us to love God and trust Him more and more. I am so grateful for the life God has given me; I am truly blessed. When Bill retired and became our teacher in our Joy Class, we were blessed in so many more ways by Bill and the Joy Class.

Julie Wilson shared these stories: *Hi Bill, This is Julie Wilson with a couple of my favorite stories for you. The first concerns my daddy, Bob Baker, and how I credit you with helping him finally come to know the Lord. When he was diagnosed with cancer, I asked you to visit him at St. Francis. He had been a Christmas-Easter guy his whole life as he didn't trust the church due to a bad experience with an unscrupulous minister when my dad was a young man. It hurt him so badly he left the church. All my life I tried to witness to him, but he basically stayed agnostic and un-committed. When he moved to Tulsa in the 90's, he started going to Christmas and Easter services with me at Asbury. He LOVED the Christmas Eve services at Asbury as well as Easter. He loved your style and the way you preached. I re-member when his doctors told him his cancer was terminal; you came to visit him regularly. He told you he didn't know how to die and didn't want to die. Here's where your amazing style came into full view. You basically got in his face, almost crawling into the hospital bed and gently but firmly said, "Bob Baker, if I could trade places with you I would in a heartbeat because I cannot wait to meet my Savior!" He was shocked and didn't know what to say. After you left, he said, "Julie Ann, I want to move my membership to Asbury [I didn't even* *know he still had one in Muskogee], and I want Bill Mason to do my funeral." The next few days went by, and your visits continued; he told me you had led him to the Lord. Praise God! We talked some more, and he couldn't say enough positive things about you. He talked openly about not wanting to die, but I said, "Daddy, you win either way. You get healed physically and stay here with us or you get healed in death and go to be with Jesus. You win either way" And do you know that's what he had us put on his tombstone.*

Bill, I thank you forever for being with my dad and helping him to learn the truth and meet Jesus, even at the end of his life. And now I know I'll be with Daddy in Heaven. I thank God for you so much!

The other story has a funny ending to it. In the 90s when I was a single adult, one Sunday you came running up to me and just gave me the biggest hug. You were smiling ear to ear and said, "I am SOOOOO glad you are you!" I didn't really know what to think about that so I said, "Well, okay..." then you said, "I've been praying for you every day for nine months and went to the hospital to see you and your new baby. When I got there, it wasn't you! I didn't know we had two Julie Wilsons in our church! I was so happy it wasn't you!" We both got a good laugh out of that. I recently met the other Julie Wilson and told her the story. She remembered when you came to see her with her new baby but didn't understand why you were so very happy. It's a small world and a story about you I've told many times. Thanks, Bill, for being truly concerned about your flock and also being able to see the funny things when they turn out that way! I can't wait to read your book when it is finished and will preorder my copy as soon as they tell us we can. God bless you! Over the years you have blessed me, Matt and his family, and my dad more than you will ever know!

I love you to death!
Julie

From John Westervelt, also known for decades at Asbury as Grandpa John (volunteer in Children's Ministries): *It was near the supper hour on a Friday night in August thirty two years ago. My wife Nelda died after nine months of extreme pain. Bill Mason came to my house. We prayed, talked, and mostly sat late into night. I shall remember forever the presence of this man of God at the time of my greatest need.*

John Westervelt

[Nelda Westervelt passed away August 14, 1987]

Jayne Mason

We had, during my tenure at Asbury, outstanding men and women on our staff who were either ministers, educators, or administrators, and I was so grateful that God led the men and women to us at the right times. I learned that if I wanted to be certain I got the right person, I would see to it that Jayne would join a prospective employee for lunch or dinner, and after the prospect left, I would say, "What do you think, Honey?" And she would tell me exactly what she thought; Jayne had excellent judgment about personalities and character.

Bumps and Joys

Even with the bumps that occurred along the road during 29 glorious years I was Senior Pastor, I do not know how any pastor could have enjoyed and learned more from the congregation of wonderful people of Asbury. John Collier, an associate for three years, told me one day, "Bill, there is only one reason I can think of why Asbury won't continue to grow, and that is if you get in the way." From that moment on, I figured out how to get out of the way since we had lay people who were exceedingly qualified and desirous to be in full-time Christian service. What a delight it always was to be Senior Pastor of Asbury United Methodist Church. And now what a joy it is to be Pastor Emeritus. God's chosen path for my life continues.

Dr. Mason standing in front of
Mason Chapel at Asbury United Methodist Church
Mingo Road in Tulsa, Oklahoma (01/09/2020)

Part IV
Retirement

1993 and Beyond

A member of Asbury and my friend came to see me one day at the church. He wanted to talk about his decision to retire for a third time. He proceeded to tell me about each job he had held previously and the process that he went through to make the decision to retire from that job. When he finished all three scenarios, I told him that I had been thinking and praying about retiring. My thoughts were to retire a year or so in the future to which Chris Parks replied, "Bill, if you are going to retire, retire. Don't dilly dally around about it." I didn't make a decision at the time of that conversation, but it certainly did focus my thoughts about retirement into a clearer picture.

One of the criteria for me in making the decision to retire is that I wanted to retire before the congregation wanted me to retire. Jayne and I had lengthy discussions about my retirement and my decision-making process. Jayne certainly had opinions and questions that we both dealt with. In the final analysis, I wanted both of us to have input and make the decision together. I had not talked broadly about my thoughts of retirement other than to Jayne. I cannot remember how long it took me to finally come to the conclusion that 1993 after 29 years was a good time to retire for the church, for Jayne, and for me.

To make a selection of a pastor to succeed me, Jayne

and I both felt at least a six-month period for the District Superintendent and the Bishop would make the process much easier to deal with. Somewhere along the way, the District Superintendent spent time with the chairman of Asbury's Staff Parish Relationship Committee. All of the negotiations and activities of the Bishop to find a suitable replacement would include conversations between the Bishop, the District Superintendent, the replacement, and the Staff Parish Relationship Committee. This should all be confidential, but it rarely is. Dr. Tom Harrison would be coming to Asbury as Senior Pastor.

Retirement Party Sunday, June 6, 1993

Phyliss Taylor recalls, "When Bill announced to the staff that he was going to retire, the staff was in complete shock. Bill was a wonderful pastor and a very good friend to my husband, Bill, and to me, which remains today."

Phyliss said that "Bill's retirement celebration was both funny and sad. We had a retirement celebration in the sanctuary with various speakers who told stories about Bill. It was a big celebration with so many people." Sue Richards remembers that the Sonshiners, under the direction of Marvin Reecher, sang in the sanctuary.

The celebration of my retirement was a wonderful occasion. We gathered in the sanctuary of the church location on Sheridan. We had a brief service, and then I was roasted by Johnna Himes. I remember A. B. Steen saying that Johnna was so funny that she could have had her own television show. During the roast, Johnna began to talk about my closet. I didn't know she had ever seen my closet, but someone may have told her about it. I had been to military school where we were expected to have our shirts hanging just so and all else in our drawers had to be folded just right. When Johnna was roasting me, she tells that all of my shirts are hanging in a row, and all of my shirts are facing south. That brought a big laugh from the crowd.

I remember that Reverend Warren Hultgren was there. He

was another faith leader with whom I enjoyed a personal relationship. Warren was Senior Pastor for First Baptist Church in Tulsa for 35 years and became Pastor Emeritus after his retirement. Warren passed away in 2010 at 89 years of age. I had met Warren at a Rotary Club meeting years before in Lucerne, Switzerland. We were both surprised to meet each other there. We became and stayed friends throughout our ministries and worked together on the Evangelistic Crusade in Tulsa.

After the festivities in the sanctuary, we moved to the Mason Center for a reception. Punch, coffee, and cake were served. A huge centerpiece came down from the ceiling into streamers. It was beautiful. The church presented the parsonage, Fair Haven, to Jayne and me as a gift for my retirement. I had gone to the trustees some time before the date of retiring to ask if Jayne and I could buy the house. Their response was quick in coming when they said, "No, you cannot buy it because we are going to give it to you." I was deeply humbled, thanked them very much, and was so very happy to tell Jayne that we were going to keep our home as a gift.

After I retired in 1993, Johnna also retired later in 1993 after working with Tom Harrison as he became Senior Pastor.

Tom Harrison, Senior Pastor, Shares His Story About Johnna

As I was preparing to move to Asbury, I shared with a friend in ministry that I've known since I was 14½ years old that Johnna Himes had been Bill's secretary for 28 years. He immediately told me that I MUST fire her. Stunned, I asked why? He said he had worked in a business setting and knew from that experience that she could never be loyal to me like she had been to Bill. When I told my wife, Dana was outraged. She said he was completely wrong. After being in my new position several months at Asbury and finding Johnna to be an invaluable asset, I felt I could tell her about this conver-

sation with my friend. She was as surprised as Dana had been at the counsel. The very next day, my friend called me at the church. Johnna took the call. I'll always remember her saying, "Tom, your FRIEND is on the line." I laughed and told Johnna, "Get him! But let me listen in." I heard Johnna ask him, "Before I let you talk with Tom, I've got one question for you. Why did you want to get me fired?" My friend could not deny what he had said to me about her. He repeated one word, "Well....well...well" about ten times all with different voice inflections. I loved overhearing the conversation; Johnna felt justice had been served, and believe it or not, my friend is STILL my friend (he is actually the one who earlier had insisted that I attend Asbury Theological Seminary). Johnna helped me tremendously over the next year to find confidence in following Asbury's legendary pastor. Johnna retired after a year. She and her succes-sor, Phyllis Taylor, were invaluable to me in their roles when Asbury was on Sheridan. I will always be grateful for those three women: Johnna, Phyllis and Dana.

When my retirement became known to the congregation, I knew that I would be questioned by a number of members and friends. Since I was the one who went through most of the decision making thought process, I determined what was important to say and let the rest of it fall away. I never did experience sadness nor regret after I made my decision. It was a new feeling to know I was not going to go to the office in June of 1993.

Phyliss Taylor succeeded Johnna in 1993 as the Senior Pastor's secretary. Phyliss had worked at Asbury in several different capacities; she retired in September, 2000. Phyliss said, "We were building the new church on Mingo, and I thought that was a good time to retire."

Sun Oil Company moved Bill and Phyliss here, and they had their daughter with them when they moved. Bill became quite active at Asbury but also the golf coach (volunteer position) at

Memorial High School. Phyllis was an important member of Asbury's staff. When Johnna retired, Tom Harrison asked Phyliss to become his secretary; she responded with enthusiasm that she would enjoy that. She quickly became Tom's right hand. We had the privilege of seeing their beautiful daughter grow up, get married, and have a family. Upon Phyllis' retirement, she and Bill continued in responsibilities in the life of the church — always making significant contributions. For years, they were responsible for the Voting Place in the Lobby of Asbury on election days. Bill worked all weddings and prepared the altar for Sunday Services and evening services. Bill counted the offering on Sunday mornings, and he was in charge of the ushers and other events in the sanctuary. Bill managed the sound for weddings, funerals, and sometimes the church services. Additionally, he prepared Communion for New Year's Eve services.

Bill Taylor also coached our son, Cameron, in football. Bill told me that on Mondays at practice Cameron would talk about "Dad's prayer on Sunday was too long." Jayne and I always attended Cameron's games, and Jayne was there with her cow bell.

Recalling Bill Taylor's involvement with Memorial High School sports brings to mind Wally and Sue Maurer. For years Wally coached track athletes at Memorial; his special interest was the long-distance runner. Wally and Sue have been involved with Memorial High School track for years attending to the myriad of details involved with a successful track meet. Sue took care of the game time administration, registration, scorekeeping, and so much more. Wally continues today to be involved as a volunteer with the Fellowship of Christian Athletes that meets at Memorial High School led by Turning Point Pastor John Plum.

When Phyliss decided to retire, she got permission from Tom Harrison to contact Victoria Williamson to see if she would be interested in the Senior Pastor's assistant position. After praying and thinking about it, she said she would. Phyliss then told her that one of the reasons she wanted to retire was the annual reports from every working part of the church would be due in about three weeks, and it is one of the toughest jobs that anyone could have. Victoria was not dissuaded and took it good naturedly.

Victoria Williamson

Victoria Williamson had been working for Dub Ambrose who was on the Asbury staff for only three months when Phyliss Taylor told Tom she wanted to retire. In Tom's concern for filling that position, Tom asked Dub if he could talk to Victoria about coming to work for Tom. Dub agreed, and Victoria agreed; she worked for Tom for over seventeen years.

When I was retired as Senior Pastor of Asbury, then as Asbury's Pastor Emeritus, Jayne and I developed a warm relationship with Victoria. I had an office at the Mingo church location, and Victoria helped me whenever I had a need. She was always supportive and helpful in countless ways; in fact she helped us in ways we didn't know about until sometime later.

Victoria worked with Jayne to plan our fiftieth wedding anniversary party in 2008, and she was of great help to me in planning and arranging Jayne's Celebration of Life when Jayne went to Heaven. Victoria continues to this very day helping me with her exceeding kindness and care in countless ways whenever needed — and sometimes I don't know about her help until later. She seems to know when I need her help, and she is always there with her smile and good nature. Victoria retired in 2017, and we continue to be good friends.

Victoria Williamson shared her thoughts: *Dear Pastor Mason, Oh how could anyone put in words what this loving, kind, sweet man means to so many of us and to me. Pastor Mason has been like a dad to me for almost 20 years. When I started working at Asbury in March of 2000, I was privileged to work with him and right away I knew I wanted to learn more from him. He is so wise and always has just the right words for whatever situation arises, and he speaks with such love and kindness.*

I'll never forget the first funeral I worked with him – it was on a Saturday only about two months after I had started working at Asbury. The very next Monday morning he came in and handed me some cash. He said, "Dear, I want to share my honorarium with you because I don't think you get paid to work on Saturday." I assured him that I did get paid, and I gave it back to him.

I have been privileged to tag along with him on home visits and hospital visits, and people are always so happy to see him. Watching him with families who were going thru the toughest time of losing a loved one taught me how to deal with grief. He truly knows how to show people the love of Christ.

Since I retired, I have been blessed to see him even more. When he gave up driving, I offered to be his (free Uber) driver, and I have lunch with him or take him to the church for lunches almost weekly. The conversations we have are so meaningful, and when I ask him to pray for me or my family, I feel with total confidence that we have been prayed for – (I think he may have a direct line to Jesus). And he always wants a follow up on the prayer requests, because he cares so much for everyone. He sometimes will ask me months later how someone whom I have asked him to pray for is doing.

I'm very thankful and appreciative of the way he and Jayne made me feel like a part of the family. I have been so blessed by the entire family. And, I truly do love Pastor Mason like my dad!

Sincerely,
Victoria Williamson

Visiting Other Methodist Churches

The first Sunday after I retired, Jayne and I attended worship at another local Methodist church. The next Sunday, Jayne and I attended worship at yet another Methodist church. We visited three Methodist churches, and on the fourth Sunday, we decided we had to go back to Asbury. We slipped into the back of the church (on Sheridan), and as we stood to sing the closing hymn, we left. For a few Sundays, we attended church at Asbury, slipping in the back, and finally decided we would sit where Jayne used to sit while I was preaching. Jayne and I made a rule that if we were going to be a part of Asbury, neither of us would ever criticize anybody or anything for any reason. We were so happy to be back among our family and friends.

Jayne and I attended the traditional worship service after the Joy Class and Mariners Class, and it was glorious to be a part of Asbury in our retirement years. Due to a change in the worship schedule, I now attend the Joy Class at 8:00, then the 9:30 worship service, then the Mariners Class at 11:00.

Teaching the Joy Class

In addition to teaching Bible study in our home on Mondays, I was asked by class members to teach the Joy Class in 1993, the year I retired. The class met at 8:00 a.m. in the Parlor at the church location on Sheridan and continues to meet at 8:00 a.m. at the Mingo location. I enjoyed teaching my good friends in the Joy Class until 2012 and remain a member of the class to this day. Dewey Sherbon teaches the Joy Class now. The class members who are like family meet for early dinners at a variety of restaurants every Tuesday; we pray, laugh, and enjoy lasting friendships and Christian fellowship.

Teaching the Mariners Class

At some point, I was asked to teach the Mariners Class at 9:30 a.m. on Sundays after teaching the Joy Class at 8:00 a.m., and I am still a member of the Mariners Class.

Playing Gin Rummy then Dominoes

At some point after our retirement, Jayne and I began to play Gin Rummy. Jayne loved the game, but when we were in ministry, we didn't have time to play. I loved playing Gin Rummy with Jayne because every time I won, I got a kiss. One evening we were with a Sunday School class party at the church, and toward the end of the evening, there was a drawing for prizes. Jayne won a set of Dominoes. That was the end of Gin Rummy but the beginning of a family love affair with Dominoes. When my girls come to see me now on Saturdays, after they do the chores that need doing, Robin will say, "Daddy, do you want to play Dominoes?" And I always do unless I am watching OU. Peggie wins more often than Robin or I.

Director of Pastoral Care at Laureate

Upon my retirement from Asbury, Laureate Psychiatric Clinic and Hospital asked me to serve as Director of Pastoral Care. I enjoyed my work there, and I served for almost two years. I met some nice people on staff there and enjoyed my association with them. It was a different environment from the church, and the staff taught me quickly and so much that I did not know.

While I was at Laureate, Tom Harrison asked me to resume my hospital visitation responsibilities that I had loved at Asbury.

Looking back, one aspect of being the pastor of a local church in a larger city was visiting the men, women, and children of Asbury when they were in a local hospital. When I was first appointed to Asbury in Tulsa, our membership was 118. It was easy to keep track of 118 members. I could go to each hospital, check the roster for Asbury members, and make note of any member or family member who was present.

As our membership grew, it was still easy to find those going to the hospital since we encouraged our people to let the church office know who would be entering the hospital, the date, and the specific hospital. I made it a practice to contact all of our families to get all of the information possible. If they were to have surgery, I asked for the check-in time and date, and I was at the hospital to greet them. I stayed with that patient until the patient left for surgery; then I stayed with the family members until the surgeon reported the surgery was over and the results of the surgery.

I quickly learned that patients and family members appreciated their pastor's presence at times like this. It was important for me to be there. If I could not be present, someone representing me was always there.

I resigned my position at Laureate in May of 1995 and was thrilled at having the opportunity to participate on a daily basis in a part of the ministry of Asbury that I truly loved and had missed upon retiring. I already had an office at the new location, so I was ready to go and visit our Asbury members at Tulsa area hospitals. I thanked God for directing my path back to Asbury.

My Mother's Stroke

A little more than two years after I retired, my mother had a stroke (September 13, 1995). Since I was retired, I would go to Oklahoma City every Wednesday morning to spend time with her. This gave my sister, Marilyn (who lived next door and who took good care of Mother), time for herself. Mother couldn't do much for herself and was dependent on Marilyn. I spent the night, and on Thursdays, I would take our son, Randy, to lunch. I would return to Mother's house, and when her favorite soap opera came on the television on Thursday afternoon, it was my cue to head back to Tulsa. Mother lived five years after her stroke. Jayne was always supportive for me to spend that time with my mother who passed away around Christmastime in 1999.

Pastor Emeritus

In December of 1998, five and a half years after I retired, Tom Harrison gave me a piece of paper one day signifying that I had been given the title of Pastor Emeritus of Asbury United Methodist Church. I had hoped for several years that this would happen, and I was so happy and honored to receive that designation.

Men's Prayer Breakfast

Since the beginning of the Asbury Methodist Men's Prayer Breakfast (on Sheridan), I have attended every Wednesday morning at 6:30 a.m. that I possibly could. It is so important to me that I do not miss it unless I am out of town or ill. It is inspiring to be in fellowship with the group who makes up the Asbury Methodist Men's Prayer Breakfast. The men from the group volunteer to make preparations for our breakfast. The cost is only three dollars for biscuits, sausage patties, gravy, scrambled or fried eggs, bowls of fruit, and often a sweet roll, coffee, tea, orange juice, or milk. Dry cereal is also available. We go right into the Christian Living Center and serve ourselves, and when everyone has had breakfast, the president calls us to order and asks for announcements that need to be made; then we have the Pledge of Allegiance. Following that, we sing a hymn (acapella). We have several men who chair the remaining part of the morning's activities to announce any praise reports or prayer requests. After the prayer part of the morning is over, we have a devotion that six men take turns leading. That is followed by closing prayer. There is time to visit with each other until all must be off to work or on to the plans for their days. There is another group of men who take responsibility for writing down what has occurred during each meeting; during the following days, a program is reproduced, and every man is aware for whom and why we prayed every week and the words to the hymn that we sing. This group of Methodist men sponsors an annual churchwide pancake breakfast and an evening meal for Methodist Men and their guests. The purpose for these events is for fellowship and to raise money for mission outreach.

Since I no longer drive, Victoria Williamson organized a group of five men who take turns picking me up early every Wednesday morning.

Tweenagers

Fred Alexander and his wife were the ones who helped organize the Tweenagers, and Fred was the first president. We chose that name specifically to represent a group of people who were between retirement and going to Heaven.

The programs did not have a particular theme; different members suggested individuals and groups as prospective speaker. The Sisters of the Skillet (Jayne was a member) made the lunches, and we enjoyed fellowship, food, prayer, and the program once a month. I attended the luncheons from the beginning as a show of support, and I continue to attend the luncheons (now prepared by Virginia and Susan) and the wonderful programs. The group started out with a handful, and there are probably seventy-five who now attend.

Boy Scouts, Troop 10, Pancake Breakfasts, and Spaghetti Luncheons

I was a Boy Scout as a youngster, and we happened to have fathers who were interested in their sons as well as the rest of us without fathers. Scouting was an important activity to me in my early years, as I've noted. We had an adequate sprinkling of campouts on weekends and always a major event during the summer months when we had more time from school. Fortunately, because of the interest of the parents, I earned the Eagle Award and am still grateful for that achievement. The last two merit badges that I needed were successfully acquired while I was a student at OMA. One of the interested fathers traveled in Northeastern Oklahoma for his employment, and he stopped twice at OMA to visit and encourage me to earn those two badges. Since I was living at the boarding school, my mother was notified when my Eagle Award would be presented, and she received my award in my absence.

A group of parents within Asbury sought to form a Boy Scout troop, thus Troop 10 was initiated and began meeting at the Asbury location on Sheridan once we had our first building completed. The parents involved in the inception of Troop 10 met on several occasions and made and conveyed the decision to any parents whose youngsters desired to join the troop that the emphasis of the leadership of the troop would be on developing the Christian characteristics of the troop members as emphasized in the Boy Scout Manual. The troop reports to the United Methodist Men. The decision to associate the troop with the United Methodist Men was a good one in that a vital part of the church has been the active sponsor and support of the troop. As a Boy Scout, it is my privilege to continue to support all activities of Troop 10 that still meets at Asbury at the Mingo location.

The Boy Scout Manual tells in detail how a Scout is to complete a badge. One of my privileges and pleasures was to be asked to listen to Scouts explain in detail how they completed their requirements of the God and Country Award. I would give approval for badge completion to those who presented before me, and it was a distinct honor.

Troop 10 is exceedingly active in campouts as well as aluminum can collection to raise money for the troop. Our daughter, Robin, is an example of an interested parent without a child in scouting but collects cans for Troop 10. She deposits the cans she collects in the recycling container in the Asbury Church parking lot.

An interesting note, Bill and Dottie Elliot (early Asbury members, both deceased) worked on developing parts of the Boy Scout Manual during the early days of Asbury.

United Methodist Women (UMW)

After Jayne and I had been at Asbury ten or fifteen years, the UMW made me a member of the group. Jayne was already a member, but since I was a man, I had not joined. I tried to attend every UMW luncheon meeting that I could, and Jayne always attended.

I am still attending the UMW luncheons and meetings. All

along my purpose has been to let the women know I support their activities; the food is always good, and the programs are interesting.

Monday Afternoon Bible Study

When I was Senior Pastor, Jayne hosted a Monday Afternoon Bible Study in our home for years, and Edie Washburn led the Bible study. Eventually, it became time for Edie to retire. Jayne announced to the large group that since I was retired, she had hired me to teach since she could fire me if I got out of line. I thoroughly enjoyed teaching that wonderful group of people in our home for years. Doode Blazer played the piano for our opening hymn, and we always said the Ten Commandments before the lesson began. Jayne led us in our opening and sometimes our closing prayers. We brought the Bible study to a close as Jayne's illness progressed but what a wonderful group that was that met on Monday afternoons at Fair Haven.

Sisters of the Skillet and Women of the Word

After we retired, Jayne remained a member of the Sisters of the Skillet. It was a wonderful group of women who prepared meals for large dinner functions at the Sheridan church. Jayne also attended Pastor Darlene Johnson's Bible Study, Women of the Word, on Wednesday mornings.

Saturday Afternoon Hot Dogs at Coney I-Lander

On rare occasions, Jayne and I went to Coney I-lander for hot dogs, and the hot dogs were so good on one particular Saturday we decided we better go back again the next Saturday. We noticed a couple, Don Betts and Hilda Knox (who were dating) always were there when we arrived. One Saturday we invited them to sit with us, and a friendship blossomed. Each of them had a spouse who was terminally ill living at St. Simeon's, and that is how they met. Each would visit a spouse, and different family members would be with their spouses when they visited. Each spouse passed away at different times but close in time. Don initiated going every Saturday with Hilda to have hot dogs which enabled us to meet them and become friends. In a short time, they became engaged. Don gave Hilda a beautiful engagement ring, and why I include this in this story, each time one of our other friends came into the Coney I-Lander, Jayne always insisted that Hilda show our other friends her beautiful engagement ring. After a while, Jayne and I started asking, "When are you going to get married?" Hilda replied, "I just had my carpets cleaned in my house, and I told Don that we couldn't get married until his dog died." Everyone within hearing distance broke out in laughter. Don grinned.

It was common for other members of Asbury to come in for hot dogs, and it wasn't long until a crowd of eight to fifteen would congregate about a quarter to noon on Saturdays. If only one person who was there had not heard the stories of the engagement ring and the dog having to die, Jayne insisted that Hilda re-tell the stories.

After leaving Coney I-Lander, we soon began to go to Braum's for single-dip sundaes to cap off a fine Saturday lunch.

I continue to go to Coney I-Lander on Saturdays. When Don passed away, Hilda continued to go to Coney I-Lander on Saturdays, and she would sit with Jayne and me. After Hilda moved to Montereau, she started trying to convince Jayne and me to move to Montereau. At that time, we neither one had any desire to move, but of course we listened to her describe life at Montereau.

When Jayne passed away, I continued to have coneys on Saturday. Hilda brought a friend, Billie Field, and we all sat together. When I stopped driving, Hilda would pick me up on Saturdays. Then Hilda quit driving in 2017, and I went with Jerry and Johnna Himes. The group who meets at Coney I-Lander on Saturdays has dwindled, but I still enjoy going. Occasionally, Hilda is able to come. My dear friends, the Himes, have both experienced health difficulties and are unable to drive an automobile to have hot dogs on Saturdays. Currently, my son-in-law, Ron Tanner, calls me on Friday evenings to offer to take me for hot dogs the following day. This has proved to be a happy arrangement for me in that we are able to sit and talk, just the two of us — an occasion that has not presented itself very often in the past. We share a love and interest in the lives of Robin's and Ron's two adult sons, Ryan and Stephen, so there is plenty of lively conversation. And Ron likes hot dogs too.

When Randy or Cameron and Adriane are in Tulsa for the weekend, we all go for hot dogs on Saturdays. Sometimes Victoria Williamson joins us. I am happy on Saturdays when I get to have hot dogs and remember the fun Jayne and I had with so many good people over the years.

Making the CD, *In This Very Room*

In 2001, when I was seventy-four, Mike and Susan Stanford approached me about making a music CD of my favorite hymns, and they served as producers. I was the vocalist, and Larry Dalton and his musician friends created the arrangements.

Part of the motivation to produce a CD was that we were building a new Asbury facility, and part of the proceeds of the sale of the CDs would go to the building fund. I told Susan and Mike that if Larry Dalton would agree to do the arrangements and the recording, I would do it. That started a one-time experience for me in that I had never made a recording before. I had fun picking out the hymns and praise songs that I love to sing, and Larry made the arrangements, went to Nashville, and rounded up some of his musician friends. They made the music and upon Larry's return from Nashville, we went to a Tulsa studio, and I sang along with the recordings made by the Nashville musicians. At one point, Larry told me that he talked to the engineer in Nashville about the purpose of the recording, and teasingly said to the engineer, "Do all you can to help this fella sound good." We did the recording for my part in two afternoon sessions." The finished recording was made into CDs, and the church sold the CDs. Occasionally, I still have a request for one of those CDs.

The title of the CD is *In This Very Room*, and the hymns and praise choruses we included are:

I Love to Tell the Story
Change My Heart O' God
Amazing Grace
Give Thanks
Great is Thy Faithfulness
Lord, I Lift Your Name on High
Grace Greater Than Our Sin
Glorify Thy Name
His Name is Wonderful
Majesty
Turn Your Eyes Upon Jesus / He is Lord

Relocating Asbury United Methodist Church

After study, meditation, and prayer, a number of us believed that the only alternative for us was to relocate the facility known as Asbury United Methodist Church. At this same time, we felt it was essential that as many members of Asbury as possible had a voice in sharing their opinions about relocation. The growth of our church had reached the point that we needed more building space and parking space, but there was no more room at 5800 South Sheridan. We invited the congregation to a congregational meeting one afternoon. It was held in the sanctuary, and the purpose of the meeting was a general discussion and a vote to move or not to move locations. Everyone who wanted the opportunity to speak was heard. After an abundance of discussion, I asked for the opportunity to speak at which time I explained to all who were present that although Jayne and I were devoted to the Sheridan facility, we both, after discussion and prayer, determined that to relocate was our only real option. I sat down, and after a quiet few moments, someone made the motion to relocate our church; a second motion was made, and only one or two members who were present voted, "No."

A Multitude of Committees

Immediately, the congregation began to form a multitude of committees. One committee, for example, was created to find prospective buyers of our current facility.

A.B. Steen remembers: *A lot of planning and action concerning a move to a new location happened during Bill's watch. We thought about building across the street, but there was not enough land. We thought about buying the shopping center (owned by George Kaiser), but it was too expensive and still not enough land. Bill and I got a commitment from Bill Lissau, chairman of the Warren Foundation, to sell us 20 plus acres along Sheridan. They withdrew the offer saying they were not going to sell any property at that time; I think Montereau was in the planning stage about this time. The Warren Foundation provided us with $10,000 for any perceived problems their decision may have caused.*

We even thought about a sky bridge letting us use current property connecting with the property across the street. Nothing we could think of for expansion at or near our current location made sense which meant we had to move. The property we bought to build on was the exact center of our congregation's residences as checked by zip codes. Our patience was a real virtue to the eventual new location on Mingo.

Gary Van Fossen, a retired architect, took it upon himself to go to the courthouse and look for available tracts of land that were large enough to meet our needs. When he would find suitable land, he would contact the owner. He called on them and would say, "I am not free to say who I represent." One day Gary called on a man named Bill Manley. When Bill found out Gary was searching for land for a church, he was interested in negotiating a sale since he thought the land would be a good fit with a church. It was apparent to Gary that Bill did not want Gary to stop pursuing the possible sale of this land, but he wanted to know what church it was. Gary had to go to the head of the building committee and tell them what he was doing with Bill Manley. The building committee had to make a decision whether or not they wanted Bill Manley to know it was Asbury United Methodist Church that was interested in his land. The committee agreed to follow up, and an agreement was reached. Each party employed an estimator, and each estimator gave his opinion as to the value of the land. They put those two figures on a piece of paper for all to see and agreed to add the two figures and divide by two to establish the sales price. Each side agreed, and a sale was negotiated.

Moving Asbury United Methodist Church to Mingo

Earl Stutzman, Asbury's Audiovisual Specialist, recalled that the dedication of the new land for the new location was held under a tent on September 24, 2000, and building site preparation started on April 18, 2002, with the erecting of steel beginning December 3, 2002. When the concrete had been poured and the steel structures were taking shape, we had a prayer service on a Sunday afternoon at 2:30 p.m. where we prayed over the building, blessed it, and over two hundred people were given pieces of chalk that they could write a prayer or scripture on the beams so that God's Word could remain on the inside of the structure forever. The beautiful facility was completed around mid-February, 2004, and the first service was held February 29, 2004. The Mason Chapel was completed about eight months later.

The building committee for the new Mingo facility wanted the chapel to look as much like the sanctuary at the Sheridan location as possible. The faceted glass windows were relocated and the chapel was named "Mason Chapel." I am gratified by and deeply appreciate the chapel being named for me. Bob Carpenter, an Asbury member and announcer for the Washington Nationals, the major league baseball team, interviewed me at the chapel after its completion.

When the new building was under construction, Jayne and I drove there often to see the progress. Then on that special day, we parked in a good spot to watch the cross be erected at the top of the new sanctuary. It was an exhilarating experience that I still remember to this day. Jayne and I returned on another day and watched the cross be erected on the Mason Chapel. What glorious experiences those were for Jayne and for me.

To celebrate our upcoming move from the Sheridan location to Mingo, Claudia Abernathy, Asbury's retired Director of Prayer Ministries, had planned and organized a "Read Through the Bible" event to begin on Wednesday, February 25, 2004, at 7:45 a.m. The event began in the Main Gathering Area of the new church building, and it ended Saturday, February 28, at approximately 11:00 a.m.

Based on a suggestion by Donna Miller, Claudia researched and planned this type of event based on other churches that had hosted similar events. Claudia established a committee of Mark Hoffman, Rod Sayler, Otis Osborn, Victoria Loy, Branda Williams, Susan and Woody Woodward, Julie Wilson, and Jan Verdi.

This event took 75 hours with 300+ people reading in 15-minute segments. Some segments of time were shared with walk-in readers since Claudia planned the event to be flexible to accommodate all Communities and Ministries and everyone else who wanted to participate in the reading. Scheduled readers were to arrive 15 minutes prior to scheduled times to receive instructions, pray for the person reading, and begin reading along in their Bibles so a smooth transition could be made from reader to reader. Volunteers were assigned as Team Leaders and as Captains to check every eight hours on readers and supplies.

Tom Harrison began reading Genesis at 8:00 a.m., and the other pastors followed. Mary Ann Smith invited several international students from the University of Tulsa to read in their native languages.

The Prayer Walk was held on Saturday morning, February 28, 2004. Pat Calhoun, Asbury member and retired Tulsa police officer, worked with Claudia to arrange all of the police support to close intersections and provide safety for The Prayer Walk. Church members, pastors, staff, and Asbury friends met in the Sheridan sanctuary for a brief ceremony and some instructions. After the benediction, Tom Harrison and I led the way out of the sanctuary. Someone had provided a staph for both of us. Tom held up my arm and said I was Moses. We led the congregation out.

The Amalekites Defeated
Exodus 17:8-16
8 The Amalekites came and attacked the Israelites at Rephidim.
9 Moses said to Joshua, "Choose some of our men and go out to fight the Amalekites. Tomorrow I will stand on top of the hill with the staff of God in my hands."
10 So Joshua fought the Amalekites as Moses had ordered, and Moses, Aaron and Hur went to the top of the hill.
11 As long as Moses held up his hands, the Israelites were winning, but whenever he lowered his hands, the Amalekites were winning.
12 When Moses' hands grew tired, they took a stone and put it under him and he sat on it. Aaron and Hur held his hands up—one on one side, one on the other—so that his hands remained steady till sunset.
13 So Joshua overcame the Amalekite army with the sword.
14 Then the LORD said to Moses, "Write this on a scroll as something to be remembered and make sure that Joshua hears it, because I will completely blot out the name of Amalek from under heaven."

15 Moses built an altar and called it The LORD is my Banner. 16 He said, "Because hands were lifted up against the throne of the LORD, the LORD will be at war against the Amalekites from generation to generation. (NIV)

As we exited the Sheridan church for the last time, Jayne and I saw our ride to the new location waiting for us in the front of the church. As it happens, Basil James called the Volkswagen dealership and made an appointment to go by and talk to the service manager. He explained to the service manager about our red 1964 Volkswagen convertible that we had owned when we first came to Tulsa. Basil asked the service manager if he knew of a client who had a 1964 red Volkswagen convertible. Immediately, the service manager responded affirmatively and remembered the name of the couple who owned a car with that description and made it possible for Basil to call them on the telephone. Basil learned the owners were members of Asbury, Tom and Hazel Robinett. The car was stored in a barn at their Grand Lake home, and the owner said he would be pleased to make this car available for Jayne and me to ride in to the new church location. I asked if the owner would be available to drive the car, and he said he would be pleased to do that. I later learned that considerable effort was put forth to make the red Volkswagen look brand new again on the day of the Prayer Walk.

Jayne and I climbed into the backseat of the red Volkswagen convertible, and we were immediately surrounded by well-wishers, members, and dear friends as we embarked on the first trip of the morning to the new church building. I say "first trip" because we made several trips back and forth to wave at the hundreds and hundreds of walkers. It was one of the most pleasurable experiences I was a part of with the body of believers called Asbury. This path that God has chosen for me continues to far exceed anything I could have ever imagined.

As we traveled back and forth making the two-and-a-half mile trip, I vividly remember thinking how much I loved all of the people who chose to walk the distance to the new church location and all who had worked behind the scenes to make it all happen. I could clearly see the love of the Lord on all of those happy faces. Each one walking carried one or more hymnals from Sheridan to Mingo. It was a perfect day and a beautiful experience.

When the walkers arrived to the Mingo location, Revelation was being read; people greeted the walkers, and the hymnals were placed where Hart and Marty Morris could get them ready for Sunday's service. Pastors were reading the last chapters of Revelation in the sanctuary:

Sonny Plischke, Chapter 12
David Thomas, Chapter 13
Patrick Jackson, Chapter 14
Todd Craig, Chapter 15
Linda Petty, Chapter 16
Dick Read, Chapter 17
Darlene Johnson, Chapter 18
Dub Ambrose, Chapter 19
Mark McAdow, Chapter 20
Bill Mason, Chapter 21

With Tom Harrison leading, we read together as a congregation Chapter 22 of Revelation.

Claudia Abernathy noted that the original plan was for the conclusion of the walk to coincide with the ending of the reading of Revelation from a balcony microphone while all walkers and readers gathered in the Main Gathering Area of the new building. However, over a thousand people came into the Main Gathering Area, so the sanctuary had to be opened to have room for everyone. After the reading of Revelation, Hart Morris led us in singing a praise hymn, and we prayed The Lord's Prayer. Tom Harrison dismissed us with the benediction.

A large Bible remains in the sanctuary that readers signed and dated next to the areas of scripture they read, and certificates were given to each reader. It was indeed a day the Lord had made that had been wrapped in prayer due to Claudia Abernathy's faithfulness.

At some point before our relocation, Phil Baxter had talked with Claudia about becoming the Director of Prayer Ministries. It so happened that Claudia was praying about the right place to serve. To focus on prayer for our church was exactly what she felt God calling her to do.

I remember going to her office that she shared with two others as she was getting settled and started in her new position. I wanted to visit with Claudia about how important prayer still was to me for every facet of our church. I was so grateful that Claudia would be helping direct and coordinate the efforts of Asbury's prayer ministries. Claudia has now retired from that full-time volunteer position, and Cheryl Stefan serves as Director of Prayer Ministries.

As I look back on giving up the Sheridan location that we worked so hard to build and moving to the new Mingo location for Asbury, it is one of my life's stories for which I am most grateful. I am genuinely filled with gratitude for the many Asburians who were involved with marketing the former location, finding the right piece of land, the right construction company, the architectural plans, the physical move and relocation of the furnishings, for the removal and reinstallation of the beautiful, faceted windows; the list goes on.

Claudia reminded me that every week on Monday mornings during construction of the Mingo facility, those of us who could gathered at the sidewalk adjacent to the furniture store to walk up and down the sidewalk and pray during every stage of construction. Claudia also recalled that Gretchen Evans was there almost every Monday morning.

There were countless committees and hardworking and dedicated members, pastors, staff, family, and friends who were involved at all levels that took such amazing care of a huge undertaking to make it all happen so smoothly. Praise be to God!

Jayne Diagnosed with Brain Cancer

In 2007, I got it in my head one day that I wanted to take Jayne on a nice anniversary trip, but it turned out that it was a nice trip in my mind only — not in Jayne's. My plan was to fly to Amsterdam, and there we would board a ship recently commissioned for a trip along the Scandinavian Coast with frequent stops along the way ending up in St. Petersburg, Russia. We would spend a few days sightseeing in St. Petersburg and return to Amsterdam. There we would stay on the new ship for a trip back to New York City and fly home from there. From the get go, Jayne was reserved in her enthusiasm for such a journey. Later, I was to learn that Jayne would be diagnosed with brain cancer. Jayne knew what was happening to her but was reluctant to talk about it. I canceled all of the plans that had been made.

I became aware in the changes in Jayne's daily activities that something was wrong. For example, when we were ready to go to bed, she would get herself ready and come into my bedroom, and she would tuck me in, give me a kiss, turn out the light, and go to her room. This routine suddenly stopped. My reaction was to think I had done something wrong, but that was not the case. She no longer felt secure in that routine since she had to step up a step to come into my room. And she would have to step down that same step to go back to her room.

Another example of becoming aware of the changes in Jayne was one night I heard her calling my name which she had never done before. I went into her room, and she had attempted to get out of bed and had fallen on the floor. I was unable to pick her up, so I called my next-door neighbor. She and a friend came over to help me get Jayne back in bed.

After that experience, I called our family doctor, Jim Mizell (an Asbury member), and he saw Jayne right away. Jim referred us to a specialist. Tests proved Jayne had brain cancer. On May 20, 2008, Jayne entered St. Francis. Her first treatment was a type of chemotherapy that fed the cancer to make it more vulnerable for radiation treatment. Jayne underwent radiation treatment, and on June 9, 2008, she went to Oklahoma Methodist Manor for rehabilitation to be able to walk again since her leg muscles had weakened. Jayne was determined to walk again in order to be able to greet our guests at our Fiftieth Wedding Anniversary Reception that was being planned. She loved the Oklahoma Methodist Manor, but she was quite happy to be able to go home after four months and resume her regular activities.

I sold Jayne's car while she was in rehab without her knowledge. With the money from the sale of that car, I had the kitchen redecorated. What is humorous about that is that neither one of us cooked anymore. I told her that I would take her any place she wanted to go at any time she wanted to go, and I kept my word. She eventually quit scolding me about selling her car.

Fiftieth Wedding Anniversary Party Summer of 2008

Mike Bennett, a trumpet player in the church orchestra, was hired, and he brought his orchestra to our Fiftieth Wedding Anniversary Reception that was held at Asbury in the Community Life Center. We invited our guests to dance, but Jayne and I didn't get a chance to dance since we were busy greeting, hugging, and kissing our guests. Virginia Huddleston, head of Asbury's catering, outdid herself in food preparation and service. Along with Virginia and Susan Effron, Victoria Williamson and Jayne planned every detail of a beautiful afternoon.

Our guests showed a good deal of patience as they waited in the lengthy line in order to greet us. In addition to all of our Tulsa family and friends, there were friends from out of state who wanted to be there. Our only regret was not having enough time to visit with the out-of-town friends we had not seen in years.

It was a wonderful experience for Jayne and me, and our adult children enjoyed the afternoon with us.

Cristina Lee shared this story in 2009: *My favorite memory of Pastor Mason was in 2009. My son heard a message at Kids for Christ at school and prayed God* *would come into his heart. I wanted to follow up his deci-sion by meeting with a pastor. We saw Pastor Mason in the church office and he immediately engaged with my son and asked why we were there. I had not really known exactly what I had hoped would happen by meeting with a Pastor until after our encounter with Pastor Mason and it was more than what I had hoped for. He celebrated his decision to follow Jesus and prayed the sweetest bless-ing over my son and that his love for Jesus would grow more every day.*

Thank you, Pastor Mason!

Love,
Michael and Christina Lee and son, Landon, [age 15]

The Making of My Bronze Portrait

In 2011, two men in the Seekers Sunday School Class, Bill Holloway and Bill Kohl, after receiving the go ahead from Tom Harrison, approached the members of the class about their willingness to provide the resources necessary to have Rosalind Cook, award-winning sculptress, make a bronze bust of me to be placed in the foyer of Mason Chapel. All of this was kept from me until the class raised the funds and en-tered into an agreement with the artist to arrange a time with me to start the process.

I knew Rosalind Cook, the artist, before she was hired since she spoke to the United Methodist Women on several occasions. She is a vivacious, outgoing personality who ex-udes the love of the Lord Jesus Christ.

Bill Holloway and Bill Kohl took me to lunch and said Tom Harrison had approved the making of the bust; the funds were raised, and an agreement had been made with Rosalind Cook to create a bronze sculpture of me. I was astounded, and I quickly wondered, "What does this require of me?" It turned out that it required several one-hour sessions, then she did the remaining work on her own. The two Bills who had started this undertaking accompanied me to the artist's studio that was located in a building behind her home along a creek in Utica Square. The two Bills gave their opinions to the artist when she would ask, "Does this look like Bill's nose?" I followed her instructions about how to sit and how to turn. She had draftsmen tools to measure every part of my face, head, neck, and shoulders. As she measured me, she transferred those measurements to the sculpting material.

Another member of the Seeker's Class, Gary VanFossen, suggested that the pedestal for the bust should match the furniture in Mason Chapel, as to style, wood, and color. Since Gary had worked with Southern Mill and Manufacturing on the chapel's furniture, Gary took on the task of working with them for the design and construction of the pedestal.

Rosalind's studio was large enough to hold several pieces she was working on, so when we were there, the two Bills and I were interested in looking at them and talking with Rosalind about them.

The completed bronze portrait of me was presented to the church at the 8:00 a.m. worship service in Mason Chapel by Rosalind Cook, Tom Harrison, and Hart Morris. Jayne and I were present for the presentation and honor.

It was an interesting experience for me to have a bronze portrait made, but due to so much attention on me, like the making of the CD, once was enough. It was amazing to me that the whole process from presenting the idea to the Seekers Class, acquiring Tom Harrison's approval, obtaining a quote from the artist, to completing the sculpture took fewer than two months' time.

Rosalind and her family moved to Crested Butte, Colorado, to retire in 2014. I heard from her in 2017, and she was enjoying retirement.

Celebration Roast by the Joy Class, 2012

The Joy Class planned and held a Celebration Dinner Roast for me that was held in the Community Life Center on October 26, 2012. After teaching the Joy Class for approximately 20 years, the members wanted to mark the occasion of my retirement as their teacher with a big celebration party. Barbara Graves played the piano, A.B. Steen was Master of Ceremonies. Barbara Graves accompanied me as I sang some of my greatest hits from my CD. Howard McCloud reflected on the occasion and blessed our wonderful dinner that Virginia and Susan catered and served of all my favorites. Then the roasting and toasting began by A.B. Steen, Dr. George Prothro, SuElla Reagan, Cal Brusewitz, Elaine Hack, Vera and Howard McCloud, Sue and Carl Richards, Mollie Achterberg, Barbara Westervelt, Jim Barrett, Helen Frymire, Dottie Schwartzkopf, Mary Paull, John Westervelt, Donna Ritchie, Judy Johnson, and Barbara and Don Thornton.

Jayne and I laughed all evening and had a great time with these dear ones who are like family to us. I remember feeling loved and grateful while hearing all the funny stories as well as the generous remarks.

Susie Barrett presented a gift from the class to the Bill Mason Scholarship and Asbury Theological Seminary. Our very own Mother Superior, Lois Robbins, gave our benediction. Deloris Messick closed the evening by singing Thanks for the Memories, and we all sang with her.

Nancy Dirks, Carl and Sue Richards, Barbara Thornton, and Judy Johnson were responsible for the setup, planning, calling, sound system, table decorations, and programs.

It was indeed a fun and memorable night of music, food, memories, and fun.

Jayne Became Ill Again in 2014

Jayne became ill with brain cancer again in 2014, and she finally reached a point where she needed onsite medical assistance. At this point her condition required intermittent hospital treatment, then she could be released. She went to the hospital for the third time for this same condition, and I said to the doctor, "I don't want to take her from the hospital until you fix this problem." The next day a member of the staff of the hospital came to inform me that I needed to find a place to move Jayne for her to go to die. I was stunned.

After some time to pray and gather my thoughts, I knew I could take her to Clarehouse, but I didn't have the heart to tell Jayne that's where we were going because Jayne knew what Clarehouse was and what that meant for her (terminal).

A social worker came to Jayne's room in the hospital to tell me that there was a bed available for Jayne at Montereau. I explained to Jayne that I had attempted to find a place for her at Oklahoma Methodist Manor, but the two people who I needed to speak with were unavailable. I told Jayne about the bed at Montereau, and she said, "Let's go there." That was a huge relief to me and to our children, and that day we moved Jayne to Montereau. She was a patient in Montereau's Chateau (skilled nursing) for two months; her care was excellent. In the meantime, I was driving back and forth from our home to Montereau, and I found caretaking to be exhausting. When at home, I would walk into a room in our home, and I would think of Jayne. I would cry if alone; if someone was with me, I gritted my teeth.

After several days of this, I decided this was no way to live, and I had better get myself moved to Montereau since I was only spending nights at home. I had been on the board of Montereau for eight years before moving there and was acquainted with department heads and people in the administrative offices. Staff helped me find a two-bedroom apartment on the second floor, and I was able to take Jayne in a wheelchair to see it. There was no furniture in the apartment, but Jayne said it was fine. I closed on our Montereau apartment, number 214, on July 25, 2014. It was like moving to be with friends. Our children were a terrific help and support on the day I moved to Montereau leaving our beautiful home, Fair Haven.

Robin had spent the night with Jayne at Montereau and had gone home after Peggie arrived. I had gone to Men's Prayer Breakfast at the church. As soon as it was over, I went straight back to Jayne's room. Peggie was with her and was whispering in her ear, "Mother, it is all right" (meaning it was all right for Jayne to go to be with Jesus). After about the third time Peggie said, "Mother, it is all right," it occurred to me that I ought to tell her that it was all right. I moved to her other side and whispered in a low voice, "Honey, it's all right." She did not take another breath.

My beautiful Jayne left us in that instant to be with Jesus in Heaven on August 27, 2014.

Jayne's Celebration of Life

Moore's Southlawn held a viewing after Jayne passed away before her Celebration of Life service. Victoria Williamson was Assistant to the Senior Pastor, Tom Harrison, at that time, and she had become concerned for me due to the extraordinarily long viewing. She didn't know how I could endure the length of time and the number of people who came to show their love and respect for Jayne. I told Victoria that I was exceedingly grateful and appreciative for the outpouring of love from this church that we had loved for well over fifty years. As Victoria continued to watch over me, I described the experience to her as one of joy to spend time with my family and my church family who loved Jayne.

The Celebration of Life for Jayne was held September 7, 2014, in Asbury's sanctuary. The Mason Chapel would have been a perfect place to hold Jayne's celebration, but it was not going to hold the numbers of people who would attend. Victoria Williamson worked with me to plan Jayne's celebration.

Rosanna Corrales, organist, played the Prelude; my family was seated; Dr. Tom Harrison made the Call to Worship, and a recording of In This Very Room was played; we stood to say the "Apostle's Creed," the "Congregational Prayer," and "The Lord's Prayer." Tom presented Jayne's eulogy; the Asbury Choir and Orchestra presented The Majesty and Glory of Your Name. Tom gave the message, and we all sang together Great is Thy Faithfulness which was followed by a video of

Jayne. Tom Harrison gave the benediction which was followed by the postlude, the Boomer Sooner Theme Song. It was a fitting and joyful celebration of Jayne's life.

The family walked to the Community Life Center (CLC) for a reception. Mike Bennett and his Jazz Band played as we greeted our guests. Afterwards, I was exhausted from the day and glad to be home at Montereau with thoughts of Jayne. My children were with me, and that always makes me happy. We rejoiced that Jayne was with Jesus and no longer in pain.

Life Would Not Be the Same for Me.

Jayne and I were married almost sixty years. We had a wonderful marriage, but I don't have any other marriage to compare it to since I have only been married once, but we literally never had a fight. If either one of us got a little testy — if Jayne got a little testy, I would walk away and come back around when things had calmed down. I absolutely saw no point at all in fussing in a relationship. God didn't give Jayne to me so that I would have someone to fuss with. I am still so grateful that God brought Jayne and me together as husband and wife. I thank God for Jayne and our children every day.

Trying to Move On

When it came time for me to sell Fair Haven, I listed our house with David Hughes, a realtor and longtime friend, who I helped raise from young boyhood. The house sold in five days.

I am blessed with two children who are good at arranging furniture and decorating. They worked hard to complete my move. We had to deal with clearing out our home of thirty years. We had a garage sale, and we left the family who bought the house some dining room, living room, and breakfast room furniture, and we gave other furniture and odds and ends to Restore Hope Ministry. Giles Gere, a member of our church, worked with a men's ministry that furnishes apartments for men coming out of prison, and we gave him furniture as well for his ministry. With the help of our children, Fair Haven was empty; we closed the deal, and I found that the new owner was the granddaughter of a former roommate of mine when I was a student at Oklahoma Military Academy. I also found out that she loved her grandfather very much. He had died several years before she and her family bought our house.

At the closing, everyone was in the room except the granddaughter, and we had not seen each other prior to this occasion of the closing until she walked into the room. She came straight toward me and gave me a big hug. She said, "I am very happy that you and my grandfather, Louis Abraham, were roommates." I appreciated her friendliness which lightened the mood of the meeting since it was a stressful room full of people sitting around a long table who were not speaking. I was happy to know that all of the children who were moving into the house would have their own bedrooms for the first time. I also learned that the children love the yard and play outside in the wintertime until their noses turn red. It was a fitting way to say "goodbye" to our beautiful home.

I think often of our home together in a nostalgic way. I am pleased the new owners have kept the home's name of Fair Haven, which means "a safe place." One of Paul's letters in Acts in the New Testament, advises the captain where they should winter. Others and the crew shipwrecked, but Paul was safe.

Paul Sails for Rome
Acts 27
1 "When it was decided that we would sail for Italy, Paul and some other prisoners were handed over to a centurion named Julius, who belonged to the Imperial Regiment.
2 We boarded a ship from Adramyttium about to sail for ports along the coast of the province of Asia, and we put out to sea. Aristarchus, a Macedonian from Thessalonica, was with us.
3 The next day we landed at Sidon; and Julius, in kind-

ness to Paul, allowed him to go to his friends so they might provide for his needs.

4 From there we put out to sea again and passed to the lee of Cyprus because the winds were against us.

5 When we had sailed across the open sea off the coast of Cilicia and Pamphylia, we landed at Myra in Lycia.

6 There the centurion found an Alexandrian ship sailing for Italy and put us on board.

7 We made slow headway for many days and had difficulty arriving off Cnidus. When the wind did not allow us to hold our course, we sailed to the lee of Crete, opposite Salmone.

8 We moved along the coast with difficulty and came to a place called Fair Havens, near the town of Lasea.

9 Much time had been lost, and sailing had already become dangerous because by now it was after the Day of Atonement. So Paul warned them,

10 "Men, I can see that our voyage is going to be disastrous and bring great loss to ship and cargo, and to our own lives also."

11 But the centurion, instead of listening to what Paul said, followed the advice of the pilot and of the owner of the ship.

12 Since the harbor was unsuitable to winter in, the majority decided that we should sail on, hoping to reach Phoenix and winter there. This was a harbor in Crete, facing both southwest and northwest." (NIV)

My Life Continues

I lost my beautiful wife, and I had moved from my beautiful home of thirty years. To the degree that I had invested my life into Jayne and into our home, it is now invested into my children and their families. My life continues to be enriched by worshiping at Asbury United Methodist Church and enjoying the lifelong friendships and relationships that I have made there. I still enjoy making new friends and new relationships.

Moving Again

I lived in my first Montereau apartment for a year. A two-bedroom apartment became available on the ground floor, and I quickly snapped it up and made plans to move again. My children were not thrilled about moving me again so soon, but they have learned to love my new location. I love my new apartment and the convenience of sitting in my living room with the ability to look out and watch who passes by and for who is coming to visit or to pick me up. My new location is easy for me, my family, and my friends to come and go. Once again, my wonderful children relocated me and decorated my new home.

The Story of the Bear Outside My Door

Several years ago, Gary Nash gave Peggie a large, five foot, stuffed brown bear for Christmas. Peggie would bring that bear to our house every Christmas and dress the bear in a Christmas-inspired costume. When I moved to the first floor of Montereau, she brought the bear to my first-floor apartment, and it resides outside my front door. Both Robin and Peggie dress this bear in holiday and seasonal costumes throughout the year. The big bear, in his or her costumes, brings laughter and fun to me and to all who pass by my door. I enjoy and love having the girls here when they decide to change the costume. For instance, today the bear is dressed for the Fourth of July, but the girls are going to put on a new costume this afternoon. I have no idea how they will dress the bear, but I do know that everyone who passes by enjoys when the bear has on a new outfit. I also know that we will laugh and have a good time being together. Peggie came up with the notion to put a container outside my door alongside the bear and filled it with individually wrapped peppermints. We often receive notes in the container thanking us for the peppermints, but one time we received a note that said, "Thank you for the candy. However, I am getting tired of peppermint candy and wish you would choose something different." I was disconcerted when I first read the note, but now I think it is funny.

The residents who live in this large complex called Montereau know me as the owner of the bear, not as Pastor Bill Mason.

Life at Montereau

Life at Montereau is certainly different from life at Fair Haven, but it has been a supportive environment whether that means being alone in my apartment at times or enjoying time with old friends and making new ones. I knew approximately one hundred people who live at Montereau before I moved in. Fifty percent of them were members of Asbury. Well-prepared meals at Montereau are enjoyable, and I always find someone to sit with when I eat at Montereau. Occasionally, I attend music programs and other special occasion programming.

Exercise Classes at Montereau

I attend Montereau exercise classes in the mornings on Mondays, Wednesdays, and Fridays. As a diabetic, I am supposed to exercise daily, and I am glad I get excellent exercise instruction three days a week. I also walk a good bit at the church on Sundays and other times at the church.

No More Driving

My dad, before he and mother married, belonged to a fraternity at the University of Oklahoma, and Chick Norton was a member of that fraternity at the same time. Coincidentally, I have had a close relationship with the Norton family since I came to Asbury. I performed the marriage for Jim and Rhonda, baptized and confirmed their children, and have enjoyed a wonderful relationship with them. A few years ago, I decided to stop driving. A man, probably forty years old, pulled up beside me at an intersection at a stop sign, and he rolled down his window so I rolled mine down. He said, "Sir, I have been following you for a few blocks, and you have almost caused three accidents." I don't remember what his exact words of instruction were, but he told me to do something about it.

I went back to my apartment, and I did some serious praying and thinking about what he said that I had almost done and what his recommendations were. Our daughter, Peggie, was in need of a car. I called her and said, "Would you like to have my car." She said she would, however, she would need to sell her car. She told me that she had heard a commercial at the Toyota place that they would buy your car whether you buy one of theirs or not, so the next morning we went to Norton's Toyota to see the people about buying her car since she was getting mine. They assigned a nice young man to take care of us. He would talk to us a while then run off somewhere then come back and talk some more and run off. Every time he would run off – this is why I am telling this story – Peggie would say, "Dad, call Mr. Norton." I said I would not call him, and lo and behold, he walked by. He took over from that point, and we all lived happily ever after. I don't know how most folks are, but I do not know the value of an automobile any more than I know how to walk like a duck, but I thought they were very generous with us.

Every now and then I feel sorry for myself since I don't have a car anymore, but I remember what that man said to me at that intersection, and I forget about no longer having a car.

Wednesday Night Dinners

When Wednesday night dinners at the church were on the schedule, Jayne and I always attended. We loved going. We enjoyed the food and looked forward to all of the people we talked to and laughed with every Wednesday night. Now, my daughter, Peggie, picks me up and we enjoy another one of Virginia's and Susan's dinners. Peggie and I usually sit with Judy Weinkauf, my daughter, Robin, and her husband, Ron, as well as Perry and Adela Mitchell. I always look forward to Wednesday nights for the wonderful food and fellowship.

Virginia, who is in charge of our kitchen, knows how much I enjoy Chicken Cordon Bleu. She keeps a reserve in the walk-in refrigerator in our church kitchen in the event that I show up for a meal and we have run out of the advertised meal. That never goes unappreciated. Virginia and Susan are wonderful servants of the Lord, not to mention wonderful people and caterers.

Reading

One of my greatest pleasures in my retirement is reading. I read one chapter of Proverbs every morning. I read five chapters of Psalms. And beginning every January 1, I start reading Genesis once again. I quickly discovered when in seminary that there is a world of knowledge available to me through books that I was required to read during my seminary days.

I used to read hoping to increase my abilities as a pastor, so I read everything I could get my hands on. Now in my retirement, I still love to read. If anyone looked in my library of books, I do not believe a book of fiction would be found. I prefer to read books by scholars or other pastors. I subscribe to and read the daily newspaper and perhaps a dozen magazines most of which are published by Christian organizations. I also enjoy magazines like Fortune, Forbes, and National Review. As a diabetic, I subscribe to a diabetes association publication, and that is beneficial to me as I desire to conduct my life in the best way possible for my health and well-being.

One day I had decided I was going to cancel my subscription to the Tulsa World newspaper, and I did. When January 1, 2019, approached, I thought, "What am I going to do in the mornings now without a newspaper?" At 7:00 a.m., I called the newspaper office and told them I had canceled my subscription but I wanted to renew my subscription right away. I received a newspaper that very day and one the next morning; they run a good circulation department.

I had a good laugh at myself thinking I could do without the morning paper.

Staff Luncheons

Since Asbury moved to the Mingo location, staff luncheons have been held once a month. The staff has a meeting before lunch, then I join them for lunch and thoroughly enjoy another one of Virginia's and Susan's meals. It is a time when I can visit with everyone on the staff and keep up with what's happening at Asbury. I enjoy the fellowship of the different ones who sit at my table or come by to see how I am doing.

Friday Morning Breakfast

Every other Friday morning, Bill Abernathy picks me up, and we meet in the home of Rex Smith who does the cooking for all of us. Rex is a wonderful cook, and he fixes something different every week. The last time we met, he made waffles and a breakfast casserole; both were delicious. We use Oswald Chamber's book, My Utmost for His Highest, as our devotional lesson, and we all make comments and observations. We voice our prayer concerns and share pertinent information. I look forward to every Friday morning.

Guest Teacher for Sunday School Classes

Although I retired from teaching the Joy and Mariners Classes, I continue to fill-in when Sunday morning classes need a teacher. It is a blessing for me to get to enjoy meeting new members of our church in that capacity as well as seeing longtime members who I do not see every single Sunday.

District Ministers' Meeting

Once a year, the fourth week after Epiphany, the Council Oak District of Tulsa pastors holds a meeting and luncheon. The most recent meeting I attended was January 28, 2019, at the Bixby First United Methodist Church. I sat with Dick Read and John Odom from Asbury. Kip Wright, founding pastor of Faith United Methodist Church, sat at our table, and he told me they had just celebrated their fortieth anniversary. Kip was gracious enough to tell me that my name was mentioned several times during their ceremony and celebration for the ways that Asbury Church had helped Faith United Methodist get started. He also included that there was never an ounce of jealousy among the Asburians who helped. He said they were all genuinely and graciously happy to help Faith start a new church.

After the meeting, we enjoyed barbequed chicken, sweet potatoes, and banana pudding with a jazz quartet that played hymns in jazz style. It was a wonderful afternoon spent in Christian fellowship with Tulsa pastors. I have been attending the annual meeting for Tulsa pastors since my early years at Asbury.

Thursday Morning Breakfast with Twelve Men

On Thursday mornings, Don Kent picks me up and we go to First Watch to meet ten others in an accountability and fellowship group — what a good time we have each and every Thursday morning.

Lunch with Bob Spears and Family on Mondays

In 2017, Bob Spears (an Asbury member) invited me to join him for lunch with his family group that includes his grown children, his grandchildren, and in-laws to have lunch at the Savoy Restaurant. Bob said, "I would like for you to come to the Savoy on Mondays for lunch as my guest." Bob went on to explain that he hosts and treats his family members who are available for lunch at the Savoy every Monday. I was free on Monday afternoons, and I enjoy Bob's company, so I agreed. He said he would pick me up about 11:30 a.m. In 2018, his daughter, Mary, a veterinarian, joined our group, and she and Bob began to pick me up to have lunch at the Savoy. Bob will always know who of his children will be at lunch since he calls them the day before to see who is coming. He tells the restaurant service person when we arrive at the Savoy how many we will need seats for. His children are all Christians, so the conversation that takes place in that hour and a half is both interesting and pleasurable for me. When it is time to go, they bring me back to my apartment, and I have had a nice lunch and a wonderful time with Bob and members of his extended family. I always looked forward to Mondays with the Spears' family, but Bob told me this week, August 26, 2019, that the Monday luncheons at the Savoy were coming to an end. I will miss seeing Bob, Mary, and all of the Spears family at the Savoy. What a wonderful family and what lively conversations I have enjoyed all this time.

Bob Spears passed away on December 17, 2019, and I attended Bob's memorial service on December 21, 2019, in the Mason Chapel at Asbury.

Billy Graham is Alive in Heaven

On February 21, 2018, Billy Graham died. His death commanded the attention of people around the world and most certainly in my house. The newspaper articles and the news channels were prompt to show segments of Billy preaching and speaking to all sizes of groups of people The fact that our government approved of Billy being honored by his body being placed in the Rotunda so thousands could show their respect for him and his life was a testament as to the dedication and passion this man had for Jesus.

I received a telephone call on February 23, 2018, from Charles Ely, news reporter for KTUL-TV. He asked to come see me to do an interview regarding my life experience with Billy Graham. I was grateful to be asked and more than willing to meet with him. Charles interviewed me, and the interview was shown on February 23, 6:00 p.m., on KTUL.

This is posted on KTUL's Web site:

Rev. Billy Graham played role in success of major Tulsa church

---

by Charles Ely
Friday, February 23rd 2018

The death of Reverend Billy Graham has been felt around the world, but it has an extra impact on the members of Tulsa's Asbury United Methodist Church. (KTUL)

The pastor who led that big congregation through much of its growth, got his calling to join the ministry at a Billy Graham Crusade. A 1983 appearance by Graham in Oklahoma City changed the life of a young office supply salesman. The next morning Bill Mason no longer cared about partying, scotch whiskey or women who made him look good.

"I felt the same way about automobiles, I wanted to drive a car that made me look better than anybody else, and clothing the same way," he [Mason] said. "All those things just changed."

Five years later he followed Graham's example and entered the ministry for life. Asbury United Methodist has grown since he took over the church in 1964. At that time, it was just a meeting inside a Tulsa grade school. But as soon as they put up a building on Sheridan, people started coming and the congregation grew. "If someone visited the church, I was in their home visiting them the next day," Mason said.

In his 29 years as a pastor, the church grew from 118 members to more than 5,000.

It has continued to grow, in its current location near 71st and Mingo. Mason credits Billy Graham for getting him started, selling a more valuable product. He also feels a real loss, with the passing of a gracious and religious man.

"I never did get the impression, in person or on TV, of an attitude of superiority or I'm bigger than you," Mason said. "He just loved people and gave me the impression, he loved me too."

A lot of people's lives are richer because Graham helped Mason follow the same path.

Reverend Mason is now the Pastor Emeritus at Asbury.

He's still active with the congregation, along with 10 different pastors continuing his work.

On July 5, 2019, this link to the KTUL video was working. https://ktul.com/news/local/rev-billy-graham-played-role-in-success-of-tulsa-church

In Part II of my life stories, I tell the story of how Billy Graham was instrumental in bringing me to Jesus.

I admired Billy for so many reasons, but I remember that he would never permit a circumstance where he would be alone with a woman; others must always be present — nor would he ride in an automobile if the only passenger or driver was a woman. Billy never compromised his commitment to never be alone with a person of the opposite sex.

Early in Billy's ministry, he and his board agreed on his salary for Crusades, and no matter how much money might come in during a Crusade, his salary would remain the amount they agreed on in that board meeting.

Sunday School Activities and Parties

Every Tuesday afternoon when I join the Joy Class for an early dinner at a restaurant, Carl and Sue Richards or Jim and Susie Barrett pick me up. Somewhere between 10 and 24 members of the class have dinner together. We always pray before we eat; we laugh and visit during our dinners together. I also attend the Joy Class Christmas parties that have been held everywhere from Barbara and Don Thornton's home, to the Lexus of Tulsa Dealership, to the Family Room at the church. Of course, I miss Jayne since we always did all of these activities together, but I have known most of the Joy Class members for over forty years.

I also attend the Mariners Class parties. The class has dinner parties throughout the year — everything from hamburgers and hot dogs to dinners at the Amish Miller's Farm. The food at Miller's Farm is outstanding, and the class fellowship can't be beat. Mrs. Miller has prepared the meal for a number of years, and she always invites some of her nieces who live on farms around her to come and help her with preparation and serving our meal.

Don and Mary Herrold were always gracious in inviting me to Wordfinders Class parties. It is a large class, and I get to see members of our church that I do not see every Sunday. The fun and fellowship with the Wordfinders are true joys in my life.

Sunday Mornings

When Sunday comes around, I have never had the desire not to go to church. I love being in church on Sunday mornings. The people with whom I associate in the two Sunday School classes I attend are like family members, and the worship service I attend is so electrifying that I am absolutely thrilled by the beautiful music that our choir and orchestra present. Singing the hymns is pure joy for me. When Sunday morning ends and my daughters and I decide where we are going to eat lunch, I have the opportunity of discussing the mornings with Robin and Peggie and hearing about their mornings. We share with each other what we learned and what inspired us. Unless I am ill or out of town, I will always be in church on Sunday mornings. The happy and joyous feelings that I have while at church and all day on Sundays are from the Holy Spirit since He lives in me.

Sigma Nu 150th Anniversary Celebration

When I attended the University of Oklahoma, I pledged Sigma Nu Fraternity. My father had been a member of that same chapter when he attended the university. My grandfather went to school in Mississippi and pledged Kappa Alpha. From the time I was a baby until my dad died when I was six years old, when my grandmother would learn that my father was coming with some of his fraternity brothers for a visit, she pinned my grandfather's Kappa Alpha pin on me. She loved to tease and have a good time. I do not remember what my dad's reaction was the first time he saw that pin on me since he was a Sigma Nu, but I do remember him laughing about it later on.

I remember being so happy to return to Oklahoma after World War II at Christmastime. I was at the University of Oklahoma in Norman. In a short period of time, however, I found myself wishing I could go to my mother's home in Oklahoma City (which had been my home before OMA and the war). It was only thirty miles up the road. I had pledged Sigma Nu, and as a pledge there was a rule that pledges could not leave campus. By the end of the first semester, I was so involved in the fraternity and multiple activities on the campus that I didn't have time to go home.

While living in Oklahoma City after graduation, I was active with the Sigma Nu Alumni Club. When I moved my family to Tulsa when assigned to Asbury, my activities with my fraternity lessened considerably. Since I continue my membership in the alumni club, I was invited to the Sigma Nu 150th Anniversary Celebration. It was held on March 8, 2019, at the Gaylord-Pickens Museum, in Oklahoma City. I invited my son, Randy, to go as my guest. He came to Tulsa to pick me up, and we attended the celebration on Friday evening and returned to Tulsa that same Friday evening, and Randy spent the weekend with me.

The celebration was attended by Sigma Nus from Oklahoma. I had hoped to see some of my classmates, but we arrived 30 minutes late, and the crowd was so large, I was not able to circulate as I had wanted. Barbie Paige from Asbury (whose husband, Dee, is a Sigma Nu) saw Randy and me when we arrived, and since there was standing room only, she graciously invited us to join them at their table. Asbury members, Peggy and Doug Walker and Dr. Ted Marshall along with Oklahoma State University's president, Burns Hargis, were at the table and all were members of the OSU Sigma Nu chapter. I was the only Sigma Nu from OU.

They served hors d'oeuvres and then a program began which included a unique experience featuring historical items from the Sigma Nu archives and a special documentary on the 150-year history of Sigma Nu Fraternity. Members were given a special keepsake memento commemorating the event.

One speaker announced that there is a movement among America's northeastern universities to establish a rule that says no organizations would be permitted on the campus that are gender exclusive. The speaker indicated that this rule has been put into effect at Harvard and Yale and the Sigma Nu chapters have closed.

92nd Birthday Celebration

Judy Weinkauf and Peggie approached me about dates to celebrate my 92nd birthday. We quickly figured that out, and from that point on, they took care of everything. The party was held at Judy's beautiful home on June 8th at 10:00 a.m. A lavish brunch was served, and about 65 guests attended. Randy was able to be there with his daughter, Jennifer, her husband, Keith, and my granddaughter, Jemma. Cameron and Adriane were in Germany and unable to attend. Robin and Peggie were there greeting, serving, and helping Judy.

An abundance of beautiful and loving birthday cards were given to me, and I enjoyed reading each and every one. Pastor Dick Read offered a blessing before we ate. He and his wife, Cindy, were to leave the next morning on one of their vacations (which have been few during Dick's time with Asbury).

The only hitch to the beautiful celebration was some people who intended to be there couldn't find the house, as it sits back on a private road. Judy's son, Kirk, and daughter-in-law were helpful in preparing for the large gathering.

Father's Day, June 16, 2019

I was surprised on June 16, 2019, Father's Day, during the Joy Class on Sunday morning. Three of my children attended class and were seated in the back of the room. Toward the end of the class, Dewey Sherbon, the teacher, asked my special guests to come to the front of the class, and Cameron and Robin appeared. Cameron talked about his perceptions of me as his dad which touched me deeply. Robin sang and led the class in Happy Father's Day to You (to the tune of Happy Birthday). It was a truly loving and genuine exchange of affection.

God's Will for My Life Has Not Changed

I set aside time each morning for Bible study and prayer as God leads me to the Bible or to my knees in prayer. God's Will and purpose for my life has not changed, and I don't expect it to change — ever. Knowing, trusting, and obeying God's Will is still my daily purpose.

Cameron called the other day and asked, "Dad, are you reading your Bible every day?" I said, "Of course I am; if we don't read the Bible every day, it is like waiting on a letter from a sweetheart that never comes." For the man, woman, or child who is genuinely desirous of knowing and gaining God's Will, reading the scripture daily is absolutely essential. I continue to read and learn from scripture every single day.

Weddings, Funerals, and Baptisms

According to the church records (kept by Johnna and Phyliss from 1964 through 2000 and continued by Victoria Williamson until 2017), I performed 1,484 weddings, 1,619 funerals, and 2,069 baptisms. Even though the total number of weddings, funerals, and baptisms is over 5,172, each and every one of them was special to me. I loved that part of being pastor of Asbury United Methodist Church.

Since my retirement, I have conducted many more weddings, funerals, and baptisms, but now, the younger pastors do most all of the weddings; David Thomas, Guy Ames, and Tom Harrison generally conduct the funerals. Tom Harrison does most of the baptisms. In my retirement, I learned that younger couples who are getting married and having babies relate better to our younger pastors. I had to give up funerals because I kept falling asleep.

Surprises

The biggest surprise in becoming a church pastor (and it was genuinely surprising) is the generous show of love by the folks in the congregation to my family and to me on the first day we arrived clear up until this very day. The showing of love was and still is sometimes a complete extravagance or a spur of the moment show of love and support in ways that are impossible to describe.

God's chosen path for my life continues to be filled with surprises, for instance the writing of this book.

Editor's Story

When I suggested to Bill in the early part of 2014 that he should write a book, I was surprised at his answer. He asked, "What would I write about?" I was surprised since Bill's life had been one of rich experiences, accomplishments, and influence. Didn't he know that his life's work was of interest to so many?

I said to Bill that he could write about whatever he wanted to write about. I could tell he was somewhat surprised at the suggestion, so I told him he didn't have to decide right there in the hallway in front of the Joy classroom, but I would like for him to think about it. He did not agree to think about it.

A few weeks later, Bill said to me, "By the way, I have decided I am not going to write a book." I was disappointed but smiled and said that it does take time and effort to write a book and maybe this was not the right time. He assured me he was not going to write a book.

Jayne passed away in August of 2014. Nine months later, Bill called me and asked if I had a video camera, and I said I did. He began to explain that he was going to be teaching some Sunday School classes (adult communities) in the summer months, and he asked if I would bring my camera to the Seekers Class the following four Sundays and tape his lessons. I said I would and asked what he would be teaching. He said, "I'm going to be talking about my life, and I want to see if we can make a book out of it."

I was happy, and I told him I would help in any way I could. When I had asked Bill to write a book, the timing was not right for Bill to spend time writing when Jayne was so very ill. I didn't know at the time I asked that the brain cancer had returned. However, In God's timing, Bill was ready.

I ran out and bought a tripod for my camera and some mini-cassette tapes. I positioned myself on the front row of the Seekers Class; Bill introduced me and explained my presence with the camera, and away he went. We all laughed and laughed at Bill's stories, and the members said they couldn't wait for more the next week.

After the month of June with the Seekers, he went to the Joy Class, then to the Mariners, and that was the end of the summer of substitute teaching. Bill and the church members were having wonderful times. I was enjoying the stories of his life and ministry along with everyone, however, for every hour that Bill spoke, it took four hours to transcribe his stories, print them out, and deliver them to Bill for review. He taught approximately twenty hours that summer.

Transcribing soon became overwhelming, and the stories had only progressed from Bill's birth to dating Jayne. Each time Bill finished with one class and began with the next class, he would start out, "My name is William Cameron Mason, and I was born June 5, 1927, in Lawton, Oklahoma." We had three versions of that along with his following experiences.

Hundreds of hours of transcribing flashed before my eyes to tell his 92 years of stories. I called Bill and discussed amending our book writing method. I suggested that we make a schedule for me to come to his apartment at Montereau for him to tell me the stories so I could type them into the software on my laptop and we could move on beyond Bill dating Jayne. He agreed.

Each hour spent working with Bill at Montereau was a joy and always a blessing, and we were making progress again. Often, I would make his lunch — usually a sandwich, soup, chips, and a cold green tea or ginger ale. I would bring soup since I could drink it from a cup and keep typing. Peggie or Robin would sometimes come by and bring Bill his groceries, a prescription, or his dry cleaning while we were working. When Bill's apartment was being cleaned on Mondays, we would raise our feet off the floor for the attendant to vacuum and keep going.

A few months down the road of making good progress (we were in Bill's middle years as Senior Pastor), my dad (96) who I spent time taking care of became quite ill. That began a series of twists and turns that delayed working on the book off and on for almost three years. We would work when we could, but Bill is busy; his telephone rings often; visitors pop in and out; his calendar is full. He is often double-booked. I teach at Tulsa Community College and have a full life as well. We both had health scares and other issues so our road to getting Bill's book printed has been long and bumpy but definitely worth the trip.

As most of us know, Bill is not boastful or self-aggrandizing. He always wants to give someone else the credit for his accomplishments. With that said, I literally had to pry much of this book out of him. However, we do realize that countless stories, names, and details are not included, but we did the best we could.

We laughed while writing this book because he is seriously a funny guy. Then I cried each time I read a letter to him from a member or friend as we worked to find the right spot in the book for each person's memories. Those letters and memories brought smiles to Bill's face while I cried. He was truly heartened and pleased to learn for the first time of the multiple ways he had touched their lives. He loves the members of his flock, and they love him. The letters were substantive, meaningful, and indicative of Bill's ministry that continues today. He is as serious today as he has always been to seek God's Will for his life and to trust and obey His leading.

Bill is always calm no matter what is going on around him. He is always wise. He is always a gentleman. Each time we sat down to write, I always felt like there were three of us at the table since prayer and the Holy Spirit are always part of all Bill Mason does or says.

Finding the right publisher for Bill's book was also a process, but amazingly the Lord led us to evangelist Aaron Jones of Bold Truth Publishing who does no advertising.

Out of the clear blue sky, God used me in 2014 to ask Bill to write a book. It has taken a while, but I do hope you enjoy learning even more about our wonderful Pastor Bill Mason as I have. To know him is to love him.

Thank you, Lord Jesus. It has been the honor of my life.

Judy

Main entry of Asbury United Methodist Church
Photo taken from in front of Mason Chapel
Mingo Road in Tulsa, Oklahoma

Part V

United Methodist Church

As I write this on December 14, 2018, for forty years there has been the constant tug-of-war between the progressives and the conservatives in The United Methodist Church. The progressives' (or liberals') desire is to change the discipline (Book of Discipline) of the church to allow pastors to conduct weddings for men to men and women to women (same-sex marriages) and allow practicing homosexuals to be ordained as United Methodist pastors. The tug-of-war has reached a point where some jurisdictions as well as some local pastors and bishops have taken the position of supporting the liberal or progressive view. Although the church law is sound and scriptural, it is not being enforced. There are too few people in the leadership of the United Methodist Church who are willing to enforce the law of the church.

A committee was established in 2016 called the Commission on a Way Forward. The purpose of that committee was to study carefully the laws of the denomination and to make recommendations to a special meeting of the General Conference to come up with a solution to this forty-year battle. The committee called "A Way Forward" has met and has made recommendations so that this may be presented and acted upon by the special-called General Conference, February 23-26, 2019. Conservatives are promoting recommendations that will be acceptable to the conservatives and traditionalists, including keeping the present scriptural standards as they are in the Discipline, and the progressives/liberals are lobbying the delegates for recommendations at the upcoming General Conference that if approved, will support their point of view.

The conservative point of view, if approved, (and I pray it will be approved), will also provide necessary legislation that will stop this debate from happening and disrupting General Conference every four years. The progressives would be provided a way that they can leave the United Methodist Church, and the conservatives would be able to rebuild the United Methodist denomination for men and women, both lay and clergy, to effectively support the Church's long-time, historic teachings of Scripture on human sexuality.

On this day, December 14, 2018, I believe the Traditional Plan will succeed (the plan supported by most all conservative and traditional United Methodists), and we can rebuild United Methodism as Scripture teaches. The proposed changes I have read as described in the Good News publication (November/December 2018), must be added to the Traditional Plan language to keep this legislative effort from being replicated every four years.

We will know the outcome after the February General Conference is held in St. Louis, and I remain in prayer that the Traditional Plan will be approved.

On March 12, 2019, I write on this day that I thank God for the Traditional Plan being upheld by the vote of the delegates at the February General Conference in St. Louis. I await the decision of the Judicial Council as that body reviews the Traditional Plan for its constitutionality.

As I write this after the April, 2019, spring meeting of the Judicial Council, the Judicial Council ruled at its April, 2019, meeting that part of the Traditional Plan concurs with the denomination's constitution; part of the Traditional Plan was stricken. As a result, a part of the plan that strengthens enforcement of the bans on same-sex marriage and the ordination of practicing gay clergy will be made a part of the Book of Discipline.

The proposed additions to our Discipline dealing with enforcement of the Traditionalist Plan that was approved will be voted on during General Conference, May 5-15, 2020. If all is accepted as proposed, then we will have to deal with the separation that must follow in The United Methodist Church. The results would be that the Traditionalist churches would remain faithful to the teachings of Scripture as currently found in The Book of Discipline, and the churches will retain the name, "United Methodist Church."

I believe the church has some rough times to go through in order to return to being faithful as Christ's Church.

Part VI
My Letter to Jayne

If I Should Die Before I Wake

"If a man die, shall he live again." - Job 14:14 (KJV)

I would like for you to read a letter which I wrote in 1982 to my wife (long before she went to Heaven).

While the approach is a little unusual, I think the point may be obvious — and I hope it will be helpful.

My dearest Jayne,

I hope and trust that this letter may be a little premature. But in view of my honest opinion that I shall not live forever on this earth, despite any pretensions I may ever make to the contrary, I have been thinking that someday I ought to write you a letter such as this in which a loving husband discusses with his beloved wife what his thoughts are and wishes might be concerning the uncertain but inevitable day of his death.

At first it seemed to me that this subject might be a little gruesome to deal with. On further reflection, I discarded that opinion. If death is a part of the Christian experience, then we ought to feel as free to discuss it and plan for it in a Christian manner as we would for any other part of life; we have freely discussed together every other major crisis, decision, or event in our lives — why not this? If we are going to discuss it together, then it ought to be at a time when we are together, and it ought to be at a time when we are likely not to be swayed by emotions or the feelings of well meaning but perhaps misguided friends, public opinion, or traditions.

Without any further explanation for the writing of this letter then, let's get on to the substance of the matter. My point in writing at all is certainly not to hasten the day of my death, because I am having the time of my life right here and now. My point is to share with you some of my living thoughts about death before it does come and also to make some particular requests as to what should and should not take place with reference to this 165 pounds when death finally does force his claim on me. The very fact that I was born makes death a certain eventuality. When this happens to me, then, what are you to think and do?

Well, the first thing I trust you will think, after any initial emotional reactions to the news, will be that while death has curtailed my physical existence, it has not ended my life. It has only brought my pilgrimage on this earth to a conclusion. The real me will no longer inhabit that mortal flesh which will have become a corpse, but the real me will not have ceased to be. I have entered upon a new existence which is what I am sure Paul meant when he wrote to the Corinthians, "For we know that if our earthly house of this tabernacle were destroyed, we have a building of God — a house not made with hands, eternal in the heavens. " He also wrote to people concerned about death, "But God gives (the dead) a body as he has chosen...if there is a physical body, there is also a spiritual body...this perishable nature must put on the imperishable, and this mortal must put on immortality...then shall come to pass the saying that is written: 'Death is swallowed up in victory. O death, where is thy victory? O death, where is thy sting? Thanks be to God, who gives us the victory through our Lord Jesus Christ! At that time, dear Jayne, that will be me he was talking about — and among your first thoughts I hope will be the thought, "Thanks be to God who gave to Bill the victory through our Lord Jesus Christ!"

So much for that — I am to be alive in a new sense, in a new dimension, so to speak, in what we call "Heaven." What is Heaven, and where is it, and what is it like? You know good and well that I don't know! My consolation is that no one else does either. I have enough certainty of its reality to affirm belief in it, for I have the word of Jesus Himself that it is like a home — "My father's house, in which are many rooms." I know, furthermore, that it is where the Jesus whom we have given our lives to serve is, and that I shall be with Him. Beyond that, none of us knows very much — but I wonder if we could understand more even if we were told? Do you remember how, as a child, you may have been told of the wonderful time you were going to have on some planned vacation — your mother could only whet your appetite for it by telling you how much fun you were going to have. If it were to be some new experience all her words could never describe the real enjoyment that finally came with the experience itself. I think Heaven is like that — so different, so grand, so beyond description, that it is just as well we know so little — we know enough to know it is good, and that is all we need to know. I don't really expect to find any pearly gates or golden streets, and I know you don't either, for those were a writer's poor efforts to describe the indescribable.

And what will life there be like? I don't know that, either, but I am sure it will be more than lying around on clouds and plucking harps. I remember reading a long time ago a book that said that the things men live by on this earth are worship, friendship, and service, and I think that is right. If there is so in this life, how much more so in the life to come, where life will be more meaningful and fruitful, filled with worship, friendship, love and service.

How can we describe it? I think it must be as impossible as it is for us to describe to a child what it is like to be an adult — or as impossible as it would be describe to a person born blind what a beautiful sunset is, or to a deaf man what a glorious experience it is to hear a great choir sing a great anthem (as we hear so often here). Just know this Jayne, I'll be busy about my Father's business and that, to the Christian, as we both know, is the only real and deep joy there is in any of life, here or hereafter.

Now let's get back down to earth! A few moments ago I was sharing this life with you, and now I am no longer — I am dead. What are you going to do with this body that I am leaving on your hands? Well, the first thing I want you to do — even before you call the funeral director — is to call a minister. No matter what time of day or night, with the possible exception of late Sunday morning. If I am retired, then call our own church's minister — but if sooner, call one of our minister friends who you'd like to direct any further funeral arrangements. I know that so often when I've gone to serve as a person's minister in such a time, there was really so little I could not — and yet, somehow God used my presence to communicate something of his love for his grief-stricken people and somehow he gave them strength when they needed it most. I believe a minister with you at that time may be of such help to you and the children.

Then, of course, you'll have to call a funeral home to come and haul me away, perhaps that is a little indelicate, but since this mortal body is really little more than excess baggage now, in reality that's all he is doing. Before he does remove the remains, one thing I definitely want you to instruct him to do is to see that my eyes and vital organs are placed in a medical bank, or whatever it is called so that they may be used for transplants to someone who might need them. If you can find a medical school that can use my body, please give it to them rather than just bury it. Remember, it is no longer the real me!

If you prefer to go the more traditional route, then there are a few things I want to say about my funeral. First, I want it to be inexpensive. You are going to need what money I'll leave you to help out with the children if we are still responsible for them — or at least to be put to better use than some vault that will be buried in the ground containing absolutely no treasure. I am not complaining about funeral costs, for funeral directors are men rendering real service to their clients, and they have their own costs and need for profit from their services; what I am saying is that I don't want you doing more than necessary. So far as this Christian is concerned, their service in disposing of this corpse does not require elaborate provisions.

Let's move on now. The funeral arrangements having been made, I want to suggest that no one else see me anymore — not even you and the children; that I'll have to leave to your discretion. This much I insist on — that the coffin is not to be opened at any public service to be held after my death, not even "lying in state" beforehand. There are a couple of reasons I believe this is right. The corpse is not me and the sooner we disassociate ourselves from that idea the better. Secondly, I know from experience that so often the last vision is a lasting one, and I don't want anyone remembering me any way except as alive — not as some lifeless corpse.

I guess the funeral is next. I like very much the idea of Elton Trueblood in his book "The Common Virtues of Life," where he suggests that the funeral per se ought to be a private family service at the grave as soon after the death as possible, with a memorial service to be held later on at the church. I would like to suggest this course of action if you will follow it.

Whether the service be held at the church without the coffin or following the more traditional pattern of having the mortal remains there present, you know that the service is to be held at the church not the funeral home. This is not just because I am a minister — this is because I am a Christian, and this is a Christian service that is being held, and so it ought to be held in a House of God, a Christian church. Of course, God is everywhere and a service of worship can certainly be held in a funeral home, a home, on a ship at sea or about any place, but you know how strongly I feel about this matter, and I trust no more needs to be said about it.

Next, I would like to request that friends be requested to refrain from sending flowers — not because I've got anything against florists, but because there are so many more meaningful ways they can express their friendship, and there are so many worthy causes to which friends might make some contribution. My own preference would be to the church, but other worthwhile causes are also in such need, and it seems a waste to see such great amounts tied up in floral offerings when these needs persist. Do not buy a spray to go on my casket, but drape it in a white cloth. No one should feel that he has to do anything along this line of flowers or contributions, but if he wants to, will you request that contributions be made to our church Memorial Fund?

Whether my body is there or not — let me remind you that the purpose of the service is the worship of our God and not the eulogizing of his servant. Prominent in the service ought to be the Word of God. You know my own pattern of service has always been to read mainly from the Scripture — the great passages that have such great significance to the Christian in his thoughts about death. I'd like some of the Psalms like the 1st, 46th, 103rd, and of course the 23rd to be read — not because they'll mean anything to me then, but because they'll mean a great deal to those present as they think on the greatness of our God. From the New Testament I'd like to suggest those portions I usually read from John 14, Romans 8. These deal with the basic Christian attitude toward death, and emphasize that death is a vanquished foe — "Thanks be to God, who gives us victory through our Lord Jesus Christ."

Those scriptures should set the tone of the prayers offered. Prayers offered at my funeral ought to be in the vein of thanksgiving to God for all his mercies toward us each day of our lives. I hope that there will be congregational singing and that the hymns sung would be stirring hymns declaring God's power, majesty, and love.

Please, Jayne, ask the minister to leave out any obituary. If our minister is given to speaking, let his speech be about God, not about me — not too long, just a reminder of the assurance of God's continued presence and goodness despite whatever circumstance may ever visit you, even the circumstance of death.

As I look back over the years we have been together, I know that my life would not have amounted to anything I would ever have wanted it to be if you have not been present with me. I have no idea how many more years we may have together, but I am sure that however long that may be, it will continue to be a life worth living because you are living with me. How can it possibly be, then, that something like death could ever really separate us, except in a sense momentarily? I know that our spirits are not now separated from one another, though we may be separated by any great distance at any time — how could they possibly be separated simply by death? Regardless of the fact of separation, we shall be one in spirit even as before — and in God's own good time I know that we shall be reunited in an even richer and more meaningful way than we have ever experienced here in this life. Don't feel sorry for me that I have gone, but think of the words of Jesus, "I have gone to prepare a place for you, that where I am you may be also."

"If I should die before I wake..." know that Elizabeth Barrett Browning was writing about us as well as about herself and her beloved Robert when she said, "I shall but love thee better after death. "

Bill

Part VII
God's Chosen Path

It was at the time of my life when I was working at my family's office supply company and before I met and married Jayne that God's chosen path for my life started to take shape. I didn't know it at the time, but while I was attending a Billy Graham crusade in Oklahoma City, I began to become aware of a change as God was making known His path for my life.

As I look back, that time at the crusade has come to mean more and more to me. There were other times that God was leading me, but the crusade is the point where I was becoming conscious of His path for my life. It was clearly God's plan for me to be at the crusade that night and hear Billy Graham's sermon from Matthew 7:13-14 about the wide and narrow gate.

The Narrow and Wide Gates
13 "Enter through the narrow gate. For wide is the gate and broad is the road that leads to destruction, and many enter through it.
14 But small is the gate and narrow the road that leads to life, and only a few find it. (NIV)

As I have written earlier, Mom and my friends had gone home after the crusade. I went to bed and my life passed before my mind's eye, and I saw all the events of my life were a part of the wide road. For the first time in my late twenties, I did not want to spend eternity in hell. I prayed asking for forgiveness and asked Jesus to come into my life. I went right to sleep, and the next day I felt on top of the world. By the third day, all of the alcohol had left my body. I felt strong and changed.

The next four years were vastly important. I began to experience the love of Jesus, and He changed my heart and my life. I continued to work hard to be successful in my job, but in my free time, I spent time growing as a new Christian by attending Bible studies and other opportunities that God put in my path.

In 1958 at 31 years old, I met and married Jayne and became a father all on the same day. I also began to assume more responsibilities at our church, and I was asked to serve as the Lay Delegate for Nichols Hills Methodist Church. I was more than aware of God's path for me, but as I dealt privately with it for me, I encountered five serious roadblocks (God didn't, but I did).

At this point in my Christian development, only prayed asking God's guidance and direction for my life when I became aware of a problem. I don't know why I wasn't praying about all matters at that time, but these are the facts.

After the birth of our fourth child, Randy, I told Jayne that God was calling me into full-time Christian ministry. For several months, I had been dealing with all of the roadblocks before mentioning God's call on my life. It never entered my mind that it was logical to pray about God's path for me regarding the five roadblocks to full-time Christian ministry.

Eventually, I looked to God to walk me through each roadblock until I was convinced that each one was not a valid objection. For example, after having our fourth child, I became concerned that I would not be able to send four children through college on a minister's income. God quickly reminded me that my maternal grandfather sent all six of his children through college or as far as they wanted to go on his preacher's income that was sometimes a chicken. By the time God patiently saw me through this issue, I was at peace and no longer saw the children's educations as a reason to not enter full-time Christian service.

It was not long until the second issue arose in my mind, but the issue of the Mike Bryan Office Supply business seemed like a huge roadblock for me. Who would succeed my uncle and mother in the business when they retired? The plan was for me to take over the management of the business at some point. Would it be honorable of me to leave? Plus, I truly enjoyed my job. After struggling with that objection as to why I could not go into full-time ministry, I finally prayed asking God's direction. In a day or two, I called my uncle to talk with him, and he swiftly and easily said that he and my Aunt Gladys would do all they could to support me. I remember to this day the joy I felt in my heart at that moment.

I won't rehash all five of the roadblocks because I no longer remember them, but what I want to point out is trusting God and following His chosen path for me has been the right way. When I am obedient to God, He opens doors that I have been unable to open to this very day. When I look back and think about how God has opened doors for me, I am always reminded of the time we couldn't find a house to live in that we could afford when we had made the decision to leave business and go to seminary in Dallas. Jayne and I had not been able to find a house for us in days and days, but when I prayed, the Lord Jesus had exactly what we needed that we could afford. We lived in that house for three years and loved it.

One of my most favorite books of The Holy Bible is Proverbs 31 beginning with verse 10, The Wife of Noble Character.

John is my favorite Gospel writer. I find wisdom in Paul's Book of Romans; I find peaceful encouragement in the Book of Psalms.

As I look back over my life, experiences and memories flood my mind and heart that show me the wisdom of asking God first. As Senior Pastor of Asbury Church, during my prayer time every morning, I always sought God's guidance in all I did or even thought about doing. The Holy Spirit was with me each and every day helping me to know, to trust, and to obey.

The longer I live, I learn to trust and obey the Lord Jesus more and more as He teaches me of His trustworthiness. At 92 years of age, I am thankful that He chose His path for my life and for all of the joy that has meant and still means to this day.

How I regret the stumbling and falling when He was urging and leading me saying, "Bill, I am the way."

Loving every person who has come into my life was not always easy, but through my trust and desire to please Him, I have learned and been able to understand the peace and wisdom in His command. It has made all the difference in my life and ministry.

I am grateful He never gave up on me. He is the way, the truth, and the life.

I love you with the love of the Lord, Bill Mason

Made in the USA
Columbia, SC
29 January 2020